BEING PORTUGUESE IN SPANISH

Purdue Studies in Romance Literatures

 volume 78

BEING PORTUGUESE IN SPANISH

Reimagining Early Modern

Iberian Literature, 1580–1640

Jonathan William Wade

Purdue University Press
West Lafayette, Indiana

Printed in the United States of America
Template for interior design by Anita Noble;
template for cover by Heidi Branham.
Cover photo:
Totius Hispaniae Nova descriptio
by Henricus Hondius and Petrus Kaerius
Johanes Janssonius, Amsterdam, 1633
Instituto Geográfico Nacional, España
12-M-13 1633 CC-By 4.0 ign.es

Cataloging-in-Publication Data on file at the Library of Congress

Paperback ISBN: 978-1-55753-883-3
ePub ISBN: 978-1-55753-884-0
ePDF ISBN: 978-1-55753-885-7

For my girls ... Em, Asha, and Lola

Contents

Acknowledgments

You never reach the end of a journey such as this without many people to thank. The point of departure was a Portuguese Baroque class at Brigham Young University with Kit Lund fifteen years ago. In that course I was assigned to complete a project on António de Sousa de Macedo's *Flores de España, Excelencias de Portugal* (1631)—a first edition copy of which resides in the university's special collections. I remember marveling at the audacity within those pages. My interest in that text eventually sparked another conversation, wherein Kit introduced me to Manuel de Faria e Sousa. He told me something of Faria e Sousa's house arrest in Madrid and the fact that it was during that time that he completed his voluminous edition of *Os Lusíadas*. A semester later I worked on a production of Ângela de Azevedo's *El muerto disimulado* led by faculty mentors Dale Pratt and Valerie Hegstrom. What I could not have known at the time, but is plain to me now, is how influential that first year of graduate school would be. Not only did these authors quickly become the focus of my master's thesis, but eventually would motivate my first conference presentation, my first peer-reviewed article, and now my first book-length study. Special thanks to Dale and Valerie for their early influence as mentors and sustained influence as friends.

During my first semester at Vanderbilt University, I had occasion to sit down with Edward Friedman one afternoon to discuss my interest in the early modern Portuguese authors who wrote in Spanish. By then I had learned for myself that Ed was as kind and brilliant as everyone had said he was, so there was no question in my mind that Vandy was the right place for me. Ed was not only supportive of my research interests, but mapped out what my years at Vandy might look like, showing enthusiasm for my topic as if it were his own. He was a dream advisor and mentor then, and has become a cherished friend since. My years working with him and Earl Fitz helped me grow in my understanding of early modern Iberia and comparative methodologies. I never really had a name for what I was doing until I heard Earl say the words "comparative Iberian Studies" one day. I took to it without hesitation. I thank both Ed and Earl for the multitude of ways they have supported me over the years, and in particular for modeling superlative scholarship, excellent teaching and mentoring, and a radical kindness that inspires and challenges me to this day.

Many individuals and institutions have supported me in different ways over the years. Summer Research Grants in 2006 and 2007 from the College of Arts and Science at Vanderbilt University helped to propel my work forward when it was still in its infancy. My fellowship with the Robert Penn Warren Center for the Humanities at Vanderbilt and my association with the other fellows and Mona Frederick was also decisive. Support from colleagues in the Department of World Languages and Cultures, deans from the School of Arts & Humanities, friends from the professional development collaborative on academic writing, and the generous support of Faculty Development at Meredith College has always kept my work moving forward. That support includes various scholarly productivity grants, a 2016–17 sabbatical, and the 2017–18 Pauline Davis Perry Award for research, publication and artistic achievement. I am also grateful to the Department of World Languages and Cultures at the University of Utah, where I was a visiting scholar during my sabbatical. I give thanks to the Association for Hispanic Classical Theater and the Society for Renaissance and Baroque Hispanic Poetry for consistently providing a welcoming and engaging environment for my research and ideas. I also wish to acknowledge the *Bulletin of the Comediantes* and *Miríada Hispánica* for publishing some of my earliest work on early modern Iberian Studies, and Joyce Detzner, production editor of Purdue Studies in Romance Literatures, for her immense help in preparing the manuscript for publication. Others provided help along the way by reading or listening to some version of this work, including Fred Williams, Carlos Jáuregui, Marshall Eakin, James Krause, Anna-Lisa Halling, David Wiseman, Christopher Lewis, Antón García-Fernández, Laura Vidler, Jason Yancey, and Jaime Cruz-Ortiz. I cannot think of anyone, however, who has shaped my academic life and this particular journey more than David Richter, whose friendship, mentoring, and overall generosity have made all the difference.

And finally, I wish to acknowledge my family: my dad for his lasting influence, my mom for her constant goodness, and both of them for their examples of teaching and learning; Rob, for always being my champion at home and abroad; all my brothers for showing up for me in so many different ways; and my sisters for always seeing me in my best light. With marriage came another mom and dad—whose love and support is beyond measure—and five more sisters and a brother. Without naming everyone, I hope all of my brothers, sisters, nieces, and nephews know how fortunate I am to call them family. But above all there's you, Emily, and our girls: Asha and Lotus. Finishing this book was only ever possible because of you. Its completion is our collective victory. Thank you for always believing in me, for picking me up when the windmills knocked me down, for sometimes going with me and sometimes sending me on my way, and for always cultivating beauty and light.

Introduction

Portuguese Pens, Spanish Words

Remembering the Annexation

> "One can change one's language as one changes
> one's clothes, as circumstances may require."
>
> Leonard Forster[1]

The year 1580 stands out as one of the most significant in Iberian cultural history. It saw the deaths of Cardinal Henrique of Portugal and Luís de Camões, the birth of Francisco de Quevedo, Miguel de Cervantes's liberation from Algiers, the first Spanish translations of *Os Lusíadas*,[2] and the dawn of the Iberian Union. The landscape of early modern Iberian literature would look much different if any one of these events had not occurred. Camões's passing in June marked the end of one of the greatest periods of Portuguese letters and foreshadowed the loss of political autonomy resulting from the crisis of succession occasioned by Henrique's empty throne. It is difficult to overemphasize the importance of these two events and their influence on the construction of Portuguese identity thereafter. In the decades following his death, Camões became the North Star for a people trying to navigate their uncertain present by mapping onto their storied past.

In theory, very little was to change for Portugal under Hapsburg rule. It was in Tomar in 1581 that a deal was made between Felipe II of Spain and a number of Portuguese representatives: "Here the *Cortes* of Tomar acknowledged Philip as the 'legitimate' king of Portugal, but only after he had agreed to major concessions and signed an agreement" (Tengwall 449). This agreement was made official in 1582 through the validation of a *carta patente* which assured that, among other things, Portuguese would remain the official language and that Portugal would maintain control over its commerce and the administration of its colonies.[3] At least on paper, then, it was business as usual—a new king, yes, but the same old kingdom. Looking at the actual paper coming off the presses, however, it is clear that Portugal was changing. As Tobias Brandenberger explains, this was a moment of great significance on the Peninsula: "Spain's annexation of Portugal and its incorporation into a new whole ... marks a political turning point of considerable importance for Iberian history and culture" ("Literature" 595). The presence of three different Castilian-born queens at the Court in Lisbon during the late fifteenth and early sixteenth centuries initiated a period in which Spanish would permeate the Portuguese literary landscape for the better part of two centuries. The control of Portugal by the Spanish crown beginning in 1580 only intensified the cultural Castilianization already sweeping across the Peninsula. The Portuguese, therefore, did not begin writing in Spanish in 1580 nor are they unique within Iberia, past or present, for choosing a language of expression other than their mother tongue. There was not much of a market for works written in Portuguese, but perhaps even more symptomatic of the decline of works in the Portuguese language was the absence of a Court and the patronage that had sustained the arts in Portugal for much of the sixteenth century. As a result of these factors and others, the frequency of Portuguese-authored works written in Spanish peaked in Iberia during the six decades of the Dual Monarchy.

The generation of Portuguese writers that emerged from the shadow cast by these events manifest a degree of self-consciousness in their writings both characteristic of and unique to the baroque literary mentality. This includes, but is not limited to, Manuel de Faria e Sousa, Jacinto Cordeiro, Ângela de Azevedo, António de Sousa de Macedo, Violanto do Céu, and Francisco Manuel de Melo—the primary authors of this study. Without specifically asking the question, many of their writings put forward a uniform answer as to what it means to be Portuguese. That they would be thus engaged is not nearly as surprising as the fact that, in general, their works cast Portugal in the same light. Within their writings we can locate the "union of volitions" that Onésimo Almeida signals as a fundamental aspect of national identity (*National* 14), and at the same time recognize in them an existence not easily reduced to a singular Peninsular identity. Overall, the unsettling of the Portuguese self-image that occurred during the late sixteenth and early seventeenth centuries produced a nation-minded generation of writers who applied their pens to the exploration, celebration, and restoration of the *patria*.

Similar to many other literary critics and historians over the centuries, Pilar Vázquez Cuesta characterizes the Dual Monarchy in terms of decline, so far as Portuguese literature is concerned: "No debe de sorprendernos el bajón que da la Cultura portuguesa durante los sesenta años de monarquía dual y los primeros tiempos de la Restauración si pensamos que mucha de la savia que en otras circunstancias habría servido para revitalizarla se emplea en enriquecer a la Cultura española" ("Lengua" 628). Did Portuguese literature really drop off as much as Vázquez Cuesta suggests in this passage? The answer to this question, of course, is a matter of perspective. If the category "Portuguese literature," only makes room for works written in the Portuguese language, then the Iberian Union indeed represents a severe drop off from Portugal's literary glories of the sixteenth century. Similarly, if "Spanish culture" necessarily includes all texts written on the Peninsula in Spanish regardless of authorship, then yes, the Portuguese contributed much to the literary glory of their neighbors. If, however, works written by Portuguese authors in Spanish, or vice versa, were integrated into the more fluid category of Iberian culture (rather than any specific national canon), we would see the annexation not as a time of artistic scarcity but as a period of plenty. Which is not to say that the late sixteenth and early seventeenth centuries produced a legitimate rival to either Gil Vicente or Luís de Camões—each of whom, lest we forget, wrote a significant amount in Spanish as well—but that does not mean that this period was as artistically bankrupt as some have suggested, and certainly not a "wasteland" as characterized by David Haberly (50).

Notwithstanding the various ways in which we might praise the Portuguese-authored works written in Spanish during the Iberian Union, traditionally both the Spanish and Portuguese literary traditions have been disinclined to allow these authors into their respective canons. Reluctance to add to an already daunting corpus of works left by Spain's Golden Age and a tendency to perpetuate the reductive readings of the past characterizes the Spanish view. As the story goes, while such texts may be in the Spanish language, they are by Portuguese authors and thus there is no room for them. The traditional Portuguese perspective, on the other hand, dismisses these authors for their willingness to abandon their native tongue and homeland at a time of national crisis. This perceived disloyalty explains why the Portuguese literary canon has closed its doors—almost without exception— to seventeenth-century Portuguese-authored works written in Spanish. Edward Glaser describes the marginalization of these works from the Portuguese perspective: "Students of Portuguese culture tend to leave aside an author who willfully neglected to cultivate the national language at a moment when its very existence as a tool of artistic expression was at stake" (Introduction 5). Santiago Pérez Isasi elaborates further still:

> En el caso portugués, la exclusión nacionalista de elementos 'extraños' en el cuerpo del canon adquiere, particularmente, la forma de una defensa contra lo español, ya sea contra las influencias estilísticas del barroco gongorino, contra el dominio político-cultural ejercido por España durante la Monarquía Dual (1580–1640) o contra los propios autores portugueses que, en especial durante los siglos XVI y XVII, compusieron su obra total o parcialmente en castellano. ("Literaturas" 26)

To Pérez Isasi's point, casting Spain's influence on early modern Portuguese letters as a foreign invasion of sorts entirely misses the mark. It is an anachronistic reading that depends on a narrow view of language and literature that does not agree with early modern realities.

In focusing on multiple authors across several different genres, *Being Portuguese in Spanish* intends to revalue what Eugenio Asensio describes as "una generación víctima de injusto desdén" ("Autobiografía" 637). Pérez Isasi connects this injustice to a systemic problem: a critical, historiographic, and epistemological apparatus that projects strict categories of nation, language, and literature onto authors whose own texts and contexts do not comply ("Entre dos" 139). At the root of both the Hispanist and Lusist perspectives that would exclude early modern Portuguese literature written in Spanish is the idea that literary canons are inherently monolingual, a position Joan Ramon Resina challenges: "the multilingual and multinational geography of the Iberian peninsula requires us to put into question the monolingual foundation of national literatures and to rethink the nature of the interactions among producers and consumers of literature" (viii).

4

Drawing all-encompassing distinctions between the early modern Spanish and Portuguese literary traditions is a critical imposition that does not serve the time period in question nor those of us who study it.

More than any other issue, questions of allegiance (based on their language of composition and where they lived) are often at the root of campaigns waged against Portuguese authors of the annexation. As Asensio points out, those who would indict Portuguese authors on account of their choice to write in Spanish are misguided: "Indignarse por esta preferencia dada a un idioma extranjero es incurrir en un vicioso anacronismo. Nacionalidad y lengua no se ligaron con vínculos indisolubles hasta la época romántica" ("Fortuna" 311). That said, many Portuguese authors were self-conscious of their decision to write in Spanish, often addressing this concern in the prologue of their published works. It is very common, in fact, to read some form of apologetics in the opening sections of a Portuguese-authored work written in Spanish during the early modern period. The explanation goes something like this: whereas writing in Portuguese would be, in effect, preaching to the choir, writing in Spanish offers the possibility of a wider readership and a deeper impact. A larger audience could serve ideological as well as economic aspirations: "al principio porque estaba de moda en la Corte, más tarde porque era en Castilla en donde radicaban los centros de decisión que afectaban a su patria y la lengua de Castilla les ofrecía mayores posibilidades de promoción social y económica" (Vázquez Cuesta, "Lengua" 601). With a slightly more nationalist slant, the twentieth-century Portuguese critic Hernani Cidade offers his view of the phenomenon:

> Prefere-se o espanhol, porque *é fácil para todos*. Para comunicar ao Mundo a admiração das façanhas dos heróis portugueses, para mostrar a superioridade portuguesa nas várias competências da vida de acção como da vida de pensamento; ou apenas ... para garantia da voga mundial, da perduração através dos séculos de uma grande criação artística, melhor seria—pensava-se—a universalidade europeia do español do que o âmbito confidencial do português. (60)

> Spanish is preferred, because it is easy for everyone. To communicate to the World admiration for the great deeds of Portuguese heroes, to show Portuguese superiority in the

> various contests of action and thought; or merely … the
> promise that a great artistic creation would matter in its
> time and in perpetuity, the European universality of Spanish
> would be better—it was believed—than the limited range of
> Portuguese.[4]

According to Cidade, Spanish was the better choice for Portuguese
writers because it made it easier to communicate Portugal's
achievements worldwide and establish her greatness in perpetuity.
While his assessment aligns with much of what Portuguese
authors of the Dual Monarchy wrote about their own choice
to write in Spanish, the perspective remains incomplete. These
authors were motivated by a multi-faceted rationale that included
social, economic, historical, and cultural factors. Neither the
loyalist nor the traitor, therefore, is an adequate descriptor for
the Portuguese author's relationship to the Spanish language
during the Dual Monarchy. Eugenio Asensio explains: "Hay en
ciertos libros portugueses una simplificación sentimental de la
época filipina que reparte los actores en vendidos y leales, héroes
y traidores. Esta visión deforma, no sólo la perspectiva histórica,
sino también la literaria" ("España" 108). While traditional criticism tends to one of two extremes, throughout this study I assert
that their relationship to Spanish, like the authors themselves, is
somewhere in between.

Even though the language of Portuguese annexation literature
is important, it only addresses the surface of the text. The body of
works of which I am concerned in this study has two constants:
Portugal and Luís de Camões. They are motivated by the *patria*,
and the model that they frequently cite is none other than
Portugal's most celebrated poet (the fatherland and the figurative
father of the land being one in the same). Even when Camões is
not specifically named, his patriotic imprint is visible within the
works of his seventeenth-century disciples. In some instances,
the references to Portugal are obvious, while at other times more
subtle, but Portugal is always there, described in virtually the
same way every time. We see an example of this in *La entrada del
Rey en Portugal* (1621), the first of many *comedias* written by the
Portuguese dramatist Jacinto Cordeiro (1606–46). He succinctly
states his purpose for writing in the play's prologue: "tenho de
eternizar grandezas de minha pátria" ("I must immortalize the
greatness of my homeland"). During the course of the play

he lays bare the virtues of his native soil, including Portugal's love, obedience, loyalty, grandeur, divine electness, and general superiority. These same characteristics recur over and over again in Portuguese literature during the Iberian Union.[5] Overall, it could be said that Portugal inspired these authors to pursue the impossible: to restore the Portuguese nation to its former glory; if it could not be done in reality, they could at least recreate Portugal's greatness in their writings.

It was Camões who captivated the Iberian world and beyond with perhaps the single most important Portuguese work ever written: *Os Lusíadas* (1572). When John de Oliveira e Silva describes the poem as "retrospective ... reflecting more on the glories that once existed than on the present reality" ("Reinventing" 103), he also identifies one of the characteristics of Camões's writing that will motivate Portuguese authors of the Dual Monarchy, who will also emphasize the past (a past that now includes Camões) in their various compositions. Camões and his epic allowed the generation of Portuguese writers that followed to see the extent to which the pen could impact Portugal's image at home and abroad. These authors took inspiration from the life and writings of Camões—wherein they found the greatest expression of all things Portuguese—as they imagined and constructed their own identity. It should come as no surprise then that Camões's name would show up in so many works written at this time. The dozens of editions of *Os Lusíadas* that appeared in the decades following his death are a testament to the importance of his poem during the Iberian Union, which explains why Vanda Anastácio describes it as a "bandeira do autonomismo" ("Leituras" 102; "banner of autonomy").[6] In sum, the early modern Portuguese authors of the annexation that comprise this study adapted to the unique conditions of their time and place by dressing themselves in the language of the empire, finding purpose in the Portugal that was and the Portugal that could be, and looking to Camões as a model of how this could be done.

One way to imagine most criticism on Portuguese literature of the Iberian Union prior to the twenty-first century is to picture a dance between understatement and overstatement where each one thinks it is the lead. When it comes to this body of works, in fact, it is easy to fall into the trap of thinking there are only two sides. Hernani Cidade, for example, claims that there was never a time of greater national pride (27), which is precisely why Glaser thinks the Spanish have generally shown little interest in these Lusocentric texts (Introduction 5).[7] No matter how one evaluates Portugal's literary output during the Dual Monarchy, the Portuguese nation was one of the most widespread topics of sixteenth- and seventeenth-century Portuguese literature; a reality augmented, not stifled, by Spain's sixty-year rule (Cidade 50). In truth, Portugal—as a place, a past, and a people—pervades early modern Iberian literature from beginning to end. More recent scholarship has had some success confronting the reductive readings of yesteryear, but relatively little has been done to revise the overall narrative that has kept Portuguese literature of the Dual Monarchy in relative obscurity since the second half of the seventeenth century. Through a close reading of the texts written by many Portuguese authors during the Iberian Union and the unique context in which they lived, however, a different story emerges.

For more than a century there have been scholars committed to what we would now call Iberian Studies. In *A intercultura de Portugal e Espanha no passado e no futuro* (*Portugal and Spain's Interculture in the Past and in the Future*) published almost a century ago, Ricardo Jorge put forward the term *hispanología* as a way of defining something similar (an intercultural, interdisciplinary approach to Iberian literature) (46). Carolina Michaëlis de Vasconcelos's preface to Jorge's study describes the scholar engaged in such criticism as a *hispanófila*:

> como quem, indagando e explorando, sempre, desde os inícios do seu labutar filológico, havia abraçado, com ardor e amor igual, *Portugal e Espanha*, estudando interessada as relações mútuas dos dois países ... no decorrer dos séculos, mas tambem as diferenças da sua psique e as exteriorizações de ódios, ciumes e rivalidades, em que a fatalidade histórica os envolveu. (Prefácio xiv)

> someone who, inquiring and exploring from the beginning of their philological labors, had always embraced *Portugal and Spain* with the same enthusiasm and love, intently studying the mutual relations of the two countries ... over the centuries, as well as their psychological differences and expressions of hatred, jealousy and rivalry, in which the fatality of history enveloped them.

While this model of reading and interpretation is not limited to the Dual Monarchy, early modern Spanish and Portuguese literature lends itself particularly well to comparative methodologies, as it was a time defined by linguistic, artistic, and political crossings. Early modern Iberia may very well be, in fact, the richest period of artistic cross-pollination the Peninsula has ever enjoyed. My choice to cast such exchanges in a positive light is intentional, as I believe that the blending of literary traditions ultimately enriched both the production and consumption of such works.

Neither Domingo García Peres's *Catálogo razonado, biográfico y bibliográfico de los autores portugueses que escribieron en castellano* (1890) nor any book-length study since clearly distinguishes between one Portuguese author who wrote in Spanish during the annexation and another. The scope of García Peres's work, in fact, is much larger, as he wanted to catalogue all of the Portuguese authors who wrote in Spanish through the late nineteenth century. This by no means lessens the value of the bibliographer's project; it simply invites future generations to discover additional ways to approach these authors and evaluate their various contributions. Unfortunately, however, literary critics and historians have homogenized these authors and their works for the better part of four centuries, casting most who wrote during the annexation as opportunists (and in some cases traitors) with little to offer by way of literary merit. In contrast, the present study maintains that during the Iberian Union a sub-set of Portuguese authors used their Spanish proficiency to construct and promote a national imaginary throughout and beyond the Iberian Peninsula. By distinguishing the present study from García Peres's late nineteenth-century work, I do not wish to distance myself from his outstanding contribution. His text is the most complete bibliography of Portuguese authors who wrote in Spanish currently available and a great point of departure for this and any other related study.

Edward Glaser, a major enthusiast of Peninsular approaches to sixteenth- and seventeenth-century Spanish and Portuguese literature, gave this assessment of early modern Iberian Studies as it stood in the mid-twentieth century: "No obstante la importancia de este campo de la investigación para mejor comprender ambas literaturas, ha despertado en conjunto escasa atención, quizá por la dificultad que ofrece localizar los textos necesarios"

(Introducción ix). By this Glaser does not mean to ignore the work of his predecessors but rather to emphasize that more needs to be done to recover this "importante rama de la investigación hispana" (xi). Clearly, as Glaser continues, there is a great need to "examinar más a fondo una faceta de la historia literaria peninsular desatendida por entero hasta hace poco tiempo" (xii). The good news is that accessibility to these texts has improved significantly over the past two decades, which explains in part why scholars have been paying more attention to this unique period of Iberian literature.[8]

Although the main purpose of *Being Portuguese in Spanish* is to advance a cohesive narrative related to Portuguese authors of the Iberian Union and their various writings in Spanish, it also means to fold into the broader field of Iberian Studies, defined by Santiago Pérez Isasi and Ângela Fernandes as "the methodological consideration of the Iberian Peninsula as a complex, multilingual cultural and literary system" (1). There is no question that Iberian Studies has taken off in the twenty-first century (Gimeno Ugalde 2; Pérez Isasi and Fernandes 3). The last decade alone has seen invaluable contributions to the field, including *A Comparative History of Literatures in the Iberian Peninsula* (2010), *Looking at Iberia* (2013), and *Iberian Modalities* (2013), among many other titles. In 2018, *Criticón* dedicated an entire issue to *Letras hispano-portuguesas de los siglos XVI y XVII*. Iberian Studies, however, has generally favored texts and contexts from the past two centuries. Esther Gimeno Ugalde explains: "en su configuración como nueva disciplina, a los Estudios Ibéricos, especialmente en su vertiente anglosajona, se les exige también un esfuerzo por superar el presentismo" (4). In a volume he edited at the turn of the century, José Miguel Martínez Torrejón put it this way: "l'absence d'une connaissance générale de ces textes est regrettable ainsi que la rareté d'études spécialisées, sans toutefois nier la valeur de celles qui ont été réalisées" (3; "the absence of a general knowledge of these texts is regrettable as is the scarcity of specialized studies, without however denying the value of those which have been realized"). There is no shortage of voices calling attention to the importance of Iberian Studies these days, with some even identifying the specific need to interpret the Dual Monarchy within the same polycentric frame (Gimeno Ugalde 4). Pursuing a generation of authors that has long occupied a space "entre dos tierras y en tierra de nadie" (see Pérez Isasi's essay by the same name) will enhance our understanding of early modern Iberia and Iberian Studies in general.

My approach to Portuguese literature of the Iberian Union is not unlike Richard Helgerson's work on the Elizabethan writing of England in *Forms of Nationhood* (1992); a work defined by crossing boundaries and analyzing discursive forms (Helgerson 6). I have identified a number of works by Portuguese authors of the Dual Monarchy in an effort to shed light on the ways in which these authors used their proficiency in Spanish to promote Portugal within and without the greater Iberian world. Despite the inherent challenges of such a position, which I will detail in the first chapter, the texts produced by these authors represent an early form of national consciousness that merits greater attention. Just as Helgerson describes in his assessment of Elizabethan literature, the Portuguese authors I consider in this study—in spite of their many differences—share a common interest in the nation: "They did not know where either they or history were going. But they did have a firm grasp on the interests they served, and they sensed that identifying those interests with the nation and the nation with those interests would satisfy several needs at once" (11). Helgerson recognizes the layeredness of the texts in question and focuses on how wrapping their ideas in the rhetoric of the nation could serve many different ends. The same can be said of the Portuguese. Writing about Portugal in Spanish was not motivated by any one factor, but by a host of possibilities which I hope to lay bare from chapter to chapter. Thus, I am not trying to make the authors of this investigation one and the same on all accounts, but am trying to highlight one of the points at which they intersect: a common interest in celebrating their *patria*. Just as Portugal is the protagonist of so many of their texts, the Portuguese nation—rather than any one author or genre—is the protagonist of this study.

The first chapter, "*Portugalidade* and the Nation: A Conceptual Framework," establishes the historico-conceptual apparatus through which I frame my approach to Portuguese nationhood. Portugal does not easily fit into general theories of nation and nationalism, especially among constructivists who insist on the modernity of the nation. The Portuguese nation boasts a stable border as early as the twelfth century and a strong sense of collective identity (what I will refer to as *portugalidade*) leading up to and following the maritime age of discovery. In order to reaffirm the national imaginary, early modern Portuguese texts repeatedly evoke a sense of collective identity through the invention and celebration of Portuguese history, language, geography, folklore, and other identifying characteristics, including *saudade*. Rather than ignore the ways in which general theories (e.g., Hobsbawm, Gellner, Anderson) challenge my understanding of the early modern nation, however, I will situate my conceptual framework in a way that allows them to work in concert with Portuguese historians (e.g., Magalhães Godinho, Mattoso, Lourenço, Albuquerque) and the early modern texts that occupy this study.

The second chapter, "Vicente, Camões, and Company: Immortalizing Portugal through the Written Word," looks closely at the two most important Portuguese authors of the sixteenth century and their influence on annexation authors. While Vicente was not the first Portuguese author to take up the language of Castile, his writings in Spanish were exceptional in both number and quality. Whether in Spanish, Portuguese, or another language, his works consistently exalt Portugal. Though the author of the well-known Portuguese tragedy *Castro* was in every way a lusophile, my focus on António Ferreira comes down to his strict views on the relationship between language and literature. Nobody left a more permanent mark on Portuguese authors of the Iberian Union than Luís de Camões, whose masterpiece, *Os Lusíadas* (1572), proved to be a powerful vehicle for nationalist expression. From the time of his death in 1580 through the end of the seventeenth century, virtually every Portuguese author had something to say about Camões and his influence on their writing and thinking. Overall, the purpose of this chapter is to emphasize the legacy of the nationally-interested literature that Vicente, Camões, and many others left for future generations to follow.

The third chapter, "The Epitome of an Era: The Life and Writings of Manuel de Faria e Sousa," questions the Castilianized view of the Portuguese historian, poet, and literary critic. The heart of Faria e Sousa's nationalism, and the central text of this chapter, is his commentary *Lusiadas de Luis de Camoens, principe de los poetas de España* (1639). My approach to this work consists of analyzing the numerous instances in the text where Faria e Sousa manifests his nationalist character, including the significance of the title page; the geographic superiority of Lisbon and the Portuguese nation; the glorification of the Portuguese language; providentialism; the loyalty, bravery, mastery at sea, and other values of the people; and the repeated references to a collective identity. It is anticipated that this will demonstrate the underlying patriotic fervor guiding Faria e Sousa's corpus of works and reveal the mechanisms at work among other Portuguese authors who construct *portugalidade* in a similar way. Beyond the analysis of his commentary, Faria e Sousa's deeply patriotic approach to historiography will also factor into this chapter. In works such as *Epítome de las historias portuguesas*, he both perpetuates and enhances Portugal's glorious past, reminding the reader at every turn of his own Portuguese roots. Although predominantly dressed in Spanish, a careful analysis of his works reveals someone deeply committed to the Portugal of his own mind and making.

Nowhere did Portuguese national consciousness take center stage more than in early modern Iberian theater, the focus of chapter four, "Staging the Nation: Cordeiro, Azevedo, and the Portuguese *Comedia*." The nation becomes an increasingly important dramatic theme in Iberian theater during the sixteenth and seventeenth centuries, not to mention an effective form of mass media. Portuguese themes, language, and history, in particular, appear in numerous plays authored by both Spanish and Portuguese playwrights. Works about Portugal by Lope de Vega, Tirso de Molina, and Pedro Calderón de la Barca alone number in at least the twenties. This chapter traces the roots of the nation-theme in Iberian theater from the works of Gil Vicente and Bartolomé de Torres Naharro onward. Despite the widespread participation of the Spanish in the dramatization of both Spanish and Portuguese themes, the majority of this chapter privileges the Portuguese playwrights Jacinto Cordeiro and Ângela de Azevedo, whose plays overflow with *portugalidade*. Cordeiro, for example, was both an accomplished craftsman of the *comedia* and a self-identified Portuguese poet-dramatist given to the praise of his *patria*, whose legacy he was committed to preserve. From beginning to end, his plays display this very objective. My analysis of Cordeiro's work focuses on two clear examples of nation-minded drama: *La entrada del Rey en Portugal* and *Los doze de Inglaterra*. Beyond Cordeiro's dramatic corpus, one of the most stimulating instances of Portuguese national consciousness in early modern Iberian drama appears in Ângela de Azevedo's three *comedias*. A close reading and analysis of her plays showcase the unique way in which her dramatic works perform *portugalidade*. While Azevedo does not openly criticize the Spanish empire in her works, they clearly establish the preeminence and uniqueness of Portugal, highlighting, among other things, geographic and linguistic superiority. Whether it is where they go or what they say, Azevedo's characters regularly manifest the Portuguese character of their creator, openly affirming a place, a history, and a language that surpass all others.

The final chapter of this study, "Anticipating and Remembering the Restoration: Sousa de Macedo, Violante do Céu, and Manuel de Melo," considers some of the key works leading up to and following the restoration of Portuguese independence in 1640. Perhaps more than any other text written during the Dual Monarchy, António de Sousa de Macedo's *Flores de España, Excelencias de Portugal* (1631) stands out for the extremity of its nationalist sentiment and foreshadows the author's active role in the defense of Portuguese autonomy in the aftermath of the Restoration. Sousa de Macedo was not the only Portuguese author actively preserving and defending Portugal's newfound autonomy. In fact, as one might expect, a myriad of works highlight the events surrounding the Restoration and support Portugal's right to independence. This is evident among poets (e.g., Violante do Céu), playwrights (e.g., Manuel de Araujo de Castro), and many others. One of the most active and important voices of post-Restoration Portugal was that of Francisco Manuel de Melo (1608–66). Manuel de Melo's subversive portrayal of Spanish decadence in his account of Spain's conflict with Catalonia, among other writings, is a clear reminder that between his Spanish mother and his Portuguese father, Manuel de Melo ultimately identified with the nationality of the latter. Overall, this chapter looks at some of the unique ways in which Portuguese authors sustained nationalist discourse in a post-Restoration Portugal.

António de Sousa de Macedo's treatise, *Flores de España, Excelencias de Portugal* (1631), closes with a question borrowed from *Os Lusíadas*. He asks the reader whether it is better to be king of the entire world minus Portugal, or to rule over Portugal alone. After hundreds of pages of superlative praise for his native land, the answer to this rhetorical question is self-evident. It could be said, in effect, that his reference to Camões is nothing more than a restatement of the thesis governing the entire work. But what, as twenty-first century readers, are we to understand from such an ostentatious proposition? Moreover, under what social, political, and historical conditions was such a question put forward in the first place? While Sousa de Macedo's answer is of interest, it is not nearly as consequential as the assertion inherent in his appeal to Camões. In a time before nations and nationalism—at least by modern standards—what are we supposed to make of the author's overt exaltation of Portugal?

During Spain's annexation of Portugal from 1580 to 1640, many Portuguese authors voiced something similar to what we find in *Flores de España*. Making sense of that voice, however, is not easy, regardless of what facile interpretations recycled over centuries may say. The writers considered in this study made their affection for Portugal known almost exclusively in the language of the empire. What does the free use of the Spanish and Portuguese languages tell us about these writers and the time in which they lived? Furthermore, annexation authors invoke a rhetoric of nation and nationalism well before the rise of the modern nation-state. They do this with a degree of self-consciousness that is difficult to define because it is attuned to a collectivity that transcends any one writer individually. Is this national consciousness? If so, what could that possibly mean in the context of early modernity? The words written in Spanish by the Portuguese during the Dual Monarchy offer a response to these questions by challenging readers to make sense of the wheres, whens, whys, and hows of its production. The fascinating intersection of identity, language, history, and politics found within these texts leads to further questions about this often misunderstood and historically neglected period of Iberian letters.

Chapter One

Portugalidade and the Nation
Toward a Conceptual Framework

The onset of the Iberian Union enabled a generation of writers to see Portugal in a new way. As Martim de Albuquerque points out, what was signified by *pátria*, or homeland, changed for many Portuguese authors during the course of the Iberian Union: "Assim como logrou ser incentivo de resistência em 1580, a ideia de pátria tranformou-se durante o jugo filipino igualmente numa arma do espírito autonomista" (166; "Along with inciting resistance in 1580, the idea of homeland during the Philippine bondage was likewise transformed into a weapon of the autonomous spirit"). Many Portuguese authors of the period brought a newfound vision of Portugal to their writing, constructing, word by word, an identity distinct from that of the Spanish empire. Rather than a disjointed view of Portugal, many of these texts establish a common vision of the "nation" consisting of linguistic, geographic, historical, religious, and ethnic characteristics. They lay bare the roots of early modern Portuguese national consciousness and contextualize the fundamental, yet problematic, relationship between language, identity, literature, and politics. Additionally, they highlight an unparalleled period of artistic cross-pollination on the Iberian Peninsula. In order to unpack the phenomena I am describing, a number of concepts will need clarification, including nation and *portugalidade* (Portugueseness).[1] Furthermore, the literature produced during the Dual Monarchy is unintelligible without a basic understanding of the history that preceded it, including the decades leading up to 1580. This chapter, therefore, puts forward the conceptual and historical framework that orients the rest of *Being Portuguese in Spanish*. In order to understand the collectivity annexation authors invoke (invent), it is necessary to understand the language of early modern Portuguese national consciousness.

The early modern brand of Portuguese identity constructed by annexation authors is based on a creative fusion of fact and fiction. Many nation theories contend that this kind of primordial identity is a far cry from the constructions of nationness emerging at the end of the eighteenth century and thereafter. That it is not modern, however, does not preclude it from being a nation nor its members from being nationalists. Which is not to say that early modern Portugal measures up to the standards applied to modern nations. What modernity offers is the possibility of forming a collectivity that seemingly includes *all* of society. The ability to reach the masses through media, education (literacy), infrastructure (transportation), and other developments sparked nationalist movements throughout the world beginning at the end of the eighteenth century. These advances made it possible for a broad range of individuals to simultaneously conceive of a collective national body, a notion well-described by Benedict Anderson as an imagined community. Even though the sixteenth and seventeenth centuries were generally devoid of these modern developments, national imaginaries of limited scale could and did exist.[2]

It would transcend the scope of this study to comb through legal archives in search of the commoner's voice in an effort to prove that all those living in early modern Portugal identified themselves as Portuguese (as opposed to residents of their particular village or region), although some have taken on this laborious task to varying degrees.[3] As far as national identity is concerned, the Portuguese historian José Mattoso acknowledges a repeated effort among the elite to identify themselves as part of a collective, but is quick to point out the demographic narrowness of this conception (97–98). At the very least, the Portuguese nation embodied in the texts of early modernity consists of the educated—what we might call a "Lettered Nation," to borrow, and slightly modify, Ángel Rama's term—although a larger cross-section of society may have participated in the construction of this collectivity. In some cases, these authors were not as removed from political activity as Mattoso suggests (98). António de Sousa de Macedo, for one, was commissioned by João IV to write in defense of Portuguese sovereignty following the Restoration. Cidade sees the Portuguese nationalists writing on behalf of their *patria* as a mouthpiece for the entire nation (8). In reality, Portuguese annexation authors writing in Spanish did not worry themselves with the collective expression of their pens as much as the widespread consumption of their ideas. Spanish was the only language that would allow them to promote their identity throughout the world. Some might take issue with the widespread use of "nation" and its various forms (i.e., national, nationalism, nationalist) in this study, hastily categorizing such an effort as misguided or anachronistic. Nevertheless, as I will detail throughout this work, nation is both the word that best captures the object of interest of so many early modern Portuguese authors and the term that they themselves often employ in their writings.

Portugal is particularly subversive in its questioning of nation theories, especially of constructivists who insist on the modernity of the nation. This may explain why Portugal is left out of many nation studies, despite the fact that many are implicitly Eurocentric. As often occurs, the "Euro" of Eurocentrism excludes the Iberian Peninsula in favor of mainstream European nations— Germany, England, France, Italy; hardly justified in any context, the least of which being the sixteenth and seventeenth centuries. Reading through many general theories of nation and nationalism (e.g., Smith, Gellner, Anderson, Hobsbawm), it appears as though the authors of these works are not familiar with Portuguese history. Portugal has an unsettling effect on a lot of the arguments put forward in such studies, so it comes as no surprise that the country is overlooked and/or superficially cast aside. While Portugal may fall outside of mainstream Eurocentrism today, there is no excuse for ignoring one of the world powers of early modernity when considering nations and nationalism before the late eighteenth century. Portuguese historians (e.g., Mattoso, Lourenço, Magalhães Godinho), on the other hand, take a more straightforward approach to the nation, unencumbered by the "modernity complex" of more recent theories. For most of them, the early modern identity of the Portuguese nation is a given, seeing that Portugal's collectivity has been developing since at least the twelfth century, when its borders were originally established. Vitorino Magalhães Godinho, in fact, *ends* his study on the emergence of the Portuguese nation in 1480. This seems to suggest that by the late fifteenth century, some form of the Portuguese nation was in place; which makes sense when one considers what happened with Portuguese literature in the sixteenth century. While it is true that many of the most significant theories published on the nation over the last few decades fail to acknowledge Portugal in their various conceptions, as Onésimo Almeida points out, "the national dialogue on identity is comprised, to a large extent, of a series of monologues, occurring in Portugal, as in other places, without a mutual theoretical vocabulary shared by its participants" (*National* 10). It follows, therefore, that a more complete view of Portuguese national identity will rely on the best ideas from within and beyond Portugal's borders.

My general conception of nation, nationalism, national identity, and national culture borrows from the extended metaphor of the *theatrum mundi*.[4] As Shakespeare's well-known verses from *As You Like It* propose, "All the world's a stage / and all the men and women merely players" (2.7.139-40). Of course, there are many different stages within this macro-vision of life, the nation being one such theatrical space. By *nation* I invoke both Homi Bhabha's narration (script) and Benedict Anderson's imagined community, the relationship of which will be discussed in detail hereafter. The identity of this community emerges from its attempts to weave characteristics into a pattern of self-definition. That is, *national identity* refers to the collective personality that evolves from performing the nation; the "list" that every nation unfailingly creates to define itself. The product of this performance by the imagined community, then, becomes the content of the *national culture*. The common element of this whole process is *nationalism*. Nationalism wants to discover the nation, define its identity, and participate in its culture. In dramatic terms, nationalism is the audience. In other words, just as there is no play without an audience, there is no nation, no national identity, and no national culture without nationalism.[5] The product of this performance is not a stable fabric, but a list of characteristics as imaginary as the nation itself, but with the potential to become a culture if the identity is repeatedly learned and performed across society. Throughout this chapter, I will lay bare the intertexts that inform the conceptual apparatus driving these definitions, including their relation to early modern Iberia.

The Portuguese nation of the sixteenth and seventeenth centuries is a nation of texts, of which I am specifically concerned with written forms. This textual revolution was not uniquely Portuguese—the printing press had this effect across Europe—but within the thousands of pages penned by the Portuguese is found a rhetoric of nationhood that clarifies what we are to understand by the frequent early modern references to the Portuguese nation. Overall, they tell a consistent story about Portugal; a narration that did not die with the birth of the Iberian Union. Indeed with the loss of autonomy that resulted from the Iberian Union came a heightened insistence on Portugal as nation in Portuguese-authored works. Benedict Anderson's discussion of simultaneity and its role in the development of national consciousness, not to mention his emphasis on textuality, provide a compelling point of contact with Portuguese annexation literature. In dialogue with Erich Auerbach and Walter Benjamin, Anderson defines time as "a simultaneity of past and future in an instantaneous present" (24). This statement captures the essence of the Portuguese authors guiding this study, each of which (re)builds Portugal's *past* (histori-cal, linguistic, literary, etc.) in a textual *present* (e.g., commentary on *Os Lusíadas, comedias, Flores de España*, etc.) in an effort to promote their autonomy in the *future*. Anderson explains that this simultaneity creates an imagined community in which a plurality of seemingly unrelated subjects collectively participate (27–32). While writing connects the Portuguese authors from 1580 to 1640, the collective imaginary defined in their works appears independently of one another. Of particular value to my read-ing of Portuguese annexation authors is Anderson's observation regarding one of Marco Kartodikromo's short stories. In reference to the repeated use of the possessive adjective "our," Anderson sug-gests that this utterance signifies a collectivity among readers that constitutes the embryo of the "representative body" (32). Textually speaking, this collectivity would appear between the lines, as evidenced, for example, in Faria e Sousa's commentary; nearly invisible on the one hand, while clearly marking the community on the other.

While Anderson certainly popularized the idea of simultane-ity in the construction of the national imaginary, similar ideas have circulated since at least the late nineteenth century. Ernest Renan's essay "What is a Nation?" (1882), for example, states that "the essence of a nation is that all individuals have many things in common" (11). He goes on to analyze several aspects that might be considered in this collectivity, most of which echo the same topics Luís de Camões emphasizes in *Os Lusíadas*, several annexation authors popularize in their works, and Portuguese writers have crystallized over the centuries. While Renan shows the insufficiencies of defining a nation by race, language, and religion, he recognizes that they all play a part in the "legacy of memories" (19) that must be in place for a nation to come into existence. Eric Hobsbawm considers all of these characteristics part of what he designates proto-nationalism, or "feelings of collective belonging" (*Nations* 46). More specifically, his model defines popular proto-nationalism in terms of religio-ethnic identification and politico-historical consciousness. According to Hobsbawm, then, early modern Portugal would be something of an early nation. The role of the individual in all of these theories is fundamental. Onésimo Almeida explains: "Ultimately, each individual creates their own interpretation of the past and constructs it in their own way ... and it is this construct that they identify with" (*National* 12). Without that self-identification, there is no participation in the nation.

Finally, and in addition to the legacy of the past mentioned above, Renan describes another critical aspect of the nation: "present-day consent, the desire to live together, the will to perpetuate the value of the heritage that one has received in an undivided form" (19). While the nation-building authors of the Portuguese annexation appear united in a common cause, the same cannot be said of the entire country; otherwise, Portugal arguably would never have lost its sovereignty. Despite the temporal distance, Portuguese annexation literature opens up a meaningful dialogue with those currently engaged with issues of nation and nationalism. That there is something deeply modern about early modern Portugal cannot be denied. Somewhere between the primordialists and the constructivists rests early modern Portugal, bursting with national consciousness at a time well before the modern nation took the global stage.

Although twenty-first century definitions of the nation certainly differ from those of centuries past, the distinction is not, as some would contend, a matter of existence. The frequent references of Manuel de Faria e Sousa to the "Nación Portuguesa" in his commentary of *Os Lusíadas*, demonstrate, for example, that the term "nation" abounded in sixteenth- and seventeenth-century Iberian texts. However, while prevalent, a consensus definition of the nation is not only difficult to ascertain from one author to the next, but sometimes even within the works of a single writer.

Contrary to Hobsbawm's assertion regarding the meaning of "nación" before 1884 (*Nations* 46–47), Sebastián de Covarrubias Orozco's *Tesoro de la lengua castellana o española* (1611) offers a distinct view of the early modern nation. On the surface, Covarrubias's definition seems to conform to the constructivist conception of the early modern nation: "reyno o provincia estendida, como la nación española" (823). While this definition limits the nation to a particular geography as Hobsbawm suggests, it is still too vague to lead to any immediate conclusions. An analysis of *nación* according to other related entries in Covarrubias's dictionary, however, opens up the seventeenth-century concept of nation significantly. In his definition of *España*, for example, Covarrubias (1) acknowledges the synonymy between Spain and Iberia, (2) mentions the three major provinces therein (Bética, Lusitânia, and Tarraconense), and (3) identifies *its* language (550–51). The inconsistencies between this definition and that of *nación* are immediately apparent. If nation, for example, is a vast province, and an example of this is the *nación española* as cited before, how can a province be composed of provinces? Are there different kinds of provinces? It would follow that while *España* normally serves as a synonym for Iberia—as both its own definition as well as the entries for Castilla, Aragón, Porto, and *Lusitânia* suggest—it can also refer to a specific part of the Peninsula. After all, Covarrubias, of all people, was aware of the many languages spoken throughout the Peninsula. Nevertheless, he refers to the single language of the *españolado*. If nation only meant Iberia in its entirety, a reference to "la lengua" would be reductive and unjustified (550).

Covarrubias defines *provincia* as "una parte de tierra estendida" (885), which hardly elucidates our understanding of nation except that it sets up a synonymous relationship between *nación* and *provincia*, in which *reyno* could also be included. Here, as in other places, Covarrubias appears trapped between etymology and contemporary usage, which is much more difficult to standardize. In his note to the reader at the beginning of the text, Covarrubias uses the word *nación* in context: "castellana antigua, compuesta de una mezcla de las que introduxeron las naciones que al principio vinieron a poblar a España. La primera, la de Túbal, y después désta, otras muchas, de algunas de las quales haze mención Plinio; conviene saber: los hebreos, los persas, los fenices, los celtas, los penos, los cartagineses" (20). In this passage *nación* represents a people more than a place, which coincides with Covarrubias's definition of *gentes*: "las naciones esparcidas por el Orbe" (636). Considered altogether, entries on *España, reyno, provincia*, and *gentes* suggest that Covarrubias's nation consists of both a place—synonymous to his entries on province and kingdom on the one hand, and Iberia on the other—as well as a people with linguistic and other identifying characteristics. On the whole, it is a flexible term with many possible meanings. In the context of early modern Portuguese literature, this amplified view of the nation stands out even more clearly.

Notwithstanding the ambivalence surrounding the term "nation" and its development since early modernity, no other word better describes the object of interest of so many Portuguese texts written during the sixteenth and seventeenth centuries. Two initial questions emerge from situating the issue of nation and nationalism within Portugal during the Dual Monarchy: what did the Portuguese actually lose in 1580 and, similarly, what did they gain in 1640? The nation, in all its complexity, is at the heart of these two questions. Developing ideas regarding nationhood made pre-annexation and post-Restoration Portugal two distinct places. Yes, 1580 was the year of the Spanish takeover, but it was really the end of something much larger that had been occurring for decades: the decline of Portugal's imperial dominance. The sixty years separating 1580 and 1640 saw a generation of writers collectively look back on Portugal's rich history in an effort to fashion something in the present that might shape the future. The consistency with which they did this will be made apparent in chapters three, four, and five. What follows in this chapter is a concise overview of some of the most important figures, places, events, and concepts of what would become *portugalidade*. They are offered by way of introduction, with more in-depth analysis coming in subsequent chapters.

As voluminous as Portuguese history is, its pre-modern identity rests primarily on the following features: its naming, the fixing of its borders, its successes in conflict, its maritime discoveries, and the development of its own vernacular. The natural point of departure for this historical journey to Portugal is the actual name of the country. While history has provided some consensus regarding the origin of the name, the "official story" behind the name of Portugal and its beginnings remains elusive. Etymologically,

Portugal apparently derives from the Roman name *Portus Cale*, with *Cale* being the name of a preexisting northern settlement near present-day Porto. Once the Romans conquered this area (around the third century BC), *Portus* (i.e., port) was added to the name. Over the next thousand years *Portus Cale* became *Portucale* and then *Portugale*. By the eleventh and twelfth centuries the area between the Douro and Minho rivers was finally known as *Portugal*. Portugal, however, was not the only name by which the country was known. By the end of the fifteenth century, and especially in the sixteenth, the name Lusitânia was used as a way of evoking Portugal's antiquity (Albuquerque 276–82). In his *Grammatica da lingoagem portuguesa* (1536), Fernão de Oliveira reflects on the mythic qualities of the names Lusitânia and Portugal:

> Luso, que também enobreceu esta terra, não foi grego, mas de Portugal nascido e creado, filho de Liceleu, e este recebeu em seu reino a El-Rei Dionísio, ou Dinis, com festas de sacrifícios e devoções, porque já desde então os Portugueses sabem conhecer e servir e louvar a Deus. E deste rei Luso se chamou a terra em que vivemos Lusitânia, a qual depois chamaram Turdugal e agora, mudando algumas letras, Portugal, não do porto de Gaia ... mas dos Túrdulos e Galos, duas nações de homens que vieram morar em esta terra, segundo conta Estrabão no terceiro livro da sua *Geografia*. E assim desta feição, já também este nome de Portugal é antigo. (2.40–41)

> Luso, who also ennobled this land, was not Greek, but born and raised in Portugal, son of Liceleu, who King Dionísio, or Dinis, received in his kingdom with celebrations of sacrifice and devotion, because ever since then the Portuguese know how to serve and praise and have a relationship with God. And this King Luso called the land in which we live Lusitânia, which they would later call Turdugal and now, moving a few letters around, Portugal, not from the port of Gaia ... but from Túrdulos and Galos, two groups of people that came to live in this land. ... And thus from this sketch, it is also clear that the name of Portugal is ancient.

Apparent in this description is the distinction between Oliveira's understanding of the name Portugal and the official version explained above. In both cases there is an effort to memorialize Portugal by situating it in antiquity. The what, therefore, is not nearly as important as the how, when, and why. Despite a differing view of Portugal's etymology, Oliveira's conception of King Luso directly coincides with the widely accepted legend of the time. Within decades of Oliveira's publication, Luso would motivate the title of Camões's epic poem *Os Lusíadas*, inspire Portuguese authors during the Dual Monarchy, and eventually become a way of speaking of all things Portuguese—a distinction it still maintains.

The political inception of Portugal came during the twelfth century, coincidentally around the same time that its name evolved into its present form. Due to his role in the Reconquest of Galicia and northern Portugal, Henrique of Burgundy (1066–1112) was simultaneously appointed Count of Portugal and married to Alfonso VI de León's illegitimate daughter Teresa in 1093. At the time, Portugal belonged to Castilla y León's large feudal network. Following Henrique's death in 1112, his son, Afonso Henriques, inherited his father's position as count. Within twenty years Afonso had knighted himself, raised an army, exiled his mother, triumphed in battle, and proclaimed himself Prince of Portugal. This independent spirit would aid Afonso in the coming decades as he declared, and eventually achieved, political autonomy through the *manifestis probatum* (1179) issued by Pope Alexander III. By the time Rome entered the picture, however, Afonso Henriques had already ruled for four decades. Perhaps more than any other year, 1139 proved pivotal to the future of Afonso and the country that would crown him its first king. During this year both the Battle of São Mamede and the Battle of Ourique took place, wherein Afonso and his outnumbered soldiers faced forces led by his mother in the first instance and the Almoravids in the second. These battles served as a prologue to the declaration of sovereignty that would come that same year and set Afonso on a course that would have him unofficially recognized as king in 1143, thirty-six years prior to the papal stamp of approval. Many of the prized virtues of Portuguese identity and the foundational myths that would come to define the nation are based on Afonso's character and the storied events of 1139.

It is not surprising to find so many Portuguese writers of the sixteenth and seventeenth centuries dedicated to the celebration and elaboration of these significant events. What existed during pre-modernity and was named during the sixteenth century, became, in the seventeenth century, the Portuguese nation. The Battle of Ourique, as Hernani Cidade explains, demonstrates this very point: "Surgira no século XV a lenda da aparição de Cristo a D. Afonso Henriques, em Ourique, mas foi a século XVII que a pormenorizou, com ela formando a Portugal a auréola de *povo eleito*" (162; "In the fifteenth century the legend of Christ's appearance to D. Afonso Henriques, in Ourique, was born, but it was the seventeenth century that added all of the details that would fit for Portugal the halo of a *chosen people*"). The development of this and other foundational fictions during the early modern period reveals the central role of myth-making in the formation of national identity. While the earliest accounts of Ourique do not even mention Christ, by the seventeenth century knowledge of the legend was so ubiquitous that an entire *comedia* was written on the subject (Tirso's *Las quinas de Portugal*).

A prominent feature of Portugal's pre-modern history and a fundamental aspect of its development as a nation is the creation of its borders, which, by the end of the thirteenth century, reflect their present-day position. Over the centuries, historians have emphasized the unique stability of Portugal's border, a characteristic commonly reserved exclusively for "modern" nations. As Orlando Ribeiro observes, no other national border in the world approaches the longstanding fixity of Portugal: "A fronteira portuguesa, fixada nas linhas gerais quando terminou a Reconquista, é o mais antigo limite político mundial, perdurando há sete séculos com essa função" (59; "The Portuguese border, fixed upon general lines when the Reconquest ended, is the most ancient political boundary in the world, a function it has maintained for seven centuries"). Those who would explain away Portugal's longstanding borders and polity as the mere product of chance, might consider the following observation by A. H. Oliveira Marques:

> A fronteira portuguesa, tal como existe desde o século XIII, não é um simples produto dos acasos da Reconquista sobre os Muçulmanos. Nem sequer se pode considerar o resultado fortuito de aventuras militares contra os vizinhos cristãos. As suas origens e características permanentes têm de procurar-se no passado remoto e explicar-se principalmente pelos sistemas administrativos romano e muçulmano, acrescidos ainda do quadro eclesiástico cristão. (25)

The Portuguese border, as it has existed since the thirteen century, is not simply a fortunate outcome of the Reconquest over the Muslims. It cannot even be considered the fortuitous result of military adventures against the neighboring Christians. Its origins and longstanding characteristics must be pursued in the remote past and explained primarily by the Roman and Muslim administrative systems, increased still within a Christian-ecclesiastical framework.

The stability and longevity of Portugal's border remain virtually undisputed from one Portuguese historian to the next and provide an important point of departure for discussing Portuguese geography in particular, and its nationhood before the late eighteenth century in general. As José Mattoso maintains, both these factors play crucial roles in the formation and solidification of national identity in Portugal (7).

Beyond the monumental successes at São Mamede and Ourique, other armed conflicts have played a decisive role in the formation of the Portuguese self-concept (16). Just as the Reconquest had a major impact on the development of Spanish identity and the patterns of conquest that followed in the New World, the Portuguese Reconquest was similarly transformative: "Portugal nasce desta luta contra os mouros. É uma guerra política e religiosa. Enquanto que se reconquista o solo da Pátria expulsa-se o inimigo da Fé" (Dias 17; "Portugal is born out of this struggle with the Moors. It is a political and religious war. While the soil of the homeland is reconquered the enemy of the Faith is banished"). Afonso's crusading successes were a catalyst for the papal bull issued in 1179, convincing the pope that he was indeed worthy to rule. The legitimization of Portugal by Rome, however, did not keep the neighboring kingdoms from attempting to retake what they felt was rightfully theirs. In fact, during the four centuries separating the 1179 decision from the annexation of Portugal in 1580, Portugal and Castile were involved in several conflicts, each of which intensified Portugal's sense of autonomy. Ribeiro describes the positive impact that these victories had on the Portuguese: "Numa época de proliferação de efémeras formas políticas, numa Península sem unidade, Portugal aparece como uma nação viável, capaz de resistir à unificação empreendida por um poderoso Estado vizinho e de ... não mais se confundir com ele" (21; "At a time of proliferation of ephemeral political forms, in a Peninsula without unity, Portugal appears as a viable nation, capable of resisting the unification undertaken by a powerful neighboring State and of ... not being confused with it anymore"). It was the outcome of these conflicts and the confrontation of the Portuguese with those of other lands that fortified their collective sense of self through differentiation: "Estes acontecimentos deram aos habitantes comuns do campo e da cidade ... a noção clara do outro enquanto oposto aos nacionais" (Mattoso 17–18; "These events gave the common inhabitants from the country and the city ... a clear notion of the other as opposed nationals"). "We" and "them" are mutually exclusive and mutually dependent, the characterization of one clarifying the identification of the other.

Peninsular history demonstrates that otherness is a moving target. The Reconquest, for example, cast the "other" in terms of faith. This shared struggle saw Christians fighting side by side against Muslims. When the Peninsula divided into competing kingdoms, political loyalties put Christians in conflict one with the other. This was especially true of Portugal and Castile. An aversion to foreigners grew out of the wars between the two kingdoms that occurred during the reign of Fernando and João I (Mattoso 17). This nationalist sentiment, however, was not limited to the upper ranks of Portuguese society: "O povo todo este tempo, ainda que nunca foy ouvido, sempre insistio em não se unir com Castela" (Albuquerque 237; "All of this time the people, even if they were never heard, always insisted on not uniting with Castile"). The single most important Portuguese victory over Castile came on the fields of Aljubarrota in 1385, the significance of which comes into view through Jorge Dias's observation: "Esta afirmação da força nacional parece ter despertado novas energias e surge a ideia de ir contra o antigo inimigo de tantos séculos. Portugal já possuía então embarcações que lhe permetiam uma expedição militar ao Norte de África e, em 1415, os portugueses conquistam Ceuta aos mouros. Era o começo da fase de expansão marítima" (18; "This affirmation of national strength seems to have awakened new energies and the idea emerges of going against the ancient enemy of so many centuries. By then Portugal already possessed vessels that made a military expedition to North Africa possible and, in 1415, the Portuguese conquer the Moors at Ceuta. It was the beginning phase of maritime expansion"). Portuguese authors of the Dual Monarchy often invoke the many layers of significance surrounding Aljubarrota in their works. Portugal's ability to repeatedly resist Castile contributed to a growing sense of national consciousness that would lead them from the battlefields of the late fourteenth century to the wave of exploration and discovery of the fifteenth (Ribeiro 60). That the Portuguese were always out-numbered and often victorious, imbued this consciousness with a sense of divine election.

Any approach to Portuguese history falls short if it fails to mention the importance of the sea, as virtually all aspects of Portuguese culture flow from the nation's rich maritime tradi-tion: "A força atractiva do Atlântico, esse grande mar povoado de tempestades e de mistérios, foi a alma da Nação e foi com ele que se escreveu a História de Portugal" (Dias 15; "The attractive force of the Atlantic, that great ocean populated by storms and mysteries, was the soul of the Nation through which the History of Portugal was written"). One of the protagonists of Portugal's rich history is the ocean, particularly the Atlantic. By virtue of its geography, Portugal was destined to stake its future on the ebb and flow of the sea. Dias explains: "A cultura portuguesa tem carácter essencialmente expansivo, determinado em parte por uma situação geográfica que lhe conferiu a missão de estreitar os laços entre os continentes e os homens" (14; "The Portuguese culture essentially has an expansive character, determined in part by a geographic location that bestowed upon it the mission of closing the loop between continents and men"). After centuries of struggle to establish sovereignty and territory, Portugal asserted its collective strength abroad, expanding her borders well beyond the confines of Iberia. Dias argues that this influenced the unification and permanence of the nation more than anything else:

> Portugal, porém, apresenta uma curiosa particularidade de unificação. Embora a origem da Nação se deva também à política, à vontade dum príncipe, que naturalmente se aproveitou de certas aspirações de independência latentes nas populações de Entre Douro e Minho, a unificação e a perma-nência da Nação deve-se ao mar. Foi a grande força atractiva do Atlântico que amontoou no litoral a maior densidade da população portuguesa do Norte. (12)

> Portugal, nevertheless, presents a curious instance of unification. Despite the origin of the Nation also owing to politics, the will

of a prince, who naturally took advantage of certain hidden aspirations of independence among the populations of Entre Douro e Minho, the unification and permanence of the Nation comes down to the sea. It was the great attractive force of the Atlantic that gathered the greatest concentration of the Portuguese population from the North to the coast.

The sea had a unifying effect on the Portuguese, bringing together those who would navigate these waters and acting as a link between those who stayed at home and those who sailed to other lands. While initially contact with the *other* would come through the establishment and defense of its borders, Portugal's maritime expansion intensified the process of differentiation, resulting in a self-definition best described as *portugalidade*: "A Expansão portuguesa, que pôs milhares de portugueses em contacto directo com outros povos e outras civilizações, veio evidentemente reforçar o sentimento nacional" (Mattoso 18; "Portuguese Expansion, which put thousands of Portuguese in direct contact with other peoples and civilizations, clearly strengthened national senti- ment.") Although Mattoso is careful not to overestimate the scale of Portuguese identity at this time, he acknowledges the wide- spread effect of the maritime expansion, emphasizing its ability to reinforce commonalities among the Portuguese: "Embora não fossem directamente vividas por toda a população nacional, sabemos que a sua experimentação envolveu, de maneira directa ou indirecta, uma porção enorme de gente de todas as condições e origens e por isso as suas consequências no processo de catego- rização da identidade nacional se fizeram sentir mesmo nas áreas rurais e no interior do País" (18; "Although they were not directly experienced by all of the national population, we know that their experimentation involved, directly or indirectly, an enormous number of people of all conditions and origins and for that reason their impact on the process of categorization of national identity was felt in rural areas and in the interior of the country.") There was nothing new about the sea itself; what changed during the age of expansion was Portugal's relationship to it. Whether by direct or indirect interaction, the Portuguese anchored their collective identity and destiny to their maritime undertakings.

For the rest of Iberia, the fifteenth century was a time of consolidation and reconquest. With the unification of Castile and Aragon in 1469 and the subsequent fall of Granada in 1492, the five kingdoms making up Iberia were reduced to three. While the nation that would eventually become Spain was beginning to take shape, however, Portugal was busy running its borders and influence far beyond the Iberian Peninsula. Exploration and conquest gave birth to the Portuguese Empire, which, in the period following the conquest of Ceuta in 1415, grew to include Brazil, parts of the Middle East and Asia, sections of Africa, and a number of islands. One remarkable aspect of this imperial expansion has to do with scale. First, there's the disparity between Portugal's population of roughly two million and the several millions they ruled over. What is more, the homeland is diminutive compared to the size of the empire. Nevertheless, the Portuguese never let their quantitative deficiency get in the way of their ambitions. As far as they were concerned, the odds were always in their favor. The Portuguese identity of previous centuries—rooted in the lands of reconquest and defense—was now inseparably connected to the timelessness of the sea. It is this feature of *portugalidade*, according to Cidade, that distinguishes Portugal more than anything else: "A independência de Portugal, não é tanto uma fatalidade geográfica ou étnica, como uma solicitação, ao mesmo tempo que oferta, do Oceano" (20; "The independence of Portugal is not so much a geographic or ethnic fatality as a solicitation, and at the same time offer, from the Ocean").

The armed conflicts that defined Portugal's territory and the exploration that expanded its reach well beyond Iberia, all form part of the shared historical experience that is central to the development of national consciousness (Gellner 43). Also of fundamental importance to the founding of a nation is the idea of a common past and shared existence:

> é fundamentalmente um fenómeno da consciência colectiva, que se baseia, por um lado, numa percepção das diferenças comuns verificadas em relação à população de outros países, ao nível das estruturas sociais, das manifestações culturais (nomeadamente de língua, dos hábitos e dos valores) e, por outro lado, de uma certa percepção do passado comum. (Mattoso 102)

> it is fundamentally a phenomenon of collective consciousness, that is based, on the one hand, on a perception of common

differences verified in relation to the population of other countries, at the level of social structures, of cultural manifestations (namely language, habits and values) and, on the other hand, on a certain perception of a common past.

By the end of the pre-modern era, Portugal had enough of a past to begin fashioning a collective identity. While this brand of national identity was not the fully-developed version that would appear during the late eighteenth century and thereafter, it contained many of the markers of a developing nation: defined territory, shared history, and a cohesive polity.

Not to be forgotten in the development of the Portuguese nation is the role of language, which plays a decisive and, at times, confusing role in identity formation on the Iberian Peninsula (especially during the Dual Monarchy). As H. V. Livermore observes, "the general replacement of Latin by Portuguese occurred in the course of the thirteenth century" (55). With the advent of the printing press, which fostered an unprecedented degree of standardization and dissemination, language became increasingly more important and complex as a function of identity. The heightened awareness of language—both native and foreign—pressed upon the late fifteenth-century European imaginary, led to an outburst of multilingualism and polyglot literature. It is within this historical moment that a Portuguese author used Castilian in his works for the first time (Vázquez Cuesta, "Lengua" 601). This type of literature, as Hugo Beardsmore explains, consists of two main variants, the second of which applies specifically to the present study. In the first group, one author uses two or more languages in separate texts, while in the second, a single author utilizes more than one language within the same text (91). The development of Vulgar-Latin and proto-Romance in the Western Roman Empire during the Middle Ages finds its echo in the subsequent emergence of polyglot literature. In *The Poet's Tongues* (1970), Leonard Forster provides a unique look at the development of polyglot texts in Europe from the medieval period to the baroque. In his work he emphasizes the prominence of bilingualism among the educated of the day: "Latin was not a mother tongue for anyone; all those who used it had to learn it. In one sense therefore the whole vast Latin literature of the Middle Ages and the Renaissance is polyglot poetry" (19). According to this criterion, one could situate the beginnings of Western European literary polyglotism with the production of texts that include both Vulgar and Classical Latin.

With the standardization of new vernaculars in Iberia came many literary innovations, including the increased production of polyglot writings. Beyond the juxtaposition of Romance and Classical Latin, some writers began to work between different Romance languages. During the thirteenth century, for example, Alfonso X de Castilla, whose native tongue was Castilian, followed the poetic current of the time and composed his lyric poetry in Galician-Portuguese. Jorge Dias sees this type of multilingualism as a longstanding characteristic of the Portuguese: "O português foi sempre poliglota. Já os nossos clássicos escreveram quase todos em mais de uma língua, e mesmo as pessoas de pouca ilustração aprendem e sabem com frequência falar um idioma estrangeiro" (31; "The Portuguese were always polyglots. Almost all of our classic authors wrote in more than one language, and even people of little erudition learn and often know how to speak a foreign language"). Although literary trends definitely popularized languages for specific uses, socio-political changes had the greatest impact on the spread of polyglotism in Iberia. The rise of empire, for instance, resulted in the growth of certain languages and the decline of others as well as a certain comingling that Forster describes as "the functional reflexion of an actual social situation" (35). From 1500 to 1700, a time spanning from the Catholic Monarchs (Spain) and Manuel I (Portugal) to the end of the Hapsburg dynasty, Iberia saw the culmination of literary polyglotism as a direct response to the many socio-political changes that occurred during those centuries. Hernani Cidade identifies Garcia de Resende's *Cancioniero* as an early example of this type of literature: "a sétima parte da poesia é em castelhano; a restante, em grande parte de influência castelhana. Domina já desde o último quartel do século XV o bilinguismo, a que darão continuidade os poetas de Quinhentos e os de Seiscentos" (23; "the seventh part of the poetry is in Castilian; the remainder, in large part of Castilian influence. Bilingualism begins to dominate during the last twenty-five years of the fifteenth century, a trend uninterrupted by poets during the 1500s and 1600s"). According to Santiago Pérez Isasi, this interplay of literature, language, and politics was systemic: "estos fenómenos de bilingüismo o diglosia dentro del sistema literario nacional no son excepcionales ni casuales, sino sistémicos: no responden a mudanzas accidentales de la voluntad individual, sino a modulaciones prolongadas en las relaciones de poder y prestigio entre las lenguas de la Península Ibérica" ("Entre dos" 140).

The period of discovery and conquest led by Spain and Portugal created an unprecedented world network that relied heavily on language and correspondence. Indeed, the various colonial encounters benefited greatly from the ability to communicate with native cultures. From Hernán Cortés and La Malinche in Mexico to Jesuit missionaries and the Tupi in Brazil, language took on a very important role in the colonization of the Americas and the development of empire worldwide. Antonio de Nebrija emphasizes this reality in the prologue of his *Gramática de la lengua castellana* (1492), stating, "siempre la lengua fue compañera del imperio" (97). Nebrija, among others, understood the inseparable nature of language and power. The Spanish, however, were hardly the first to discover this reality. In fact, studies on virtually every European language—as well as several indigenous languages of the Americas—popped up throughout the sixteenth century. Language, however, always held the promise of power, so it would be wrong to say that humanity figured this out at the beginning of the early modern period. What made the difference, or rather, the reason why Nebrija's work was not conceivable a century previous, was because the printing press had not been invented. Among the many ways Gutenberg's invention changed the world was the revolutionizing effect it had on language (i.e., its standardization, the subsequent assimilation and identification of diverse groups of people, etc.). This is what Nebrija addresses in his prologue. Given that his work was published the same year that Granada fell and, consequently, the *Reconquista* ended, not to mention the "discovery" of the New World by Christopher Columbus, perfectly illustrates the relationship between language and politics.

In addition to these socio-cultural changes, the political landscape changed drastically in 1516 as power shifted from the homegrown Catholic Kings to the foreign Hapsburgs, beginning with the polyglot king Carlos V. These changes intensified relations between Iberia and the rest of Europe and, consequently, amplified the Peninsula's exposure to other vernaculars. Improvements in communication and the spread of imperialism, not exclusively independent of one another, led to an unprecedented degree of literary interaction that crossed both political and linguistic borders. In consequence of these developments, multilingualism spread among the educated throughout Europe, with certain languages often assuming specific roles in society. Forster captures this in a well-known anecdote attributed to Carlos V:

> The idea that certain languages were specially proper for specific purposes lasted into the sixteenth century when Charles V, King of Spain, Emperor of Germany, and Duke of Burgundy, maintained, so it is said, that French was the language to speak with one's ambassadors, Italian with one's women, German with one's stable boys (according to another version, with one's horse) and Spanish with God. (17)

Similar passages frequently appear in the literature of the time, often expressed in an apparent effort to exalt one's native tongue and, in some cases, degrade another. While the specificity of vernaculars changed in a general sense as Forster suggests, the widespread use of Spanish by the Portuguese in the literature of the annexation demonstrates that such ideas concerning the appropriate use of language did not disappear entirely. That is, the idea that a particular language was uniquely suited for a specific function (e.g., writing a *comedia*), persisted until the end of the seventeenth century.

An intriguing collection of sixteenth-century anecdotes provides the perfect context for framing this reality. In one of them, Pedro de Alaçova Carneriro, a Portuguese ambassador living at the Court in Madrid, apparently speaks Spanish with everyone except the king, Felipe II, whom he always addresses in Portuguese. Perplexed by this phenomenon, the king finally asks him why he never speaks to *him* in Spanish. The Portuguese diplomat replies, "porque com vossa magestade falo de sizo, e com os mais de zombaria" (*Anedotas* 145; "because with your majesty I speak of prudence, and with the others of foolishness"). This passage links Portuguese to good sense and judgment, while referring to Spanish in terms of mockery and the mundane. In other words, important and sacred matters addressed to high profile individuals require a language worthy of such topics—echoing the previous passage attributed to Carlos V. According to this particular anecdote, Spanish only measures up to common, menial matters. Although comical, this slight is significant due to the clear relationship it draws between language and identity. It would follow that an affront to the Spanish language was an affront to its native speakers.

A resurgence of the Portuguese language as a means of identification accompanied the Renaissance and continued well into the seventeenth century. Fernão de Oliveira's *Gramática portuguesa* (1536) and João de Barros's *Diálogo em louvor da nossa linguagem* (1540) helped trigger this revaluation of language. In actuality, praise of the Portuguese language became a standard fixture in the prologues of many Portuguese texts produced during the sixteenth and seventeenth centuries. This occurred, in part, because of the mixed feelings that many had about writing in Spanish instead of their native Portuguese. In the prologue to Fernão Álvares do Oriente's *Lusitânia transformada* (1607), for instance, the author explains that part of his motivation for writing in Portuguese is to offset the proliferation of texts in Spanish that, in his view, discredit his native tongue (9). Albuquerque points to Oliveira and Barros's profound awareness of the political value of language as one of the main factors motivating their active defense and preservation of the Portuguese language (93). In chapter four of his *Gramática,* Oliveira argues that empires of the past (e.g., Greek and Roman) maintain a certain degree of relevance in the sixteenth century because they spread their respective languages in oral and written forms. Rather than perpetually glorify their languages, the grammarian insists on the dissemination of Portuguese throughout the world instead: "tornemos sobre nós agora que é tempo e somos senhores, porque melhor é que ensinemos a Guiné que sejamos ensinados de Roma, ainda que ela agora tivera toda sua valia e preço. E não desconfiemos da nossa língua porque os homens fazem a língua, e não a língua os homens" (4.42–43; "Let us turn to ourselves now that it is time and we are lords, because it is better that we teach Guineans than be taught by Rome, even with all of its value and worth intact. Let us not distrust our own language because men make the language, and not the language men"). Among the many ideas put forward in this passage, the relationship established between identity and language stands out. Oliveira's well-known statement suggests that a language cannot surpass the source of its utterance. That is, only a great people are capable of cultivating a noble tongue.

Of all the aspects of the Portuguese language one might consider in an effort to understand the connection between the Portuguese people and their language, nothing stands out more than *saudade*: the most triumphant single expression of *portugalidade*. Despite its longstanding place within Portuguese language and identity, the etymology of *saudade* is somewhat obscure. In the *Dicionário etimológico resumido* (1966), for example, Antenor Nascentes traces the origin of *saudade* to the Latin *solitate* through the archaic forms *soydade* and *suydade*, attributing some influence to *saúde* (677). Francisco da Silveira Bueno, in his *Grande dicionário etimológico-prosódico da língua portuguesa* (1967), concludes more or less the same. While most accept this etymology, others diverge from the work of these two important Portuguese etymologists. João Ribeiro, for one, links *saudade* with the Arabic *saudá*, "which in Classical Arabic means 'black bile,' 'hypochondria,' 'melancholy,' related to the adjective *aswad* 'black'" (cited in Pap 99). Leo Pap, borrowing from Ribeiro, explains, "*saudá* literally refers to the 'blackened' or 'bruised' blood within the heart, and figuratively, to a feeling of profound sadness" (99).

The twenty-fifth chapter of Duarte Nunes de Leão's philosophical essay *Leal conselheiro* (1438), titled "Do nojo, pesar, desprazer, avorrecimento e suydade" ("On disgust, grief, disdain, irritation and *suydade*"), includes a lengthy treatment of *saudade*. His is the only known definition of the word to predate the Portuguese Renaissance. The brief chapter summarizes what are still considered the most fundamental characteristics of the term: that it originates in the heart; is untranslatable; relates to people, places, and/or things; and produces anything from happiness to sadness to melancholy. Among the most important passages in the work is the following excerpt concerning the uniquely Portuguese nature of *saudade*: "me parece este nome de suydade tam proprio que o latym nem outro linguagem que eu saibha nom he pera tal sentido semelhante" (129; "*saudade* seems so unique to me that neither Latin nor any other language that I know of can match its likeness"). For our present concerns, it is of little importance whether *saudade* really is translatable or not. What matters is that, beginning in the fifteenth century, the term is presented by the Portuguese as inexpressible in any other language. This could be seen as an attempt to differentiate Portuguese and its speakers from other languages and peoples. Returning to Oliveira's statement about the relationship between a people and their language, one might suggest that *saudade* came from the need to express something uniquely Portuguese—perhaps the collective feeling of a people reacting to an unprecedented age of exploration, and the inevitable comings and goings that resulted. The full significance of *saudade* as a trope of *portugalidade* begins to emerge in the sixteenth century, bearing even more fruit during the Iberian Union and the period of self-definition and nationhood that followed the Restoration.

Notwithstanding the importance of Portuguese as a literary language and identity marker, a series of events during the late fifteenth and early sixteenth centuries had a direct impact on Portugal's eventual loss of sovereignty. The intermarrying between the various Peninsular kingdoms left Portugal a tragedy or two away from political chaos. More than anything else, King Sebastião's unexpected death in 1578 at the Battle of Alcácer-Quibir (in Northern Africa), set Portugal on a path of political ruin, as his successor—Cardinal Henrique—was not able to marry before his death in 1580, leaving Portugal with a crisis of succession that would see its political autonomy slip away for the next six decades. Portugal might have maintained control of its own destiny had either of the homegrown candidates—António, Prior do Crato (1531–95), or Catarina de Portugal (1540–1614)—succeeded in their claims to the throne. Felipe II of Spain, however, had the support of the Portuguese elite (nobility, clergy, upper bourgeoisie), and managed to orchestrate his rise to power and the subsequent unification of Iberia (Vázquez Cuesta, "Lengua" 577–84). After more than five hundred years of sovereignty, a foreign ruler would assume control of the Portuguese nation, the seemingly inevitable consequence of the frequent intermarrying among the Spanish and Portuguese royalty (577).

While changes across many parts of society were minimal, the annexation of Portugal in 1580 greatly intensified the cultural Castilianization that had been escalating in Portugal for most of the sixteenth century. Ana Marías Carabias Torres describes some of the ways in which these two Iberian cultures converged: "la difusión de los gustos y los modos que, a pesar de las peculiaridades regionales, generaliza influencias y estilos artísticos, literarios, musicales ... que conduce al bilingüismo y al nacimiento de nuevas modas" (31). Although this convergence happened at many levels of society, linguistic developments especially stand out. Not only did the two languages influence each other, but, among the Portuguese, bilingualism was spreading rapidly. Carabias Torres signals several reasons for the widespread knowledge of Spanish among the Portuguese:

> La proximidad semántica de ambas lenguas, la contigüidad de las regiones geográficas en las que se afincaron y las circunstancias político-sociales derivadas de la presencia constante de castellanos en la corte lusitana—por un lado—, y de la unificación de los reinos bajo los Felipes—por el otro lado—, han sido los argumentos fundamentales esgrimidos como justificación del bilingüismo portugués, donde el castellano se convirtió en la segunda lengua. (38)

Naturally, the growth of bilingualism led to an increasing number of Portuguese-authored works written in Spanish. In fact, as Stanley Payne observes, "Castilian was the language of the majority of literary works published in Portugal during these decades" (245). Pilar Vázquez Cuesta takes it one step further: "el cultivo del castellano se había generalizado tanto por esta época entre los escritores portugueses que lo verdaderamente excepcional es encontrar quien no haya sucumbido nunca a la tentación de emplearlo" ("Lengua" 605). Indeed, the "who's who" of seventeenth-century Portuguese literature—Manuel de Faria e Sousa, Francisco Manuel de Melo, Violante do Céu, António Vieira, etc.—all published in both Spanish and Portuguese, generally favoring the former over the latter.

Even though writing in Spanish was a widespread phenomenon among the Portuguese during both the sixteenth and seventeenth centuries, authors from both centuries have been judged very differently. As Vázquez Cuesta explains, the politicized eyes of history hold annexation authors to a standard that does not pertain to their literary predecessors:

> Ya en el período de la monarquía dual, cuando la opción lingüística cobra aún mayor significado porque no se trata sólo de emplear o no un idioma extranjero, sino precisamente el de los que estaban robando sus libertades a la patria, esa mayor universalidad del castellano y la conveniencia de aprovecharla para dar a conocer en el exterior las glorias portuguesas será lo

> que aleguen muchos de los que han puesto su pluma al servicio
> de una tradición literaria extraña para probar a los demás, y
> sobre todo demostrarse a sí mismos, que actúan como buenos
> patriotas. ("Lengua" 613)

The applause they enjoyed in their day has been silenced by a centuries-old misconception: that annexation authors dishonored themselves and their works by writing in Spanish during a time of national crisis and, therefore, should be erased from the archives of literary history. With or without the crisis of succession resulting from King Sebastião's death and the Hapsburg rule that followed, Spanish was the literary language of prestige in early modern Iberia. There is no question that political developments on the Peninsula impacted this phenomenon, but Spanish was a major aspect of Portuguese literature before the annexation and it maintained its prominence through the end of the seventeenth century.

The point is not that Portuguese authors writing in Spanish during the Iberian Union were loyalists after all. One of the issues that makes these authors and body of works worth studying is the ways in which they navigate their complex identities. The question is not whether their works demonstrate a commitment to Portugal or not. It is clear that they do. What is perhaps most fascinating about these texts is what they have to say about language, identity, and literature. These Portuguese authors clearly lay claim to their Portuguese heritage, but this will always be questioned on account of the times in which they lived. To be Portuguese during much of the sixteenth and seventeenth centuries is to inherently participate in a series of crossings. Portuguese language, politics, and literature were absolutely heterogeneous. These writers were Portuguese and they were Spanish. Each author seems aware of their mixed state of being, manifesting this through an unyielding insistence upon their *portugalidade*. That is why I say that they *lay claim* to Portuguese identity. While it was, in part, their birthright, it was also a choice. The increased mobility of early modern Iberia, resulting from the unique socio-political circumstances of the time, left Portuguese authors with a number of options. Some writers elected a Castilianized existence (e.g., Juan Matos Fragoso). Others—as we will see in chapter two with António Ferreira—remained strictly Portuguese and demanded the same of their compatriots. A larger number of the Portuguese, including many of the authors I highlight in this study, walked the middle ground.

Among other ways, they reconciled their Spanish and Portuguese identity by writing about one in the language of the other. The balance tips in favor of their native Portugal, but the dominant culture left an indelible mark as well.

The texts produced in Iberia during the early modern period capture the social, political, and cultural landscapes converging on the Peninsula at the time of the Iberian Union. While I am clearly not the first to put forward this idea, what I offer readers is a fresh vantage point from which to see these converging landscapes. I have selected a sample of works written by Portuguese authors in Spanish because I believe that they can speak in ways that other literature from the time cannot. It is not that they are offering entirely new ideas. In many ways they merely tell a story. The early modern Portuguese nation was born out of this telling. Manuel de Faria e Sousa, Ângela de Azevedo, and António de Sousa de Macedo, among many others, infuse their works with various aspects of Portuguese identity, including the legendary moments of Portugal's storied past.

Chapter Two

Vicente, Camões, and Company
Immortalizing Portugal through the Written Word

From their allegorization of the nation to their creative constructions of Portuguese history and identity, Gil Vicente (c.1465–1536) and Luís de Camões (c.1524–80) pioneered a way of writing about Portugal that thrived during the Iberian Union. Vicente's dramatic works of the early sixteenth century and Camões's poetry thereafter left Portuguese authors of future generations a literary inheritance rich in nationalized themes, cross-cultural exchange, and linguistic diversity. What began predominantly as a literary trend among these pre-annexation pioneers and their contemporaries evolved into something much more political by the time of the Hapsburg era of Portuguese cultural history. This chapter offers an analysis of a number of works by Vicente, Camões, and some of their contemporaries as an introduction to the literary techniques and writing strategies that will be on full display in subsequent chapters that deal directly with Portuguese authors writing during the Dual Monarchy. Faria e Sousa, Azevedo, Cordeiro, Sousa de Macedo, and others build upon the artistic foundation established in the sixteenth century, ultimately resignifying the practices that led to its founding in an effort to (re)invent the Portuguese nation.

Among other legacies, Portuguese annexation authors inherited their predecessor's proficient and, sometimes, playful use of Spanish. The use of Spanish among Portuguese authors during much of the early modern period reflects an artistic and historical phenomenon that began in the fifteenth century. Tradition holds that the first Portuguese author to incorporate Spanish into his writing was Pedro, Condestable de Portugal (1429–66), author of *Sátira de felice e infelice vida*.[1] By Pedro's own admission, the choice to write in Spanish was born out of necessity and not personal preference, as fortune's wheel had forced him into exile where he would have to write in the language native to his surroundings (9).[2] Spanish had become the *lingua franca* of his writings. This would also be the case for the proliferation of talented authors emerging at the turn of the century: "Poetas como Duarte Brito, el conde Vimioso, don João Manuel, Luis Anriques, Henrique de Sá, Fernão Brandão, João Rodrigues de Castelo Branco, el propio Garcia de Resende, Gil Vicente, Sá de Miranda, etc., alternan las dos lenguas sin que debamos buscar para este fenómeno explicaciones de carácter personal" (Vázquez Cuesta, "Lengua" 601). With these authors, however, Spanish did not replace Portuguese but became another means of expression; often one that would be employed in concert with their native tongue. This phenomenon reflects the broader cultural alchemy that defined Iberia at the time: "una situación de constantes interferencias culturales y lingüísticas" (López Castro 45).

With the many inter-dynastic marriages between Portugal and Spain during the early sixteenth century came an extraordinary level of linguistic proficiency among educated Portuguese and, consequently, an increase in Portuguese-authored works written in Spanish. As in the case of the Portuguese-born Jorge de Montemayor (or Montemor; changed by the author) and *La Diana*, these works occasionally brought writers notoriety and widespread acceptance throughout Iberia. The Spanish language thrived in the Portuguese Court of Manuel (1469–1521), as all three of his wives were Castilian and spoke little if any Portuguese. This includes, in succession, Isabel de Aragón (1470–98) and María de Aragón (1482–1517), both daughters of the Catholic Monarchs, as well as Leonor de Austria (1498–1558), sister of Carlos V. As Tobias Brandenberger explains, "the role of these women as cultural mediators must not be underestimated" ("Literature" 596). Isabel's predecessor Leonor de Avis (1458–1525), in fact, is partially responsible for the "birth" of Portuguese theater: "Conta a tradição que Gil Vicente, poeta-ourives favorito da rainha viúva D. Leonor, entrou na noite de 7 para 8 de Junho [sic] de 1502 pelos aposentos da soberana reinante D. Maria adentro para improvisar, junto do berço de D. João III, recém-nascido, o *Monólogo do Vaqueiro*, tendo 'inventado' ali mesmo o teatro português" (Stegagno Picchio 25; "Tradition holds that Gil Vicente, the widowed queen D. Leonor's favorite poet-goldsmith, entered the room of the ruling sovereign D. Maria the night of June 7 to 8, 1502, to improvise, next to the cradle of the newborn D. João III, *Monólogo do Vaqueiro*, having 'invented' right there Portuguese theater"). Gil Vicente's famed literary career can be traced to this initial encounter with nobility, with João III's birth the catalyst of a nascent dramatic tradition of which Vicente would become first captain.

As Vázquez Cuesta points out, these Castilian queens wanted a court made in their own image, and not one that required them to adapt to Portuguese customs: "estas cuatro reinas—orgullosas del prestigio y el poder de la familia en que habían nacido—no se adoptan dócilmente (como sería de esperar, dada la sumisión femenina de la época) al modo de vida y la cultura de su patria de adopción, sino que tratan de configurarlas a imagen y semejanza de la de origen" ("Lengua" 587). Given these circumstances, it is not surprising that the Spanish language would become an integral part of Vicente's dramatic corpus; his success depended on the creation of a theater that would be familiar enough to these queens to find favor in their eyes. He followed the success of *Visitação* (another name for *Monólogo do Vaqueiro*) with *Pastoril Castelhano* (also in Spanish),[3] becoming thereafter a regular at the Royal Palace where he would have the opportunity to develop his genius for more than three decades. The diverse nature of the Court for which he wrote and the society from which he came was not lost on his writings, wherein we discover the constant "interacción de lo popular y lo culto" (López Castro 15); an alchemy formulated at the cultural crossroads of fifteenth- and sixteenth-century Iberia.

The confluence of cultures that defined Vicente's time and place is never more evident than within the realm of language: "En el apreciamos una triple herencia cultural: la lengua portuguesa unida a la propia tradición; el castellano, que revela, en ese momento, la influencia artística de un país sobre otro; y el latín, vinculado a una común tradición europea" (López Castro 13). Of Gil Vicente's forty-six dramatic works, twelve are exclusively in Spanish, including his first five.[4] Altogether, Paul Teyssier calculates that thirty-six percent of Vicente's literary corpus is in Spanish, which amounts to more than 14,000 lines (296). In addition to the works comprising his *teatro castellano*, Vicente has nineteen other dramatic works in which some characters speak Spanish and others Portuguese (and here I am referring to both languages in the broadest possible terms, since Vicente's writings explore the plurality of possibility within each vernacular). As Luciana Stegagno Picchio observes, languages are at the heart of Gil Vicente's theater: "o bilinguisimo, ou melhor, o plurilin-guismo, em seguida será sempre um dos traços característicos da obra de Gil Vicente" (45; "bilingualism, or better yet, multilin-gualism, straightaway will be one of the enduring character traits of Gil Vicente's work"). Polyglotism appears in Vicente's plays not only to perpetuate the same comical effect that had inspired playwrights to do the same during the Middle Ages (Sletsjöe 989), but also as a way of holding up a mirror to the world in which he lived. Although there is no evidence that he ever left Portugal, influences from throughout Iberia had a direct impact on his life and learning. This is especially true of the Iberian vernaculars that show up in his plays, all of which coalesce to make him one of the founding fathers of Iberian theater as a whole.

Vicente's vast literary corpus offers many avenues of critical inquiry, but the unique view of sixteenth-century Portuguese society, culture, and history that his polyglot plays offer continues to motivate important questions about language, identity, and empire. Most critics concur that Vicente uses lin-guistic distinctions primarily as a technique of characterization, although many diverge in their interpretation of this convention. According to Márcio Ricardo Coelho Muniz, there are some discernable patterns regarding Vicente's overall use of Spanish: "língua ... privilegiada pelo dramaturgo nas moralidades, de assuntos elevados, e no denominado teatro hierático (comédias, tragicomédias e fantasias alegóricas), particularmente quando versavam sobre temas cavalheirescos, e nas personagens de rasgo mais culto e aristocrático" (80; "the language ... privileged by the playwright in his moral plays, regarding higher matters, and in the so-called hieratic theater [comedies, tragicomic and allegorical fantasies], particularly when dealing with chivalric themes, and with more aristocratic and educated characters"). Some critics, however, see in Vicente's use of Spanish and his characterizations a distancing from and subversion of Castile. Adrien Roig, for one, suggests that Vicente had very little regard for his Iberian neighbors, citing the many villainous, despoiled, and seductive characters who speak Spanish in his plays (129–33). In support of this particular interpretation are the many instances where Vicente casts Castile in an unfavorable light. We can see this, for example, in the words pronounced by the *vilão* Jan'Afonso in *Festa*: "Todo bem e a verdade / neste Portugal nasceram, / e se há i alguma ruindade / de Castela a trouxeram" (476–79; "All that is good and true / was born in this here Portugal, / and if there is any wickedness / they brought it from Castile"). These lines attribute, rather simplistically, all that is good to Portugal and all that is foul to Castile. But Jan'Afonso is not done yet: "É a mais ruim relé / esta gente de Castela / que juro pela bofé / que milhor é a de Guiné / setecentas vezes que ela" (481–85; "They are the worst of the worst / these people of Castile / such that I swear in good faith / that the people of Guinea / are seven hundred times better"). Here he compounds Castile's decadence further by saying that the people of West Africa are infinitely better than them, an insult José Camões describes as "feroz anti-castlhanismo" (17; "savage anti-Castilianism"). While the purpose here may be humor and not subversion or slander—lest we forget the Castilian-born queens for whom many of these works were written and performed—even a comical jab at their longstanding neighbors (and rivals) is suggestive.[5] That many shady characters within Vicente's works also speak Portuguese, however, not to mention the positive treatment Castile receives in other instances, should temper the conclusions to which we might jump regarding Vicente's use of language. This is Coelho Muniz's contention at least, which he puts forward in order to demonstrate that Roig's interpretation may be overstated (or at least narrowly conceived).[6] Overall, there is more of a critical consensus surrounding the socio-political context to which we can attribute Vicente's diverse language choices than what those choices do or do not mean, or what they tell us about how he viewed the intersection of society and politics. What is beyond question is Vicente's ability to explore the dramatic potential of language on the stage. His works demonstrate the artistic richness of introducing more than one vernacular to theater—a legacy he passed on to the Iberian dramatists that followed.

What may be most fascinating about Vicente's dramatic corpus is the fact that, as Armando López Castro explains, "no revela una dirección única, sino una interrelación de distintas perspectivas, que se combinan y potencian mutuamente" (13). This is particularly true when trying to interpret the various ways that Vicente's works cast Portugal and Spain; both are elevated and debased at different times and in different ways. To make matters more complicated, some of the positive references are ironic or satirical, making their interpretation even more of a challenge for readers. Vicente was not afraid to shine a light on the growing decadence within Portuguese society, sometimes even doing so by contrasting the Portugal of yesteryear with the Portugal of his day. Notwithstanding these observations, the pages that follow detail a certain inclination within Vicente's plays to exalt Portugal and put forward an intelligible rhetoric of nationhood.

In reference to Vicente's plays, Roig explains: "de ninguna manera, en los numerosos paralelos establecidos entre ambos pueblos, pueden los españoles equiparse con los portugueses. Portugal se lleva siempre la palma" (135). A comical exchange between Apolo and the Portuguese *vilão* Jan'Afonso in *Templo d'Apolo* gets at both the issue of language and a high regard for Portugal:

> APOLO. A qué vienes di grosero
>   piensas que estás en aldea?
> VILÃO. … acho-me enganado
>   porque Deos nam é castelhano
>   nem viera eu cá este ano
>   se disto fora enformado
>   mas nam é nada um engano.
>   Nunca vos eu darei bolos
>   porque como a noz é noz
>   Deos naceu em Estremoz
>   e sa mãe em Arraiolos
>   e esta é a minha voz. (571–85)

> I think I've been deceived
> because God is not Castilian
> nor would I have come here this year
> if I had known this
> but nothing is by accident.
> I will never give you the time of day
> because what's ours is ours
> God was born in Estremoz
> his mom in Arraiolos
> and this is my witness.

Here we see Jan'Afonso react to Apolo's use of Spanish by citing this as evidence that he cannot be God. Although he now considers his pilgrimage to see Apolo time ill-spent, he still uses the occasion to inform Apolo of God's Portuguese origin. He will go on to claim several saints; the heaven, earth, and sea; and more for Portugal as well (586–95). His words culminate thereafter:

> Todo bem e a verdade
> neste Portugal naceram
> também dele procederam
> todos reis da cristandade
> porque os mais dele vieram.
> Eu nam vos hei d'adorar
> porque Deos é português. (595–602)

> All that is good and true
> was born in this very Portugal
> from which proceeded
> all the kings of Christendom
> because most are from there.
> I will not worship you
> because God is Portuguese.

It should not be lost upon the reader that these words come from a simpleton. That does not mean that they are meaningless, but it does put them into perspective: that first and foremost they would be for comic effect; "apresentada com uma naturalidade que confere aos versos um tom hilariante" (J. Camões 17; "presented with a simplicity that gives the lines a hilarious tone"). Beyond the humor, however, a number of possibilities emerge. For one, what Jan'Afonso says about the relationship between Portugal and goodness is exactly what the character of the same name says in *Festa* (minus the dig at Castile) (476–77). Also worthy of consideration is what these lines seem to be saying about the human propensity toward self-centeredness and hyperbole; that, in this case, all things orbit in relation to Portugal, the source of everyone and everything that is good. And yet in early modern Iberian literature the simpleton is often a messenger of truth and wisdom (e.g., *graciosos* in the *comedia*, Sancho Panza, etc.). Under any circumstance, the affirmation that God is Portuguese is a superlative that should not go unnoticed, which may be why Roig, in reference to this line, states that "no puede haber mayor encarecimiento de la suma excelencia de Portugal" (136). The final say may go to the actor whose delivery of the line will ultimately tell the audience whether laughter or national pride is the proper response.

The analysis that follows chases a theme as it persists in many of Vicente's plays: the glorification of Portugal. Although a number of works (e.g., *Auto da Índia*) reveal the imperfections of sixteenth-century Portugal, the Portuguese nation of the past (i.e., Lusitânia) usually occupies a place of privilege therein. Perhaps more than any other pre-Lope playwright, Gil Vicente mastered the art of dramatizing the nation—a legacy that many Portuguese playwrights would emulate during the annexation. While not all of his works focus on the Portuguese nation, the sustained interest in Portugal that characterizes many of his plays serves as a standard for the nation-minded *comedias* thereafter. In some instances the author dedicates entire works to the veneration of Portugal (e.g., *Lusitânia*, *Fama*), whereas in others the reader experiences a variety of patriotic outbursts (e.g., *Festa*, *Exhortação da Guerra*) that are not necessarily connected to the work's motif. Altogether, the influential Portuguese dramatist's creative use of allegory, personification, and linguistic flourishes establish a pattern for staging the nation that Spanish and Portuguese playwrights echo during the late sixteenth and seventeenth centuries. The point is not that the Portuguese themes within Vicente's works can only be read as a glorification of Portugal, but that they do offer this possibility.

In *Fama*, Gil Vicente exalts his native land through the allegorization of Fama, a beautiful young shepherdess whose devotion to Portugal comes at the expense of her other potential suitors: France, Italy, and Castile. One by one these admirers attempt to woo Fama away from Portugal, but none of them can persuade her to descend from her *portugalidade* to a lowlier state of national existence. Despite their repeated advances, Fama affirms that "esta moça é portuguesa" (*Fama* 60, 284; "this girl is Portuguese"). The spirit of competition at the heart of this play prefigures the many Golden Age texts that likewise pit poet against poet, text against text, and nation against nation. The work begins with the unsuccessful attempt of a Frenchman: "Y por qué no seréis vus francesa?" he asks, to which she coolly replies, "Porque nam tenho razão" (61–62; "Because I have no reason to be"). Despite his advances, Fama finds no reason to assume another identity. This happens, in part, because France has nothing to offer Fama that she does not already have in greater quantity and quality. She finds his plight amusing: "Isso é cousa pera rir" (66; "This is laughable"). By the end of their exchange, she tells him that his efforts are futile: "Francês i-vos muito embora / que isto é tempo perdido" (79–80; "Get out of here Frenchman / this is all a waste of time"). The comicity here is not limited to Fama's view of France's humorous attempt at her affection, but extends to the audience's broader understanding of allegory and the self-fashioning performance of each nation.

Next on the scene is the Italian. While Fama initiates the dialogue by asking who he is, as soon as the answer comes she asks him to leave. Just to emphasize the difference between Portugal, her true love interest, and Italy (or any of the three pretenders, for that matter), Fama asks what he has to offer by way of riches: "e que riquezas tendes vós?" (*Fama* 185; "and what riches do you have?"). Similar to the others, the Italian has much to say about his riches, although it ultimately falls short of Fama's expectations. This is important because it provides a valuable point of contrast between Portugal and the other characters, each instance giving Fama cause to describe the supremacy of her one true love. Fama seems to shirk at the others, as if to ask "what can you offer me that I do not already have?" After Italy gives his answer to the question, Fama offers a brief lesson in greatness, ("eu vos ensinarei logo" [195; "I will show you now")]) Portugal acting as the case in point. Fittingly, her tour of Portuguese glories will be a sea navigation—"Começai de navegar" (196; "Start sailing")—leading the Italian from place to place, glory to glory, fame to fame (200–13). After taking a figurative cruise around the world, visiting some of Portugal's greatest maritime successes, all the Italian can say is "Ó Diu" (231; "Oh God"). Fama, however, is just getting started: "Esperai vós / que ind'eu agora começo" (231–32; "Hold on / I am just getting started"). She contends that wherever you go, you will find "gente português" (248; "Portuguese people"). When the Italian and the Frenchman get together to lament Fama's disdain for them, the Frenchman observes, "la famosa portuguesa / no le pude far francesa" (304–05), and then adds that she has defamed him (313). The Italian echoes his words, also suffering from the effects of unrequited love (311).

Last on the scene, and with arguably the best chance to win her favor, the Castilian takes his shot at Fama, entering with a little more confidence than the others: "Cúya sois linda pastora?" (*Fama* 328; "whose are you lovely shepherdess"), followed by a smooth "Sois de aquí deste casal?" (330; "you from these parts"). Fama comes back quite self-assured: "Daqui fui sempre e agora" (331; "I was and always will be from here"). The Castilian seems to be a bit full of himself, a smooth talker, and a lover of his own voice, which Fama picks up on right away: "Oh Jesu vós falais tanto / que já estou enfastiada" (380–81; "Oh Jesus you talk so much / I am already bored stiff"). As is the case with the Frenchman and Italian, praises for Portugal roll from the Castilian's tongue. He exalts Portugal, for instance, when he says "y sois vida de las glorias / y corona de las gentes" (348–49), and "tan alta y preciosa cosa / como nel mundo ha nacido" (353–54). What he also accomplishes here is an established hierarchy among European nations. Despite Castile's compelling credentials, in the end he is left wanting, unworthy of Portugal's grandeur. The Castilian cannot imagine anyone eclipsing his own glory, which leads him to ask Fama about Portugal's quality. In response, Fama illustrates the true meaning of fame and glory by describing the exalted reputation of the Portuguese across the globe (400–08). One of the main ideas she establishes is that Portugal's presence reaches every corner of the earth—an idea that Portuguese authors will explore more fully during the Iberian Union. After a long description of Portugal's worldwide presence, Fama concludes where she ended up with everyone else: "Bem e é rezáo que me vá / donde há cousas tam honradas / tam devotas tam soadas? / O lavor vos contará. / I-vos embora" (436–40; "Does it not make good sense for me to go / where things are so honorable / so devout so renowned? / It is not that hard to figure out. / Off with you"). The Castilian's previously longwinded ways are silenced by Fama's unyielding commitment to Portugal, whose glory cannot be surpassed.

As France, Italy, and Castile get together to discuss their failures in courting Fama, all three conclude that God must be on the side of the Portuguese. The Castilian explains that for this reason, among others, he did not insist: "Por eso no porfié / con ella ni es razón / porque sus vitorias son / muy lejos y por la fe" (*Fama* 479–82). After the Italian adds his voice of agreement, the Castilian once again speaks of the Portuguese in terms of providentialism: "El muy alto Dios sin par / la quiera siempre ayudar / y nos vámanos de aquí" (485–87). In case there remains any doubt as to the greatness of the Portuguese, Vicente concludes his play by sending

Fé and Fortaleza to pay tribute to Fama, reinforcing, through the final lines of the play, Portugal's superiority:

> FÉ. Vossas façanhas estão colocadas
> diante de Cristo senhor das Alturas
> vossas conquistas grandes aventuras
> são cavalarias mui bem empregadas.
> Fazeis as mesquitas ser deserdadas
> fazeis na igreja o seu poderío
> portanto o que pode vos dá dominio
> que tanto reluzem vossas espadas.
> Porque o triunfo do vosso vencer
> e vossas vitórias exalçam a fé
> de serdes laureada grande rezão é
> princesa das famas por vosso valer
> nam achamos outra de mais merecer
> pois tanto destrocós fazeis a Ismael
> em nome de Cristo tomai o laurel. (*Fama* 500–14)

> Thine achievements are placed
> before Christ the Lord on High
> thy conquests, great odysseys
> are of the highest order.
> Thou makest of mosques a ruin
> and of the church your stronghold
> therefore let thine dominion spread
> that thine swords shine forever.
> Because thine triumphant gains
> and thine victories exalt the faith
> all the more reason to praise thee
> princess of fame for thine worth
> we cannot find another more worthy
> as you bring so much destruction to Ismael
> in the name of Christ take your laurel.

The electness of Portugal takes center stage in these concluding lines. Fé and Fortaleza come in Christ's name to honor Fama and Portugal, who are treated as one. Looking back on the entire work, it is interesting to note Vicente's use of language. While there is certainly some overlap between the vernaculars spoken, each suitor speaks his respective language.[7] The characters not innately associated with a particular tongue—Fama, Fé, Fortaleza, and the author—all speak Portuguese. This kind of linguistic posturing is significant in a work whose primary aim seems to be the divinization of Portugal. Altogether, *Fama* cleverly weaves allegory, language choice, and providentialism into a single fabric of early sixteenth-century national consciousness. While Golden Age playwrights relied much less on allegory in their attempts to stage the nation, in this play Vicente offers a model of characterization and competition that will receive much attention by dramatists of the seventeenth century seeking to establish national preeminence.

Lusitânia (1532) also makes use of allegory and suggests a similar purpose to that expressed in *Fama*, although the overall approach is unique. *Lusitânia* presents a national protagonist through which Vicente personifies many of the fundamental characteristics he attributes to his native land. His play defines the Portuguese nation by inventing a foundational myth about the marriage of Lusitânia and Portugal, the two main characters of the work. A close reading of Vicente's allegory, however, reveals that the protagonist of the work is neither the beautiful young Lusitânia nor the Greek soldier Portugal. Instead, the author incorporates these and other characters into the larger national identity his work casts. *Lusitânia* is unique compared to Vicente's other patriotic plays, in that the work characterizes the Portuguese nation through the creation and mythologization of a collective national protagonist. Thus, rather than a synecdochic view of Portugal through the eyes of a "moça portuguesa" ("Portuguese maiden"), as in *Fama*, Vicente portrays the nation through a number of characters who collectively represent Portugal. That is, it is not just the actual character, Portugal, but the blend of identities within the work that embodies the collective protagonist. While I agree with the critical consensus that the play lacks unity of action, time, and place, I disagree with those who claim that the work lacks unity altogether (Zimic 359). The unifying element of this metatheatrical work is, in fact, the nation. Not that all parts of the play figure in to this greater whole, but the majority of them do, from the principal allegory guiding the play within the play, to the classic dialogue between Todo o Mundo (Everybody) and Ninguem (Nobody).

The first scenes of *Lusitânia* revolve around a Jewish family. Lediça, the daughter, is busy with domestic concerns when a courtesan appears on the scene and tries to woo her. He immediately disappears as soon as Lediça's father returns home. Jacob, a

Jewish friend of the family, then engages in a conversation with the father about the proper way to commemorate the birth of Prince Manuel.[8] They decide that the best way to celebrate this event is to stage a work of drama. Naturally they go to the theater to receive inspiration for their work, where they are to enjoy an *auto* by Gil Vicente (Zimic 359). These initial scenes, as Ronald Surtz explains, have a specific function: "The pseudomythological plot which forms the play proper is framed by what the Elizabethans would have called an induction, i.e., an introductory scene with multiple characters that develops a situation more or less complete in itself" (42). Before the actual play within the play begins, the audience is given the basic story-line (which I paraphrase):

> Three thousand years ago the generous nymph Lisibea, daughter of the queen of Berbéria and a sea-prince, lived in the mountains of Solérica (near Sintra). Lisibea was so beautiful that the Sun, who witnessed daily the perfections of her undressed body and the beauty of her gentile soul, elected her daughter, Lusitânia, goddess and lady of the province. At the same time there was a famed and amorous knight and hunter from Greece by the name of Portugal, who comes from Hungary to the Solérica Mountains in search of game. Upon seeing the supernatural beauty of Lusitânia, Portugal immediately falls in love. Lisibea, who has developed deep feelings for Portugal, dies of jealousy and is buried at the Félix Mountain, later to be named Lisboa in memory of Lusitânia's mother. (appears between lines 460 and 461 of the play)[9]

My analysis of this work considers the following themes: the love triangle of Lisibea, Lusitânia, and Portugal as a collective characterization of the Portuguese nation; the use of myth in the invention of history;[10] and the ways in which the metatheatrical structure of the work supports the content. These three topics illuminate the national protagonism at work in *Lusitânia* and reiterate the primacy of the Portuguese nation in Vicente's dramatic corpus.

The layered structure and the allegorical nature of the work, not to mention its general lack of unity, leave *Lusitânia* somewhat fragmentary. While dialogue predominates and characterization is fairly straightforward, it is difficult to configure all of the parts into a single whole. This has led at least one critic to conclude that almost any of the parts could have been developed into separate dramatic works (Parker 96). Stanislav Zimic, on the other hand, sees in *Lusitânia* an allegorical comedy, "cuyo sentido fundamental se desprende precisamente de la relación lógica y significativa entre todas sus 'partes'" (360). While he argues that the unifying element of these parts is the interaction of past and present, fantastic and real (362–63), I contend that a proto-nationalist impulse to characterize Portugal motivates Vicente in this work. Lisibea, Portugal, Lusitânia, and others, then, come together as the invention of a collective self, a national protagonist. Reis Brasil describes the participation of each of the three main characters in the birth of *portugalidade* as follows: "Um príncipe vindo de longes terras, de nome 'Portugal,' casou com 'Lusitania,' dando origem â portugalidade, mas o nome de 'Lisibea' ficou inmortalizado na cidade de 'Lisboa,' que deu origem à portugalidade, mas que quis morrer, como parte independente, para ficar a fazer parte integrante dessa mesma portugalidade" (121; "A prince, named 'Portugal,' coming from distant lands, married 'Lusitania,' from which *portugalidade* originates, but the name 'Lisibea' immortalized by the city of 'Lisboa,' which gave life to *portugalidade*, wanted to die on her own terms in order to remain an integral part of that same *portugalidade*").

In order to set up the national character of the entire work, the play within the play begins with a statement by the *Lecenciado argumentador* that aims to communicate its leitmotif: "Em especial / o antigo de Portugal: / Lusitânia que cousa era / e o seu original / e por cousa mui severa / vo-lo quer representar" (440–50; "In particular / the antiquity of Portugal: / what Lusitânia was / and its origin / and on account of its gravity / I am going to want to stage it"). If the subject matter of the work is not enough to convince spectators of Vicente's allegiance, the *Lecenciado* goes on to speak of "este mui leal autor" (457; "this very loyal author"). In context, it is hard to imagine this verse referring to anything but the dramatist's loyalty to Portugal. Once he has underlined his own fame and fidelity, Vicente moves on to Lusitânia, Portugal, and Lisibea, each of whom contributes to our overall understanding of the national protagonist. In the following passage, for instance, Vénus offers her description of Lusitânia (in Spanish), which not only applies to the beautiful girl, but by extension to the entire nation:

> VÉNUS. Oh Lusitania señora
> tú te puedes alabar

de desposada dichosa
y pámpano de la rosa
y serena de la mar.
Frescura de las verduras
rocío dell alborada
perla bienaventurada
estrella de las alturas
graça blanca namorada. (*Lusitânia* 889–98)

What make these lines particularly insightful are the multiple references to the natural world, which would seem to support the claim of Lusitânia (the character) as the embodiment of Portugal (the nation). Similar portrayals of Lusitânia appear throughout the play. Another example occurs shortly after Portugal first meets her: "Solérica que vou buscar / senhora hei de preguntar / se as que nacem nesta terra / tem o céu a seu mandar / que em Grécia nem ultramar / tal fermosura nam vi" (539–44; "I am searching for Solérica / and will ask you my lady / if those born in this land / have the heavens at their command / for in Greece and overseas / I have never seen such beauty"). Here Portugal extends his awe of the surrounding beauty to all natives of this exotic land. Once he has met Lusitânia, however, he exalts her above all others from this most choice of places: "Pois das lindas sois rainha / das fermosas gram supremo" (563–65; "For among the beautiful you are queen / amid the lovely you reign supreme"). The glorification of her beauty is important, since it emphasizes her supremacy. The idea of Portuguese preeminence frequently arises in early modern Portuguese literature and is a key aspect of Portugal's self-concept at this time. While this feature of Portuguese identity did not originate with Gil Vicente, clearly he furthers the argument in his play. One of the primary rhetorical strategies in the play, therefore, is synecdoche, which sees Vicente constantly praising Portugal in its entirety through the exaltation of its various parts.

In contrast to his focus on Lusitânia's physical beauty, the author's descriptions of Portugal focus on his nobility, honor, valor, and amorous nature. It is significant to note that Portugal is a noble knight from Greece. This likely hearkens back to the fictionalized founding of Lisbon by Homer's Ulysses, one of the clearest intertexts informing Vicente's allegory. While this popular myth may be his point of departure, what the author accomplishes in the dramatization of Lusitânia, Lisibea, and Portugal is completely innovative, as Zimic describes: "nuestro autor inventa totalmente la leyenda de Portugal y Lusitania que dramatiza en su obra—no hay evidencia alguna de su existencia en la tradición folklórica o literaria" (360). Thus, the allegory at work in this play is actually a fiction within a fiction, another example of Vicente's literary layering. Within this frame of understanding, the unity of Portugal and Lusitânia within the work acts as a symbol of the mixing of foreign and native identities that mark the founding of Portugal and the way it would understand its identity thereafter (Zimic 365). Fundamental to our consideration of Portugal as a collective identity in *Lusitânia*, then, is the marriage of the native and the foreign, the land and the sea.

Toward the end of the play, before the couple is married, one character compares the virtues of Portugal to those of Lusitânia's other suitor, Mercúrio:

> VERECINTA. Que este nobre Portugal
>   es fundado sobre amor
>   y es marido natural
>   estotro es un bestial
>   una siba sin sabor
>   un caldo de briguigones.
>   Y Portugal si crer me quieres
>   es varón de los varones
>   servidor de las mujeres
>   más que todas las naciones. (*Lusitânia* 1051–60)

Within this short passage Portugal is celebrated for his nobility and love, as well as for his superlative nature; all of this in contrast to Mercúrio, who is seemingly the worst of his kind. As if to validate the qualities stated above, Mercúrio himself tells Lusitânia that if he were her, he would take Portugal over him (1076). Hence, in the same way that Lusitânia exceeds the beauty of all other women, Portugal stands above all other men. Therefore, the only possible way to surpass either is to bring them together. This is precisely what Vicente seems to postulate with his allegory. He creates a national protagonist by bringing his characters together into one great whole. In this way his glorification of Lusitânia and Portugal extends beyond the characters of this specific work to the Portuguese nation in general.

The national protagonist, however, is incomplete without considering Lisibea as well. After all, it is her character that inspires—at least according to Vicente's legend—the name Lisboa, the famed city the author and his literary compatriots immortalize throughout early modernity. While Lisibea is not as central of a character as Portugal and Lusitânia, her death is important to any consideration of Portuguese identity. One of the most highly esteemed and essentialized characteristics of the Portuguese is their loyalty. Lisibea's cause, like that of the nation Gil Vicente describes, is Portugal. Her commitment to Portugal eventually costs Lisibea her life, bringing to mind another characteristic commonly, and sometimes comically, associated with the Portuguese: their profound love. While the play specifically depicts the love of Lisibea for Portugal, the general love of the Portuguese for their nation is also present in the allegory. Lisibea's final words confirm the inevitability of her death, a fate the character seems willing to accept: "Minha morte é cerca e certa / e eu dou-te vida escura / vou-me à minha sepultura / que está na serra deserta / feita per mão da ventura" (*Lusitânia* 587–91; "My death is nigh and certain / as I give into the darkness / I am going to my grave / in the solitary sierras / undone by the hand of fate"). The personification of ventura (fate, fortune) at the end of this passage is revealing. Although not a comprehensive registry of all Portuguese letters from the 1200s to 1900s, according to the Corpus do Português "ventura" appears in the 1500s more than any other century. More than 20% of the 870 instances registered by the Corpus come from the works of Gil Vicente. In some cases it is simply an expression of chance (e.g., por ventura); more often than not, however, it is personified in one of two ways: either as a deliberate act of Christian deity or as a reference to the errant hand of the Roman God Fortuna.[11] Camões's sonnet "Grão tempo ha ja que soube da Ventura" ("Long has it been since I last knew of Fortune"), clearly depicts an example of the latter, where Ventura (as well as Fortuna) are capitalized to highlight their personification.

The "mão da ventura" ("hand of fate") reference is not the only instance in which Vicente alludes to the hand of providence in *Lusitânia*. In fact, there are a number of times in which Vicente makes reference to God's divine purposes for Portugal. When the *Lecenciado* states, for example, that his purpose is to "trovar e escrever / as portuguesas façanhas / que só Deos sabe entender" (421–23; "compose and write / Portuguese achievements / that only God can understand"), he lays bare the guiding principle of the work (the glorification of Portugal), and also manages to connect the designs of the Portuguese nation to providence. That is to say, only God can fully comprehend Portugal's superlative deeds because he is their author. The title of *Lusitânia*, therefore, does not point to the beautiful young girl that eventually marries Portugal so much as to the antiquity and collectivity of the Portuguese nation as a whole. Vicente has set his sights much higher than love and marriage, with the final outcome being the personification of the national imaginary with which he identifies. What the work does not clarify, however, is whether this imaginary only exists through the lens of nostalgia and *saudade* or if it has some semblance to the context of its creation (i.e., 1530s Portugal).

Fama and *Lusitânia* are particularly relevant works for considering Vicente's interest in nationalized themes. In light of Benedict Anderson's claim that "nationalism thinks in terms of historical destinies" (149), it is not a stretch to think of both works in terms of the nationalist values they espouse. Each puts forward a foundational allegory that promotes an essentialized Portuguese identity. The collective protagonist resulting from the allegory in *Lusitânia* is unmatched in beauty, valor, loyalty, fame, love, and divine favor. In these and many other plays by Vicente, "la preeminencia de Portugal está claramente afirmada en los viajes marítimos, las conquistas ultramarinas, la defensa y la propagación de la fe, la fama universal y la predilección de Dios" (Roig 136). Through his characterization of Portugal, then, Vicente successfully establishes a view of the nation that only intensifies during the century-and-a-half following his death. Moving into the late sixteenth and early seventeenth centuries, we discover an abundance of dramatists who likewise create myth and manipulate history to fit their concepts of national identity. In fact, "proto-nationalistic historical drama" (68), to borrow Cory Reed's useful term, abounds in Iberian drama of the early modern period. From Spanish-authored *comedias* such as Lope de Vega's *Fuenteovejuna* to Portuguese-authored *comedias* such as Jacinto Cordeiro's *Los doze de Portugal*, it is apparent that Golden Age playwrights throughout Iberia maintained Vicente's early sixteenth-century fascination with the nation.

Gil Vicente, however, is not the only sixteenth-century Portuguese author whose writings exhibit a strong degree of national consciousness nor the most recognized. In the first full century following the invention of the printing press, many

Portuguese authors of the 1500s made sure that Portugal received her deserved attention: "esforçaram-se por construir uma imagem nacional própria, que permitisse distinguir Portugal e os portugueses de todos os outros países e de todas as outras gentes" (Albuquerque 273; "they worked hard to construct a national image of our own, that would allow Portugal and the Portuguese to distinguish themselves from other countries and all other people"). More than anyone else, Portuguese authors of the late sixteenth and early seventeenth centuries frequently call upon Luís de Camões in an effort to construct and fortify Portuguese identity. As Vergílio Ferreira explains, Camões "é a expressão melhor de todos nós" (13; "he is the best expression of all of us"). This is evidenced, for example, by the fact that one of Portugal's most important national holidays—*Dia de Portugal, de Camões e das Comunidades Portuguesas (Day of Portugal, Camões and the Portuguese Communities)*—is celebrated on June 10, the same day of Camões's passing. It was not until the twentieth century that this day was baptized as such, but there are clear indications of Camões's importance to Portugal from before his death to the present day.[12] Portuguese writer Agustina Bessa-Luís sees in Camões a certain transcendence that typifies the Portuguese self-concept: "representa ... o português de todos os tempos. É poeta, soldado, aventureiro; intelectual e mundano; vítima e herói; experiente e desprecavido" (121; "he represents ... everything the Portuguese ever were. He is a poet, soldier, adventurer; intellectual and worldly; a victim and hero; experienced and reckless"). Finally, Teófilo Braga describes Camões's intimate link to Portuguese identity as follows: "Quando em qualquer paiz da Europa se falla em Portugal, confundem-nos inconscientemente com a Hespanha; mas ao dizer-se—sou da terra de Camões—immediatamente a individualidade nacional é reconhecida" (*Os centenarios* 6; "When in any European country Portugal comes up, they confuse us unconsciously with Spain; but upon saying—I am from the land of Camões—immediately our national individuality is recognized"). The above quotes help to introduce or remind the reader of the synonymous relationship between Camões and Portugal, but nowhere is this more evident than in his actual writings. The works themselves, as well as the ways in which they were read by subsequent generations, illustrate the connection between the poet and the *patria.*

Although his complete works reveal a prolific writer of several literary forms (especially lyric poetry), his epic poem, *Os Lusíadas,* defines Camões's iconic status and his formative role in the development of Portuguese national identity more than any other work. It captures Portugal at the height of its glory—Vasco da Gama's successful passage to India—describing within this context the roots of the Portuguese nation by referencing some of the most significant people, places, and events of Lusitânia. Da Gama's enterprise, which brought good hope to a place that had only known storms, was considered the greatest voyage of its time:

> Columbus's New World may have loomed larger to Europe since. At the turn of the fifteenth century da Gama's discovery was held much the greater, and with reason. For the spices and precious stones he brought back from India symbolized not merely the ruin of Venice, the turning of the Mediterranean into a backwater, and the emergence of Portugal, a country insignificant in size and population, as the richest nation in Europe. (Atkinson 12)

Camões's undertaking, therefore, would be to compose an epic that could ascend to the heights of the historical record, if not surpass it. Mattoso describes the relationship between the two: "O seu fundamento não era o mito, mas a História, tal como na sua época ela se entendia. A transposição da História para a epopeia deu-lhe, porém, a força do mito" (103; "Its foundation was not myth, but History, as it was understood in its time. The transposition of History to the epic poem gave it, nevertheless, the force of myth"). Accordingly, one of the strengths of *Os Lusíadas* resides in its brilliant blend of historicity and artistry. It is based on real events, yet it is more than mere history. The poem, as well as the rest of Camões's works, is also more than mere glorification. The definition and exaltation of the Portuguese is a prevalent theme within his writings, but to reduce his *corpus* to that or any other single theme is reductive and misplaced.

Hernani Cidade sees in Camões's most famous work an immense contribution to the development of *portugalidade*: "Surja o poema para os Portugueses o que a *Ilíada* e a *Odisseia* haviam sido para os Gregos e o que a *Eneida* foi para os Romanos, pois nem estes nem aqueles elevaram tão alto e projectaram tão longe o heroísmo" (31; "The poem becomes for the Portuguese what the *Iliad* and the *Odyssey* had been for the Greeks and what the *Aeneid* was for the Romans, yet neither the ones nor the others elevated heroism so high and projected it so far"). Cidade pulls a nice rhetorical trick in this passage by first associating Camões with some of the greatest epics of all time, only to explain that none of these works were able to achieve what Camões did with *Os Lusíadas*. As William Atkinson observes, Camões was well aware of the famous epics of the past: "Virgil, to the Renaissance the greatest among the poets of antiquity, had sung of arms and the man. The *Aeneid* was to Camoens at once model and challenge, but from the opening words he made clear that his would be an *Aeneid* with a difference. 'Arms and the men' was his theme, the epic exaltation of a whole race of heroes" (20–21). In his assessment of the value of *Os Lusíadas*, José Mattoso admits that the impact of the epic on the national imaginary is difficult to exaggerate (35). The collective protagonist that Gil Vicente brilliantly explores in *Lusitânia*, among other works, finds even greater expression in Camões's work. Mattoso explains:

> O povo, que até então fora apenas uma massa cinzenta e ignorada, cuja existência só se percebia como suporte da autoridade régia, passa para o primeiro plano das acções mais heróicas, independentemente de qualquer chefe. É um colectivo, e por tanto um ser abstracto, mas, ao tornar-se protagonista de uma história gloriosa, adquire personalidade, isto é, uma identidade compreensível para as mentes mais simples ou mais rudes. (36)

> The people, who until then were just an obscure and disregarded mass, whose existence was only acknowledged as a support of royal authority, move to the foreground of heroism, independently of any superior. They are a collective, and therefore an abstract being, but, upon becoming the protagonist of a glorious history, they acquire personality, that is, an identity comprehensible to the most simple and uncultured minds.

At the same time that Mattoso underscores the collectivity that Camões's work imagines, he likewise acknowledges that this would not have been a collective personality with which all of Portugal identified for the simple reason that widespread knowledge of the poem among all walks of Portuguese society is unthinkable (37).

It is important to recognize the double-edged success of *Os Lusíadas*. It cuts both ways, brilliantly exalting the achievement as well as the achievers, making it "the best possible introduction to Portugal and the Portuguese" (Atkinson 7). What lends more weight still, as Christopher Lewis explains, is that Camões speaks as one who has lived in the epic world that he recreates in his poem: "Camões's own experiences at sea imbue *Os Lusíadas* with a verisimilitude that Virgil, inventing Aeneas's journey from the comfort of Rome, could never have hoped to grasp. The sea influences the tale in a very tangible sense, reflecting an authenticity that extends to its characters as well" (354). By fictionalizing the heroic deeds of Vasco da Gama and his fleet, Camões managed to package Portugal in a way that would allow the Portuguese to better identify themselves and be identified by others (which is why we can equate the Land of Camões with Portugal, as Teófilo Braga's anecdote illustrates). *Os Lusíadas*, then, is the realization of what every literary epic promises: the consolidation of an identity (Lewis 353). Indeed Camões's work became a Portuguese constitution of sorts to which many Portuguese authors of the the Dual Monarchy pledge allegiance in their own works. In the remaining chapters of this study, in fact, I will put forward several examples of authors who appropriated Camões and his epic in defense of their individuality as a nation. For Portuguese authors of the annexation, *Os Lusíadas* was the culminating expression of the *portugalidade* they sought to preserve and promote in their writings. Consequently, prominent features of the poem, such as *saudade*, providentialism, and the characterization of a collectivity, as well as direct passages from the work, frequently appear in Portuguese texts of the Iberian Union.

Camões's death in 1580 marked the beginning of what would be a haunting year of loss for Portugal, culminating a few months later with the onset of the Iberian Union. As the epitome of Portuguese identity, it was only natural for seventeenth-century authors to return to Camões and his epic to reconstruct their national imaginary. As Fernando Namora recalls, "Camões e *Os Lusíadas* foram, nos momentos de angústia histórica, a chamada às armas para a renovação espiritual e política da Nação" (61; "Camões and *Os Lusíadas* were, during the times of historical distress, the call to arms for the spiritual and political renewal of the Nation"). Teófilo Braga agrees: "Todas as vezes que essa liberdade esteve em perigo, Camões e o seu poema foram o palladio em volta do qual se congregaram todas as energías da independencia" (*Os centenarios* 31; "Every time that that freedom was in danger, Camões and his poem were the safeguard around which all of the energies of independence were gathered"). Faria e Sousa's immense critical commentary on Camões's work may be the most patriotic text published by a Portuguese author in the seventeenth century. As detailed in chapter 3, the commentary contains numerous references in praise of Portugal, but, more importantly, it exalted Camões's place in Iberia, Europe, and, eventually, the world. Altogether, thirty-six editions of *Os Lusíadas* were published in the decades of the annexation (more than one every two years). That extraordinary number reflects some of what the epic meant to the early modern Iberian world, particularly to Portuguese authors writing during the annexation (Namora 57).[13] A recent article by Catarina Fouto and Julian Weiss argues that while Spanish translations of the epic were meant to serve imperialist ends, "they also disseminated throughout the Habsburg Empire a text that would become a symbol of Portuguese autonomy" (9). Camões and his epic enabled the generation of Portuguese writers that followed to see the impact of the pen within and beyond Portugal's borders. As Portuguese authors paid tribute to their homeland in the decades of the Dual Monarchy, Camões's name unfailingly appears.

Camões's influence on Portuguese authors of the Dual Monarchy and beyond, however, was not limited to *Os Lusíadas*. Similar to much of Gil Vicente's literary corpus, Camões's three dramatic works, found in *Teatro completo—Auto chamado dos Enfatriões, Auto de Filodemo,* and *Comédia d'el rei Seleuco*—alternate between Portuguese and Spanish according to the character speaking.[14] As Vanda Anastácio observes, "o castelhano é usado no teatro camoniano como um traço caracterizador. Falam-no grande parte das personagens secundárias" (Prefácio 30; "Castilian is used in Camonian theater as a characterizing trait. It is spoken by many of the secondary characters"). Camões not only follows Vicente's conventional use of Spanish as a tool of characterization, but also echoes his patriotic zeal. What is more, Camões adds a touch of subversion to his theatrical works by assigning Spanish to the devils, fools, and other inferior characters more consistently than we see in Gil Vicente. Camões's suggestive characterization was not overlooked by Portuguese authors in the decades following the poet's death. For example, in his edition of *Os Lusíadas*, Manuel de Faria e Sousa, perhaps Camões's most enthusiastic admirer, refers to the degraded role of Spanish-speakers in Camões's drama:

> [E]l Poeta avia seguido en esto lo que hizieron todos los Autores Portugueses en las Comedias antiguas, que era, luego que se introduzia en ellas Diablo, Moro, Adivino, Fantasma, Bobo, i semejantes, casi siempre hablavan en Castellano, siendo todo el resto de la obra en Portugues, como si el Bobo, Fantasma, Adivino, Moro, o Diablo, no pudiessen hablar, sino en Castellano. (7.29.257)

In this passage, Faria e Sousa goes beyond mere observation, insinuating, by the end, that Camões's use of Spanish in his characterization of the profane reflects, in some way, the very nature of the Castilians.

While qualitatively he mirrors Vicente's occasional antagonism toward Castile, the frequency of occurrence is much higher in Camões, as his three dramatic works reveal. His characterizations build on Vicente's conventional use of various linguistic registers, but Camões ultimately establishes something that his precursor only managed to intimate. In *Filodemo*, for example, the shepherd Doriano and his foolhardy son Alonsillo are the only two characters that speak Spanish (1148–1236; 1502–90; 1774–1963). The list of characters on the title page of the manuscript does not even make use of the designation Alonsillo, preferring, instead, "Hum Bobo filho do pastor" (Anastácio, Prefácio 77; "the shepherd's fool of a son"). The body of the work maintains this preference, always listing his speaking parts under the familiar title of *Bobo*. Camões assures his reader that the name befits the character. In their entertaining first scene together, Doriano laments that he cannot seem to silence the babblings of his son:

> MONTEIRO. Dar-m'eis novas ou sinais   Will you let me know if
>   De um fidalgo português,   A Portuguese nobleman,
>   Se passou por onde andais?   Happened to pass by here?
> BOBO. ¡Yo soy el hidalgo portugués!
>   ¿Qué manda su senhoría?
> PASTOR. ¡Cállate! ¡Qué nescio es!
> BOBO. ¿Padre, no me dexaréis
>   Ser lo que quisiere un día?
>   ¡Oh Santo Dios verdadero!

¿No seré lo que otros son?
Digo agora que no quiero
Ser Alonsillo, el vaquero.
PASTOR. ¿Pues qué quieres ser?
BOBO. Burrón.
PASTOR. Cállate agora, ignorante!
BOBO. Quiero dezir dos palabras
　Digo que si soy possante
　Soy cabrón: des hoy adelante
　Quiérome andar con las cabras.
PASTOR. Cállate ahora un poco.
BOBO. Ha de ser quanto yo quisiere.
PASTOR. Señor, diga lo que quiere,
　Que este muchacho es loco,
　Y muero porque no muere. (1175–97)

This dialogue continues in much the same way through the end of the scene—the *Bobo* speaking nonsense, the father unsuccessfully quieting him—not to mention the other two scenes in which the Spanish-speaking duo appears. Altogether, *Filodemo* succeeds as a perpetuation of Vicente's conventional switches between languages at the same time that it assigns the unfavorable role of the fool to the Spanish-speaker (a choice that Camões replicates in his other two works).

In *El rei Seleuco* (*King Seleucus*), for example, and not unlike *Filodemo*, Camões limits his use of Spanish to Físico and his cross-dressing, servant-fool, Sancho. While the connection appears coincidental, Físico and Sancho's exchanges are reminiscent of a later Sancho and his master Don Quijote. Físico and Sancho's interactions are the most humorous of the entire work. When, for example, Sancho is suddenly torn from his slumber by his master and told to dress quickly, Sancho appears in just that, a dress, claiming that it was the quickest thing he could find. Físico objects to his appearance, but Sancho calmly replies: "parezco un gavilán, / Hermoso como una dama" (697–98). In their relatively few lines together, Físico calls Sancho a "vellaco/velhaco" (678/737), "ladrón" (680), "necio" (726), and "bovo" (728, 734). Rather than ennobling Sancho with his higher social status, Físico, instead, ends up nearly as degraded as his servant. The fact that Sancho and Físico, the clowns of the work, are the only ones who speak Spanish, seems to reflect more than mere dramatic convention.

Unlike the author's approach to characterization in *Filodemo* and *Seleuco*, Camões maintains a suggestive step beyond convention in his use of Spanish in *Enfatriões* (*The Two Amphitryons*). Karl von Reinhardstoettner, in his assessment of the play, calls the text "profundamente nacional" (cited in M. Braga 41). That the protagonist of this work finds himself in the familiar context of the sea, the same place of so many other fictional characters of the time, hardly justifies von Reinhardstoettner's claim. A brief look at the use of Spanish in the work, however, shows that there was more behind Camões's appropriation of another tongue than mere convention. *Enfatriões* revolves around the mischief of two gods, Júpiter and Mercúrio, who take full advantage of Enfatrião's absence at war by assuming the appearance of the absent soldier and his servant. Camões lets Júpiter and Mercúrio's alternation between Portuguese and Spanish speak for itself. While as gods Júpiter and Mercúrio consistently speak in Portuguese, in the commoners guise of Enfatrião and Sósea they elect Spanish (which is confusing considering that the real Enfatrião speaks Portuguese). Echoing the anecdote previously discussed, Camões manages to deify his native Portuguese and debase Spanish through this simple, yet significant technique of characterization. The real Sósea, whose role parallels that of the *Bobo* in many ways, also speaks Spanish. The exchanges between Júpiter, Mercúrio, Sósea, and Enfatrião capture the brilliant play on doubles found in Camões's work as well as the author's playful use of Spanish in the depiction of these two characters.

From *Os Lusíadas* to his plays, Camões's works are manifestly pro-Portuguese. It is tempting to say that Camões's theater constructs something ultimately more defiant than Vicente's by consistently debasing his Spanish-speaking characters. Scale, however, is important to keep in mind. After all, Camões's three plays represent only a small fraction of what Vicente composed in Spanish. Even if you include his lyric poetry, Camões wrote relatively little in Spanish. When considering their legacy within the context of the Dual Monarchy, then, it is important to think of the works of Vicente and Camões in terms of what they suggest and not what they consistently and definitively say. That many of their writings are not Lusocentric and that some of what they say about Portugal is unflattering does not erase the reality that certain texts advance a coherent national discourse. As a literary practice, Vicente's works anticipate the Portuguese preference for writing in Spanish that characterizes the Iberian Union (Camões's to a much lesser extent). The two authors epitomize sixteenth-century Portuguese letters and are foundational figures within the Portuguese canon. Their works bear the imprint of a century marked by intense linguistic, cultural, and political exchange. Vicente dominated the first decades of the century with an unprecedented use of language and nationalized themes in his plays. Camões punctuated the latter part of the sixteenth century with one of the most important Portuguese works ever written.

There is more to sixteenth-century Portuguese literature than Vicente and Camões, even if they are perhaps its greatest expression. Of the many other prominent Portuguese authors of the 1500s, one is particularly relevant to this study because his views on the relationship between language and literature anticipate the way Portuguese-authored works written in Spanish during the Dual Monarchy were remembered from the late seventeenth century onward. Based solely on his most well-known work (*Castro*), it would seem that the focus of António Ferreira's writings aligns well with Vicente and Camões's.[15] John R. C. Martyn sums up the tragedy's legacy: "Ferreira was the first to put it on the stage, and more successful than any contemporary or later imitators. In fact, the intellectual courage and inventiveness of Ferreira need to be stressed, in staging a play not only based on Portuguese history, rather than on the Bible or a Classical theme, but also written in Portuguese, a language as yet untried for high drama" (4). Nothing from his life or work would lead a reader to question Ferreira's commitment to Portugal. His approach to *portugalidade*, however, is markedly different than Vicente and Camões's in at least one important way: his insistence that the Portuguese should write exclusively in their native tongue. In a number of different poems, Ferreira pushes back against the tide of Castilianization inundating Portuguese letters by injecting the conversation with questions of loyalty, a reality that has long troubled Portuguese writers of the Dual Monarchy.

In reaction to the increasing preference for Spanish as the literary language of choice during the sixteenth century, many intelectuals, including António Ferreira, reacted: "No es de extra-ñar, pues, que algunos intelectuales más conscientes comenzasen a advertir el peligro que corría su lengua de verse suplantada por una extraña dentro de su propio territorio y tratasen de conjurarlo contando sus excelencias, al mismo tiempo que indagaban las causas de este hecho" (Vázquez Cuesta, "Lengua" 606). No amount of publications in favor of the Portuguese language, however, could slow down the Peninsular move toward Spanish. The language of Castile took over in much the same way that Galician-Portuguese had previously dominated the literary landscape. Although Ferreira did not want to see his native tongue discarded in favor of Spanish, his views were broader than his own immediate context. According to "Soneto XXXII" from Livro II of Ferreira's posthumous poetic anthology *Poemas lusitanos* (*Lusitanian Poems*) (1598), what might be good in a foreign language, is always better in the mother tongue:

> Por ventura que em quanto â estrangeira
> lingua entregas teus doces accentos,
> Não he tua voz com tanto effeito ouvida.
> Dà pois â dor sua lingua verdadeira,
> da os naturaes suspiros teus aos ventos,
> Por ventura será tua dor mais crida. (9–14)

> By chance as soon as you surrender
> your delightful words to a foreign tongue,
> Your voice is not heard with as much effect.
> Give pain, therefore, its true expression,
> lend your native sighs to the winds,
> And perchance your pain will be credible.

Aside from the many other points he will make elsewhere, in these lines Ferreira's focus is on the inherent superiority of writing in one's native language—the strongest place from which one can speak. Doing so makes the pain more painful and the sweetness sweeter still. Thus, the affective potential of the written word is diminished by writing in any language other than the mother tongue. His overall point, then, is not that everything is better in Portuguese; it is if you are from Portugal, but if you are from somewhere else you should write in the language native to that location.

Among the poems that comprise Ferreira's *Poemas lusitanos*, are several that directly oppose the increasing Castilian influence in Portugal. Ferreira does not call out Portugal's neighbor by name, but the identity of the elephant in the room is clear. As

Albuquerque explains, Ferreira symbolizes a larger movement that was occurring among some of the Portuguese at this time: "Foram, contudo, os homens do século XVI, a quem se deve o primeiro grande combate pela ilustração a defesa da língua. ... esses homens profundamente conscientes do valor político do idioma" (93; "It was, however, the men of the sixteenth century, to whom is owed the first great erudite fight in defense of language. ... those men profoundly aware of the political value of language"). Ferreira's odes are particularly zealous in their patriotic expression. They are dedicated to past and present nobility; political, religious, and literary contemporaries; and even a ship of the Portuguese Armada. The first ode, however, is an invocation in which he calls upon the muses for help to sing Portugal's glories ("nossos bons passados" [*Poemas lusitanos* 6], "Portuguesas conquistas y victorias" [15]). Not lost in this preliminary ode is the opportunity to address the issue of language:

> Lingua aos teus esquecida,
> Ou por falta d'amor, ou falta d'arte,
> Së para sempre lida
> Nas Portuguesas glorias. (20–23)

> Language forgotten by your own
> Either for lack of love, or skill,
> Be forever read
> In Portuguese glory.

Here Ferreira asserts that Portuguese authors who disregard their mother tongue do so because they are either deficient in their patriotism or in their literary skill. While these words, in isolation, come across as somewhat self-serving, looking at all of his poetry two things stand out: first, he genuinely believed that everyone should write in their native language; and second, he practiced what he preached.

Perhaps the most pronounced example of Ferreira's belief that everyone should write in their native tongue is "Carta III," a long poem in *terza rima* that he addresses to his friend and fellow poet Pêro d'Andrade Caminha (1520–89). The poem offers an unmistakable view of Ferreira's rigidity concerning the relationship between language, literature, and identity, as well as a clear sense of his esteem for Portugal. He begins by emphasizing that anciently, the highest literary achievement was to honor one's own language (*Poemas lusitanos* 1–3). While he offers Virgil as a classical example of this practice, he also mentions Boscán and Garcilaso (7–15). With these and other cases, the poet repeats the same idea—it is the duty of every writer to celebrate his native land in his native tongue: "nascem, vivem e morrem para os seus" (33; "they are born, they live, and they die for their own"). It would follow that to reject this honor is to bring shame to one's literary accomplishments and blur their commitment to the *patria*. Ferreira jumps from this general introduction to the specific case of his friend, Andrade. His accusation is clear: "Mostraste-te tègora tão esquecido, / Meu Andrade, da terra em que nasceste, / Como se nela não foras nascido" (52–54; "So far you have shown yourself so forgetful / My Andrade, of the land of your birth / As if you were not born there"). He questions why Andrade would waste his "doces versos" ("sweet poetry") on another language and people, thereby robbing his Portuguese tongue and land of such sweet enrichment (55–60). Ferreira wants Andrade to recognize that this choice shows disdain for his native language; that he shares in a collective responsibility to elevate Portuguese to her rightful place. Having stated the problem, Ferreira beckons to his friend, "Volve, pois, volve, Andrade" (64; "Return, then, return, Andrade"), encouraging thereby the prodigal to return. He expresses his confidence that Andrade will put into practice the "correct" behavior he has described and abolish "essa língua estrangeira" (62; "that foreign tongue")—presumably Spanish. He threatens his friend with the hatred of his compatriots and rejection by the muses if he insists on writing in another language (70–72). Furthermore, he explains that every writer has the duty to glorify his homeland—"Demos a quem nos deu e devemos mais" (75; "Let us give back to whom we owe so much")—due to its implications in the present and the legacy it leaves future generations.

To what, exactly, does Ferreira want his friend to return? ("Volve, pois, volve"). He seems to be nostalgically holding on to a past that may no longer exist; longing for a simpler time when the world was smaller and everything had its right place (not that such a world ever existed). The linguistic tidiness that Ferreira endorses, however, hardly matched the times in which he lived, and certainly not the fast-approaching period of unification. With the annexation came a shift in perspective, among many, as to the author's responsibility to publish strictly in their native tongue. Ferreira's unequivocal plea to Andrade is to not let go of yesterday's literary values. He warns his friend of the consequences that will surely come if he continues to neglect Portuguese in his writing. His appeal to loyalty reads convincingly, but Ferreira was ultimately up against a complete socio-cultural shift. Portuguese annexation authors did not have the luxury of writing and publishing in their native language as freely as Ferreira. Unfortunately for those authors, the standard against which history has judged their choice to write in Spanish reads much like Ferreira's rebuke of his friend.

While his incrimination of Andrade is significant in isolation, it is especially meaningful when considering what occurred in Portugal in the century following Ferreira's death, during which time it is difficult, if not impossible, to find a Portuguese author who did not cultivate the Spanish language. What would these writers have thought about Ferreira's powerful injunction?

> Floreça, fale, cante, ouça-se e viva
> A portuguesa lingua, e já, onde for,
> Senhora vá de si, soberba e altiva.
> Se tèqui esteve baixa e sem louvor,
> Culpa é dos que a mal exercitaram,
> Esquecimento nosso e desamor. (76–81)

> May the Portuguese tongue flourish, speak,
> Sing, live and be heard, that where'er she go
> She goes as the lady she is, high and mighty.
> If until now she was lowly and unlauded,
> Those who poorly applied her are to blame,
> Our forgetfulness and disaffection.

Ferreira fears for a future in which the Portuguese language is not held in the same regard that she enjoyed during his lifetime. Were this to happen, he argues, the Portuguese lettered community would be at fault. It is worth noting that in using the possessive adjective "nosso" ("our") he includes himself among those to whom the credit or blame would fall.

Ferreira's philosophy of writing does not permit the commemoration of Portugal by Portuguese authors in any language but Portuguese, seeing such attempts as contradictory— a contradiction annexation authors either rejected or with which they made their peace. Ferreira's opinion may have fallen out of favor during most of the seventeenth century (at least in practice), but literary history traditionally evaluates seventeenth-century Portuguese letters according to Ferreira's rubric, discarding almost any text not written in Portuguese. The authors whose works occupy the remainder of this study consistently employ a rhetoric of nationhood to describe their choice to write in Spanish; that Spanish allows them to spread the glories of Portugal to a broader audience. Of course there is more to it than this or any other single factor, but the wider circulation afforded by the Spanish language cannot be discounted. Traditionally, this explanation, no matter how well-substantiated, has not been sufficient to significantly alter the longstanding, negative view of any author willing to abandon their native tongue during such a crucial moment in Portuguese history.

António Ferreira validated his strict view of language loyalty by refusing to publish anything outside of his native Portuguese tongue.[16] While this is certainly the case throughout *Poemas lusitanos*, nowhere does Ferreira prove his friendship with the Portuguese language—"Ah Ferreyra, dirão, da lingua amigo!" ("Ode I" 30; "Ah Ferreira, they will say, language's friend!")—more than in *Castro*. It is Ferreira's work par excellence and a masterpiece of the Portuguese literary canon. What is more, *Castro* is the first tragedy written in the Portuguese language and one of the first in all of Europe. This historical work centers on Inês de Castro, her amorous relationship with D. Pedro, and the intervening power of D. Afonso IV (the State). The subject-matter is well-suited for someone of such clear nationalist leanings as Ferreira. While mentioned by Garcia de Resende, and famously alluded to in a section of *Os Lusíadas*, Ferreira's dramatic work is the apogee of the Inês de Castro theme in the sixteenth century.[17] Basing his text on this well-known episode of Portuguese history gave the author the opportunity to not only highlight this specific occurrence, but also to invoke many other aspects of his "grande Portugal" (1.39; "great Portugal"): *saudade* (3.9, 62, 154; 5.31), the divinity of the *Quinas* (2.286–87), and the collective identity of Portugal (2.71, 93, 104). Beyond these explicit references, however, is a work beautifully crafted in the Portuguese language that has left an enduring mark on European drama, especially on the

Iberian Peninsula. Indeed, the greatest manifestation of Ferreira's commitment to the Portuguese language was the writing of *Castro*.

Ferreira's tragedy is both the final and ultimate work to appear in *Poemas lusitanos*. T. F. Earle explains: "*Castro* and *Os Lusíadas* are the two greatest achievements of Portuguese classicism. Ferreira and Camões proved that the Portuguese language could be used for the literary genres regarded as the most noble and the most difficult, tragedy and epic" (68). While *Castro* has stood the test of time, it would take Miguel Leite Ferreira three decades to see his father's collected works published. Both the title of the volume and its prologue reiterate what I have tried to demonstrate with my brief analysis of Ferreira's poetry: that he was similar to Vicente and Camões in his passion for all things Portuguese, and different from them in his strict adherence to writing in his native tongue (which he expected of his compatriots as well). By favoring Portuguese themes and history, dedicating many of his poems to his compatriots, and—above all else—writing entirely in Portuguese, no title seems more appropriate for his collected poems than *Poemas lusitanos*. Whether his son was involved in the naming of the volume is unclear, but the prologue Miguel Ferreira penned leaves no doubt as to whether he understood how important Portugal and the Portuguese language were to his father.

The prologue begins with a reference to language: "Esteve a lingua Portuguesa não conhecida no mundo, por causa dos ingenhos Portugueses não terem experimentado nella, o que outras nações mostraram nas suas" ("The Portuguese language was unknown in the world because Portugal's brightest were not experimenting with it the way other nations were with theirs"). Immediately he picks up where his father left off, the difference being that what António Ferreira saw as a real possibility, his son experienced as a living reality. By the late sixteenth century, the Portuguese language was in severe decline; Spanish was overwhelmingly preferred by those writing in all genres. Having laid blame upon his countrymen for the current state of the Portuguese language, he goes on to single out his father for his efforts: "meu pay ... pretendeo com a variedade destes seus manifestar como a lingua Portuguesa, assi em copia de palavras, como em gravidade de estylo a nenhuma he inferior" ("my father ... tried to show in a variety of ways how the Portuguese language, as much in its abundance of words as in its dignity of style, is inferior to no other"). Fittingly, he mentions his father's positive contribution to the standing and esteem of the Portuguese language in his brief prologue. The most provocative part of the entire section, however, is what follows: "Esteve este livro por espaço de quarenta annos, assi em vida de meu pay, como despois do seu falecimento, offerecido por vezes a se imprimir, e sem se entender a causa, que o impedisse, não ouve effeito. Agora que com a idade foy crescendo a razão, conheço qual era" ("Over the course of forty years, both during my dad's life and after his death, this book was presented many times for printing, and without ever understanding what was holding it back, nothing came of it. Now that with age came maturity, I know what it was"). Why did it take so long to see *Poemas lusitanos* published? He speaks of a cause (*causa*) that he only came to understand as an adult, but never elaborates on what motivated decades of rejection. The argument cannot be made that the collected poems were not worthy of publication, so what was it? Peter van Crasbeeck (1572–1632)—or Pedro Craesbeeck, as he was known in Portugal—established his publishing house in 1597, issuing Ferreira's poetry within his first year of operation. Had Ferreira's work been snubbed by the other publishing houses? If so, for what reason? Did it have anything to do with his insistence that his compatriots write in Portuguese? Or was it related to the fact that many publishers would not publish texts in Portuguese?[18] Whatever the actual reason, Miguel Leite Ferreira credits Phillip I of Portugal for his intervention which ultimately resulted in *Poemas lusitanos*.

There is no all-encompassing explanation as to why Portuguese literature did not continue in the seventeenth century as gloriously as it had in the sixteenth with Gil Vicente, Bernardim Ribeiro, Sá de Miranda, Luís de Camões, António Ferreira, and others. Perhaps the inevitable decline of empire is also the fate of literature (at least in the short term). Seventeenth-century Portuguese literature could not escape the shadow cast by the sixteenth, just as the Spanish Enlightenment had little hope of producing an encore worthy of the Golden Age. By this I do not mean to suggest that seventeenth-century Portuguese literature lacks its literary giants—the remaining chapters offer some examples— only that these authors (and others) are generally understudied and underappreciated. Several socio-political factors reshaped

Portuguese literature for the better part of two centuries. While this phenomenon culminated after Ferreira's death, Portuguese-authored works written in Spanish were already commonplace during his lifetime (e.g., Vicente and Camões), making the monolingualism of his literary corpus all the more unexpected. While overshadowed in many ways by his contemporaries, nothing can obscure Ferreira's important contribution to the literary landscape of Portugal in the sixteenth century. Few subscribed to his rigid view of language and literature in the century that followed, but many shared his zeal for Portugal and his desire to glorify the *patria* in his writings. Vicente, Camões, and Ferreira were not alone in their efforts either. Other Portuguese writers actively participated in the invention and preservation of *portugalidade* (e.g., Fernão de Oliveira, João de Barros). During the baroque, many Portuguese authors affirmed an autonomous Portuguese identity in their writings, extending the legacy left by the pioneers of the sixteenth century.

Chapter Three

Epitome of an Era

The Life and Writings of Manuel de Faria e Sousa

As a pioneer of comparative Iberian studies, "patriarca da camonologia" (Sena 56; "patriarch of Camonology"), and one of the most prolific writers of early modern Spain and Portugal, Manuel de Faria e Sousa (1590–1649) is a central figure in this study; indeed, a book of this kind would be inconceivable without him. While the majority of his adulthood was spent in Castile—where he would eventually die—Faria e Sousa's body ultimately returned to the land with which he most identified: Portugal.[1] He wrote the major part of his critical and literary work, however, in Spanish and cultivated relationships with some of the most prominent artists in Madrid during the first half of the seventeenth century. It may seem to follow, therefore, that Faria e Sousa abandoned his native land and tongue for a more accepted language and centralized place on the Iberian Peninsula. After all, this is the information that most literary critics and historians have recycled during the past four centuries. Notwithstanding its recurrence, this approach to Faria e Sousa is both superficial and reductive; it only tells part of a complex Iberian story of which he is one of many main characters. Although his writings were dressed in Spanish more often than not, they reveal the work of a Portuguese enthusiast committed to promoting Portugal within and without Iberia. Rather than perpetuate past misconceptions of his life and works, or read Faria e Sousa from the opposite extreme (as some kind of *pure* nationalist), this chapter puts forward a perspective of him that embraces the complexity of the world he inhabited and the costumes (linguistic, national, literary) he donned throughout his life.

Faria e Sousa's literary corpus consists primarily of poetry, historiography, philosophy, and literary criticism. He did not simply experiment with these genres as he had with chivalric and pastoral romances in his youth (*Fortuna* 140). He composed more than six hundred poems in at least fifteen different poetic forms, focusing primarily on the sonnet. While impressive, his poetic production defers to his immense body of historical works and literary criticism, where the Iberianist dedicated more than five thousand pages to the glories of Portugal and Luís de Camões, his beloved poet. Whether a sonnet, a literary commentary, or a history of Portugal's successes at home and abroad, his work leads to at least one definite conclusion: Faria e Sousa was not only innocent of disloyalty, but guilty of nationalism. As it happens, Faria e Sousa has a nationalizing effect on virtually every literary project he undertakes. Jorge de Sena sees this as an obsession: "chega a ser obssessiva a insistência com que a Portugal, como entidade autónoma e bem definida, ele se refere" (17; "the insistence with which he refers to Portugal as an autonomous and well-defined entity becomes obsessive"). In Faria e Sousa's criticism, poetry, and historiography, the Portuguese nation consistently emerges as the protagonist. Many have downplayed his literary contributions by scrutinizing what they see as his political allegiances, often focusing on the fact that he lived most of his adult life in Castile and published the majority of his work in Spanish. As I will demonstrate in this chapter, however, the Spanish language masked the Portuguese identity of his works, allowing Faria e Sousa, like many of his contemporaries, to promote a patriotic agenda in the language of the Empire and spread the glories of his native land across the globe.

In highlighting the various ways in which Faria e Sousa affirms his Portuguese identity, it is not my intention to understate Faria e Sousa's Spanishness. To ignore his multilayered connections to Spain would be to commit the same error that others have maintained in regards to his commitment to Portugal, when in actuality the author and many of his Portuguese contemporaries may very well be something closer to an Iberian blend than either Spanish *or* Portuguese. Covarrubias's entry on *España* is useful in understanding Faria e Sousa's relationship to Spain. The lexicographer concludes the passage by introducing the word *españolado*, which he defines as "el estrangero que ha deprendido la lengua y las costumbres y traje de España" (551).[2] The cross-cultural proficiency of the early modern lettered Portuguese would appear to demonstrate precisely what Covarrubias designates as *españolado*. From language to literature, Spanishness is a learned identity, a performance many Portuguese authors seem to have mastered during the Dual Monarchy. *Portugalidade*, however, is also a costume—an emerging set of characteristics that only become the basis of Portuguese national identity as they are performed. Within this heterogeneous world, I am particularly interested in the author's consistent choice to masquerade a Portuguese identity, which underscores the performativity of national identity altogether.

The heart of Faria e Sousa's nationalism, and the central text of this chapter, is his commentary *Lusiadas de Luis de Camoens, principe de los poetas de España* (1639). All citations used here are from the facsimile edition of 1972, *Lusíadas de Luís de Camões, comentadas por Manuel de Faria e Sousa.* My approach to this work consists of analyzing the numerous instances in the text where Faria e Sousa manifests his nationalist leanings. This includes the significance of the title page, the geographic superiority of Lisbon and the Portuguese nation, the glorification of the Portuguese language, providentialism, his essentialized approach to Portuguese virtues (e.g., loyalty, bravery, love, mastery at sea), and the repeated references to a collective identity. This demonstrates the underlying patriotic fervor guiding Faria e Sousa's corpus of texts and reveals the mechanisms at work among other Portuguese authors writing with a similar aim during the Iberian Union. Beyond the analysis of his commentary on *Os Lusíadas*, this chapter also looks closely at the ways in which Faria e Sousa articulates his nationalism through historiography. I will focus most of my attention on his condensed version of Portuguese history titled *Epítome de las historias portuguesas* (1628), although I will also look briefly at *Asia portuguesa* (1674), *Europa portuguesa* (1678), and *Africa portuguesa* (1681). My reading emphasizes the various inaccuracies and exaggerations within *Epítome*—much of the same evidence other critics have used to disparage his contribution to Portuguese historiography. As I will argue, however, nationalism has less to do with truth and accuracy than it does with imagining the past in a way that casts the nation in the best possible light.

Faria e Sousa and Criticism

With some notable exceptions, critical reception of Faria e Sousa's works can be divided into three general stages: a favorable view during the seventeenth and eighteenth centuries, with progressive decline; indifference or hostility during the nineteenth and early twentieth centuries; and an awakening and revaluation from the mid-twentieth century to the present. To begin with, Faria e Sousa was considered extremely gifted in the eyes of many of his contemporaries. The list of his Iberian admirers includes Baltasar Gracián, António de Sousa de Macedo, Juan Pérez de Montalbán, Manuel Severim de Faria, Miguel Botelho de Carvalho, Francisco Manuel de Melo, and Lope de Vega, among many others. When Faria e Sousa broke onto the literary scene in 1623 with publications in Madrid and Lisbon, he dedicated one of his works, *Narciso e Echo*, "A Lope Feliz de Vega Carpio, Prodigio dos engenhos passados y presentes." ("To Lope Feliz de Vega Carpio, Prodigy of geniuses both past and present") Lope answered this dedication with the following *Décima*, which appears in the introductory section of Faria e Sousa's *Noches claras* (1624):[3]

> Peregrina erudicion
> De varias flores vestida,
> Enseñansa entretenida,
> Y sabrosa correcion:
> Fuerças de ingenio son
> Dulce pluma docta mano
> De un Filosofo Christiano
> Sosa de las letras sol
> Demosthenes Español,
> Y Seneca Lusitano. (n. pag.)

Beyond the general praise of erudition, wit, and religiosity found in the above poem, Lope associates him with Demosthenes, the famed Greek orator, and Seneca, one of the great writers of the Roman tradition.[4] As this poem suggests, Lope held Faria e Sousa in very high esteem. Their relationship, in fact, has been the focus of a number of critical studies.[5] In the dedicatory section of his tragedy *El marido más firme* (1627), "dedicada a Manuel Faria de Sosa, noble ingenio Lusitano," Lope specifies some of what he admires in his Portuguese friend. He extols *Narciso e Echo*, stating that if his own work could match the quality of Faria e Sousa's, there is no question that it would be published. He speaks of "la erudicion del arte y la excelencia del ingenio" that characterize Faria e Sousa's works overall and mentions that his writings are continually nourished by the homeland from which he never strays. Given these antecedents, it is not surprising to find that in *Laurel de Apolo* (1630) Lope crowns Faria e Sousa as Portugal's finest poet and historian (3.155–59).

Faria e Sousa, however, was not universally praised by his contemporaries. Among some of his compatriots, in particular, Faria e Sousa faced strong opposition. This may explain, at least in part, why he spent so much of his life away from Portugal. He alludes to this in his dedication to Lope in *Narciso e Echo*, in which he speaks of a friend "que dexò a sus naturales por huir su veneno." In the context of the entire dedication, it is clear that this "friend" is as real as Cervantes's in the prologue to *Don Quijote*. In Faria e Sousa's case, however, it is not merely a literary device, but an early modern example of the "I Have This Friend" trope, he being the one who left Portugal because of the toxic environment he found there (presumably among the lettered community of Lisbon).[6] It is not clear to what or to whom these words are specifically directed, but they would certainly apply years later to Agostinho Manuel de Vasconcelos, Manuel de Galhegos, and Manuel Pires de Almeida,[7] who, among others, initiated the processes by which Faria e Sousa would have to face the Inquisition both in Spain and in Portugal on account of his published commentary on *Os Lusíadas*. In the "Advertencia" section of his written defense titled *Información en favor de Manuel de Faria i Sousa ...* (1640), he refers to his accusers as "zelosos de si" and "los que se aquilan por todo ruido," and calls into question their integrity for putting forward a denunciation of his work the same week of its publication. With some comic incredulity he explains: "Esto fue cosa digna de admiración, porque efte Volumen para ser leido de un estudioso, avia menester siquiera medio año: i dellos, a lo menos un siglo: de que se infiere claro, que quien le pudo acusar fingiendo piedad, no le pudo ser para acusarle con fundamento." In a subsequent section of *Información* addressed to Don Álvaro de Costa, he refers to his accusers and their accusations as "profundissimos Amusos" (or profoundly contrary to the Muses). All in all, he sees them as "ministros de la envidia, i de la inquietud, i de la ignorancia" (*Información* 6).[8] Despite this specific opposition, the balance of seventeenth-century criticism tipped in his favor: "Su obra vastísima tuvo numerosos panegiristas y detractores ... Sin embargo, abundaron más los elogios que las censuras, como era justo, y por eso son incontables las alusiones que sus contemporáneos y posteriores le dirigieron" (Martínez-Almoyna 151).

At the turn of the seventeenth century, there were at least two clear indications that Faria e Sousa's legacy would continue in a positive trajectory. On the one hand, his many seventeenth-century admirers left a well-marked paper trail of praises;[9] on the other, some of his most important publications appeared in the fifty years after his death, including English translations of *Asia portuguesa* (1695) and *Europa portuguesa* (1698) by John Stevens. The eighteenth century would see new editions of *Asia portuguesa* (1703), *Europa portuguesa* (1730), *Historia del Reyno de Portugal* (1730, 1779), *Imperio de la China* (1731), and *Fabula de Narcisso e Echo* (1737), as well as an English translation of *Europa portuguesa* (1705, 1713). Add to this editions of Camões's collected works from 1779–80 and again from 1782–83 (which are based in part on Faria e Sousa's earlier editions), and you begin to see a modest yet substantive place for the author during the 1700s. Of course none of this takes into account the many editions of *Os Lusíadas* in Portuguese and in translation that borrowed from Faria e Sousa's monumental edition in one way or another without attribution.[10] By comparison, Francisco Manuel de Melo, perhaps the most critically-acclaimed seventeenth-century Portuguese author of the past century, barely even registers among eighteenth-century publications.

Beyond these editions and reprints, two other works stand out for what they reveal regarding Faria e Sousa's eighteenth-century stature. In 1733, Francisco Xavier de Menezes issued a reprint of Franciso Moreno Porcel's eulogistic biography *Retrato de Manuel de Faria y Sousa* (1650), to which he appended an eleven-page "Juizio Historico." Among his stated objectives for the addition, Menezes hopes to correct the misconception that by staying in Castile after 1640 Faria e Sousa demonstrated a lack of patriotism. His matter-of-fact explanation that Faria e Sousa remained in Madrid as a spy of sorts for João IV has been debated by many critics and historians since.[11] The endgame here is of less importance than the fact that Menezes raises the issue in the first place, especially when considering that loyalty becomes one of the touchstones of Faria e Sousa criticism thereafter. Dîogo Barbosa Machado (1682–1772), however, avoids the question altogether in his four-volume *Bibliotheca Lusitana* (1741–58)—still considered an invaluable bibliographic source. The entry on Faria e Sousa is extensive, covering seven pages. It offers a short biography, a run-down of what his peers thought of him, and a list of his collected writings. By way of evaluation, Barbosa Machado describes Faria e Sousa as follows: "A natureza se empenhou a formar na sua pessoa hum exemplar de todos os dotes scientificos concorrendo a viveza do engenho, a felicidade da memoria, e a vasta lição da Historia, e Poesia para ser venerada por Oraculo" (250; "Nature worked over-time to create in his person a model of all scientific gifts through which keenness of intellect, abundant memory, and significant training in History and Poetry all vie for Oraculo's admiration"). He later states that "seu nome celebraõ as pennas de doutissimos Escritores como merecido tributo ao seu incomparavel engenho" (253; "the pens of such gifted Writers celebrate his name as a well-earned tribute to his incomparable genius"). It is worth noting that there are no statements of censure to balance out the acclaim. Barbosa Machado's "library" of Portuguese authors does not make any distinction between those who wrote in Portuguese versus those who wrote in other languages, a reality that Fidelino de Figueiredo would underscore almost two centuries later: "convém recordar que estudar a elaboração literária em português não é possuir ìntegramente o génio literário português, porque Portugal também se expressou literàriamente em latim, em castelhano e em hebreu" (*História* 55; "it is worth remembering that studying the literary process in Portuguese one cannot fully appreciate the literary genius of the Portuguese, because Portugal also expressed itself literarily in Latin, in Spanish, and in Hebrew"). All of this does not mean that the eighteenth century had anything to say by way of reproof, only that the positive overall perception of Faria e Sousa coming out of the seventeenth century remained in place going into the nineteenth.

Everything changed for Faria e Sousa's legacy during the nineteenth century.[12] A newfound concept of nation gave rise to a new brand of nationalism in Europe that would impact, among other things, literary canons. Whereas Barbosa Machado's encyclopedic text allows for Portuguese authors regardless of the language in which they wrote, the nineteenth century would raise the issue of language loyalty in its assessment of Portugal's literary past.[13] What is more, with Romanticism came a significant shift in aesthetics that is discernible both in its own expression as well as in its evaluation of previous literary movements. José Maria da Costa e Silva (1788–1854) illustrates this very point in the opening paragraph of his chapters on Faria e Sousa in *Ensaio biographico-critico sobre os melhores poetas portuguezes*: "Poeta, crítico, historiador, moralista, e erudito … gozou no seu tempo de uma grande reputação literaria, que longe de conservar-se intacta, tem consideravelmente diminuido com o correr dos tempos, e o progresso do bom gosto literario" (7:96; "Poet, critic, historian, moralist, and scholar … he enjoyed a great literary reputation in his day, though far from remaining intact, having diminished considerably over time and given the development of good literary taste"). Costa e Silva sees the decline of Faria e Sousa's standing as a sign of progress; the inevitable outcome of superior literary tastes. The conceit in this passage, however, is mild compared to the outright arrogance that would follow in some of what Camilo Castelo Branco, Teófilo Braga, Álvaro J. da Costa Pimpão, Marcelino Menéndez Pelayo, Wilhelm Storck, and Carolina Michäelis de Vasconcelos would write about Faria e Sousa during the late nineteenth and early twentieth centuries.[14] In his preface to *Fortuna*, Edward Glaser takes on Castelo Branco's particularly hostile attitude toward Faria e Sousa (Introduction 11–13). As he summarizes, "Castelo Branco's piece attests to his formidable skills as a polemicist as well as to his unfitness for the calling of a literary historian" (Introduction 12).

Characteristic as it is of the time in which it was conceived, on the whole, Costa e Silva's assessment of Faria e Sousa's literary output is fairly well-balanced.[15] His primary contention is that Faria e Sousa underachieved:

> Parece que a natureza se havia esmerado em enriquecer Manoel de Faria e Sousa de todos os dotes, e prendas necesarias para fazer brilhante figura na republica das letras, engenho agudo, amor do estudo, comprehensão fácil, imaginação viva, e sobre tudo tenaz, e prodigiosa memoria, que é o primeiro, e mais eficaz instrumento do saber humano, e sería hoje um dos escriptores mais estimados, e conhecidos da nossa patria, se o pessimo gosto do seculo, em que viveu, não tivesse corrompido, e quasi inutilisado tão felices disposições naturaes. (7:97)

> Nature seems to have worked extra hard to bless Manoel de
> Faria e Sousa with all of the necessary gifts and abilities to cut
> him a brilliant figure in the republic of letters, including a sharp
> wit, love for study, quick intellect, vibrant imagination, and
> above all tenacious and prodigious memory, which is the first
> and most effective instrument of human knowledge, and today
> he would be one of the most esteemed and well-known writers
> of our homeland if the awful taste of the time in which he lived
> had not corrupted and almost rendered useless the delightful
> capacities that were his birthright.

Although this may come across as harsh, Faria e Sousa's autobiographical writings communicate a similar sense of frustration; not
that he was born at the wrong time, but that he did not attain the
level of greatness that his natural gifts and work ethic promised.
For Costa e Silva, he was just too baroque (7:107). That said, there
are no shortage of redeeming passages in Costa e Silva's criticism:
"Si exceptuarmos Calderon, e Lope de Vega Carpio, parece-me
que sem escrúpulo poderemos considerar Manoel de Faria e Sousa
como o Escriptor mais fecundo, e variado, que tem produzido a
Peninula das Hespanhas" (7:151; "Not counting Calderon and
Lope de Vega Carpio, without hesitation I think we can consider
Manoel de Faria e Sousa the most prolific and varied writer that
the Iberian Peninsula has produced").[16] It is important to remember that Costa e Silva is the exception. The fairness with which
we might characterize his critical appraisal of Faria e Sousa is
tempered by the hostility of Costa e Silva's contemporaries, who
saw him as a "self-seeking eccentric whose critical judgments are
of dubious value" (Glaser, Introduction 5). Sena puts nineteenth-
century criticism in its proper context: "A obra de Faria e Sousa
... tem de ser julgada no contexto político-cultural do seu tempo,
e não com os anacronismos de nacionalismo burguês e romântico
que ainda tanto pesam nos prejuízos historicistas portugueses"
(16; "Faria e Sousa's work ... has to be judged within the politico-
cultural context of his time, and not by the anachronisms of a
bourgeois and romantic nationalism that still weigh so heavily on
Portuguese historical prejudices"). Overall, Sena attributes Faria e
Sousa's decline to "uma confusa reacção antibarroca" (39; "a confusing anti-baroque reaction").

If the nineteenth and early twentieth centuries were the
undoing of Faria e Sousa's legacy, criticism since has gradually been

fixing an image of Faria e Sousa that is not merely a throwback to yesteryear, but an enhanced perspective that restores him "to the pre-eminent place which rightfully should be his in the history of Iberian culture" (Glaser, Introduction 6). It is precisely within the Iberian frame, in fact, that Faria e Sousa is best contemplated. During the second half of the twentieth century perspectives on Faria e Sousa began to shift, with Glaser among the scholars most committed to reevaluating the author's contribution to seventeenth-century Iberian letters.[17] More than forty years ago, Glaser signaled three major causes for the "prevailing misconceptions" surrounding Faria e Sousa's life and work (Introduction 5–6): first, that writing in Spanish put him in a "no-man's land of literary history" (5); second, the difficulty of gaining access to his writings; and third, the lack of accurate biographical information. Significant improvements in each of these areas has resulted in the critical attention that Glaser hoped to facilitate through the publication of Faria e Sousa's autobiography in 1975, among many critical works authored by Glaser (still the greatest Faria e Sousa scholar).[18] Knowingly or not, scholars have answered Glaser's call to "come forth" with new research to support or contradict his own ideas (6). Some (Asensio, Costa Pimpão, Pierce, Sena) were Glaser's contemporaries, but many more have emerged in the decades since his passing, and with them a new era of Faria e Sousa scholarship.[19] Despite this swell of interest, no one has put forward a study focused entirely on the *portugalidade* that permeates Faria e Sousa's collected works.

For centuries, the majority of critics and historians within and beyond Iberia have reduced Faria e Sousa to what they see as a contradiction.[20] While on the one hand many acknowledge his exaggerated love for Portugal, on the other they reject his national pride due to his residence in Castile and overwhelming literary production in Spanish. Domingo García Peres sees the situation as an obvious case of paradox: "Faria y Souza tuvo la mala suerte de ser sospechoso á la mayor parte de los españoles por ser portugués, y a los portugueses por escribir en castellano, y seguir residiendo en Castilla después de la emancipación" (208–09). Consequently, as Arthur Askins observes, "he is allowed an easy home in neither tradition" ("Manuel" 245). Rather than inciting a critical tug-of-war over which literary tradition can claim Faria e Sousa and his Portuguese contemporaries writing in Spanish, most critics have simply discarded their contributions altogether. Some of his contemporaries, not to mention most critics and historians since, have managed to see past Faria e Sousa's Castilian mask. Rather than overemphasize the Spanish exterior of his works, my reading of Faria e Sousa uncovers the Portuguese identity at the heart of his literary corpus. By this I do not mean to say that by stripping away his Spanish identity one arrives at a true, Portuguese persona, only that the deep structure of his literature reveals the latter as his identity of choice. He self-identified as Portuguese, and as a result he consistently lays claim to this national collectivity in his works (at the same time that he contributes to its invention). None of this, however, erases the Spanish part of his identity. That he often affirms the former over the latter does not give the reader permission to ignore neither the one nor the other. The author defies, therefore, either/or criticism, embodying, instead, a blend of Iberian identities ("Iberian," by its very nature, suggesting such a mingling). It is precisely the fluidity of identity among early modern Portuguese authors that has stifled many scholars over the centuries.

Traditionally, critics have either obsessed over Faria e Sousa's connections to Castile or oversimplified his literary contribution. This tends to include some reference to his lengthy stay in Madrid and/or the fact that he wrote predominantly in Spanish—as if either of these realities say anything about the content of his writings—and some flippant allegation concerning the quality of his work (inaccurate, exaggerated, imitative).[21] I will argue that these frequent indictments merely serve as red herrings, leading the reader to reject Faria e Sousa's works on account of a perceived disloyalty. These slippery issues, in fact, prove very little concerning the author's devotion to Portugal and even less about the quality of his writing. If Faria e Sousa is to claim his deserved place within Iberian letters, the role of the Portuguese writer during the Dual Monarchy will have to be considered with greater impartiality and attention to the text. Following a brief contextualization of Faria e Sousa's residence and choice of literary language, my investigation will lead to the author's literary criticism and historiography, thereby allowing the text and the context to work together to demonstrate his *portugalidade*.

Faria e Sousa's long-time residence in Castile (1619–28, 1634–49) is one of the most misunderstood aspects of his life and one of the reasons for which he has been disparaged by the Portuguese lettered community throughout history. An association fallacy fueled the view that because he lived in Spain for so many years (and remained there after 1640), he was therefore a traitor and not worthy of inclusion in Portugal's literary heritage. There are at least two things wrong with this perspective. First, it is a clear case of ad hominem to discount Faria e Sousa's writings on account of a perceived character flaw. Second, the character flaw in question makes assumptions about Faria e Sousa's intentions that cannot be corroborated by the historical record. By his own admission, Faria e Sousa wanted to return to Portugal almost as soon as he had arrived in Madrid (*Fortuna* 171). This is made abundantly clear in his autobiography, wherein the author repeatedly describes unsuccessful efforts to return to Portugal, making him a sort of anti-hero who cannot complete the journey home. Eugenio Asensio keys in on this trope in his assessment of the autobiography: "Cuando escribe la *Fortuna* imagina al panorama de su vida como una aspiración frustrada de regresar a la tierra natal de Entre-Douro-e-Minho donde él y su mujer poseen tierras. De hecho no la vuelve a ver más que durante una fugaz visita en noviembre-diciembre de 1629. Es un Ulises que, con cualquier pretexto, retrasa la vuelta a la tierra soñada" ("Autobiografía" 633). This citation takes on Faria e Sousa's apparent duplicity. While he desires to return to Portugal, his pride will not allow him to return a failure. He insists on achieving the success he set out for in the first place: symbolic capital sufficient to hold the respect of his countrymen, and enough actual capital to provide for his wife and children (*Fortuna* 159). It would be wrong, however, to read this duplicity negatively. It is not about the author falling short as either a Portuguese patriot or a converted Castilian, but about the ways in which he asserts *portugalidade* within the broader context of his Iberian identity.

Faria e Sousa's self-writing offers much more than unfulfilled desire to return to Portugal. Many other passages shed light on the author's living situation, clarifying his purposes for leaving his native land on the one hand, and capturing his state of mind while living in Spain on the other. In the following selection, for example, Faria e Sousa juxtaposes his allegiance with that of some of his compatriots: "En Castilla entré pero ella nunca pudo entrar en mí; por más y más que después viese en Madrid a muchos portugueses olvidados de su patria y aun de su honra (si honra puede haber en quien se olvida de su patria), que parecía que al pasar los ríos que se pasan de Portugal a Castilla, habían pasado el Leteo" (*Fortuna* 160–61), which, according to Greek mythology, is the river of forgetfulness located in Hades. Here Faria e Sousa distinguishes between the physical and the metaphysical. That is, the author would have the reader believe that *where* he was did not change *who* he was. What can be destabilizing about Faria e Sousa is that he lives *both* lives, although clearly favoring the one (Portuguese) over the other (Spanish)—at least on paper. Accordingly, a rewriting of the first part of the above passage could easily read, "I left Portugal but Portugal never left me." Those who would have Faria e Sousa pursue a writing career in his homeland ignore the realities of the Iberian Union, when "o centro de gravidade da vida política e da cultura desloca-se inevitávelmente para Madrid" (Sena 13; "the center of gravity of political and cultural life inevitably moves to Madrid"). As Faria e Sousa sees it, the duty of the Portuguese is not to stay home, but to remember Portugal while living abroad; that the give-and-take of cross-cultural experiences never justifies the desertion of one's native identity. Among the many Portuguese who fit the mold (i.e., having remained in Castile after the *Restauração*), history has been especially harsh in its treatment of Faria e Sousa:

> foram muitos os "grandes" de Portugal e seus servidores que não regressaram senão depois de garantidos os seus privilégios pelo tratado de paz de 1668, e não pesa sobre eles o mesmo anátema, nem eles, que se saiba, tiveram—no defender e apresentar internacionalmente, na língua franca da Europa seiscentista que o castelhano era, as glórias e a dignidade de Portugal—papel semelhante ao que Faria e Sousa desempenhou com os seus trabalhos de historiografia e a sua actividade de polígrafo. (Sena 10–11)

> Many of the "greats" from Portugal and their followers never returned until after their privileges had been guaranteed by the peace treaty of 1668, and the same anathema does not afflict them nor have they, as far as I know—introduced and defended internationally in the *lingua franca* of seventeenth-century Europe which Spanish was, the glories and dignity of Portugal—had a similar role to the one Faria e Sousa carried out with his historiographical works and myriad activities as a writer.

Here Jorge de Sena points out the irony that Faria e Sousa is more shunned than his Portuguese contemporaries who also stayed in Spain after 1640 even though none of them can compete with the Lusocentrism of his writings and their international influence.

In 1631 Manuel de Faria e Sousa accepted a position as secretary to the marquês de Castelo Rodrigo, D. Manuel de Moura Corte-Real (1590–1651), who had been appointed ambassador to Rome. Within a few years, however, he would abandon Italy and his patron in order to return to Madrid. His unexpected appearance in Castile led to suspicions of treason and imprisonment at the hands of the Inquisition (Barbosa 251). Although liberated from this confinement after three months, Faria e Sousa lost the right to freely leave the capital, thus eliminating any possibility of a return home (Glaser, Introduction 74). According to his autobiography, he spent the next five years seeking permission to return to Portugal. By his own admission, the erudite dedications to Felipe IV and the Conde Duque de Olivares in his commentary on *Os Lusíadas* were actually crafted with this purpose in mind: "el premio que yo esperaba … era la licencia solicitada, por el discurso de cinco años y nunca alcanzada, para irme a mi casa" (*Fortuna* 375). His city arrest reminded him that, while he may have lived in the heart of the Spanish Empire, he was still an outsider; his life story would always begin with "Once upon a time in the kingdom of Portugal." To complicate matters even more for the Portuguese living in Spain, after the Restoration of 1640 Portuguese soldiers were permitted to leave Spain only to perform military duties, at which time many would desert to England and make their way back to the newly freed homeland (T. Braga, *História* 303). Even if the excitement of the Restoration had motivated Faria e Sousa enough to convince him to leave his failures behind and return to Portugal, and supposing that he were able to somehow orchestrate this flight home, the poor health and destitute living conditions facing the ailing author overwhelmed any chances of this happening. Suffice it to say, then, that while many factors kept Faria e Sousa in Castile, disloyalty to his native Portugal is not one of them.

Even though many have cited Faria e Sousa's residence in Madrid before and after 1640 as proof of his lack of patriotism and justification for marginalizing his works, his choice to write in Spanish has fueled just as many—if not more—of his detractors over the centuries. More than four hundred years after his birth, Faria e Sousa still maintains the distinction, or for some, the infamy, of having published more in the Spanish language than any other Portuguese author in history. Many question Faria e Sousa's commitment to Portugal, given his decision to write predominantly in the Spanish language. This choice, however, is far too complex to be reduced so easily. A number of different factors motivated Portuguese authors to write in Spanish, including economic opportunism, literary prestige, and a larger reading audience. What is more, writers had to conform to the demands of the market, which at that time favored literature published in Spanish. Faria e Sousa describes this reality in his autobiography: "Todos mis escritos, antes de pasar a Castilla, fueron en portugués, si no eran algunos pocos versos; porque siempre tuve por absurdo el hacerse un portugués castellano en Portugal. Después que pasé a Castilla, fue preciso hacerme castellano, porque como ya escribía para imprimir, no me imprimieran acá lo que escribiese en portugués" (*Fortuna* 156). These words capture the fluidity of identity among Faria e Sousa and many of his contemporaries. Rather than cast aside his Portuguese identity and become Castilian as market forces required, Faria e Sousa resisted the homogenizing effects of imperial rule and cultural hegemony by expanding his concept of self to include more hybrid categories (bilingual, multicultural, Iberian). The author never stopped writing in Portuguese, choosing instead to translate his writings from Portuguese to Spanish in order to publish them in Madrid. That is to say, he chose to work from within the imperial system to spread the glories of his native land rather than putting down his pen altogether.

In addition to the publishing standards of the time, writing in Portuguese severely limited the reach of a particular work because the target audience was comparatively small.[22] Works authored in Spanish, on the other hand, could circulate throughout the Iberian Peninsula, not to mention many other parts of Europe and the world. Simply stated, "el castellano le era necesario, como lengua internacional, para hacer llegar a España y a la Europa culta su inmenso alegato en defensa y gloria de Portugal y de su poeta Camões" (Asensio, "Fortuna" 318). Faria e Sousa himself describes the relationship between language and readership in the prologue of his commentary on *Os Lusíadas*: "Valganme los expositores Latinos de textos Griegos; i de textos Latinos me valgan los expositores vulgares en diferentes lenguas" (*Lusiadas* 13).[23] The point here is that Faria e Sousa wants to extend to others the same benefit that he has enjoyed from reading works that would otherwise be inaccessible given his limited knowledge of Greek and Latin. We should agree with Eugenio Asensio, then, that writing in Spanish served a performative function; a costume necessary to fulfill a role: "sirviéndose del castellano como instrumento, [Faria e Sousa] reveló al público de la Península y de más allá la genialidad de Camões y las glorias heroicas de Portugal" ("Autobiografía" 630). Esther de Lemos agrees: "o seu amor pelas coisas portuguesas não fica, porém, em causa: antes pelo contrário, pois tratar delas numa língua então de tão larga audiência, era a melhor forma de lhes assegurar universalidade de expansão" (4; "his love for all things Portuguese is not the issue: quite the contrary, since speaking of them in a language with such a large readership was the best way to assure their worldwide expansion"). Speaking specifically of Faria e Sousa's edition of *Os Lusíadas*, Jorge de Sena adds: "o facto de esta obra dele ter sido publicada em espanhol—para mais directamente influenciar a cultura hispânica e mais largamente difundir Camões na Europa—não a faz menos um monumento da cultura portuguesa" (9; "the fact that this work of his was published in Spanish—in order to more directly influence Spanish culture and better publicize Camões throughout Europe—does not make it any less of a monument of Portuguese culture"). Fouto and Weiss underscore the bilingual nature of Faria e Sousa's edition—with analysis and a prose translation in Spanish to go with the original Portuguese—their point being that the former exists to promote the latter (10–11). Spanish, then, is a means to a Portuguese end.

One may scrutinize the effectiveness of Faria e Sousa's strategy, but that it is a legitimate approach to promoting Portugal during a very fluid time in Iberian history cannot be denied. Eduardo Lourenço observes the delicate nature of this endeavor: "Faria e Sousa celebra em castelhano as glórias lusitanas, sem ver nisso contradição alguma, e, o que é mais importante, sem que os espanhóis com elas se apoquentem" (*Labirinto* 27; "Faria e Sousa celebrates Lusitanian glories in Castilian, without seeing in this any contradictions, and, what is more important, without the Spanish feeling less than"). Here Lourenço acknowledges that what subsequent critics and historians might see as a contradiction (i.e., Portuguese authors celebrating Portugal in Spanish), did not register as such in Faria e Sousa's mind (or in the mind of his contemporaries, for that matter). Lourenço also recognizes the risk Faria e Sousa undertook in writing such Lusocentric works. At what point does writing about Portuguese greatness in the dominant Iberian language of the time (i.e., Spanish) begin to undermine Spanish hegemony? Though it is difficult to imagine anyone exalting Portugal to greater heights than Faria e Sousa did in his writings, he managed to do so without retribution from his Spanish contemporaries. One could argue then that rather than a sign of some kind of disloyalty, writing patriotic works in Spanish may have been the best way to promote and preserve the Portuguese imaginary. This may be what Asensio had in mind when he crowned Faria e Sousa "el más patriota de los portugueses" ("Autobiografía" 635). It can be said, therefore, that while Faria e Sousa dressed the majority of his works in the Spanish language, the substance of his works is overwhelmingly Portuguese. The ever-popular attack on Faria e Sousa's loyalty, based primarily on his choice to write in Spanish, is misguided and, as we will see hereafter, cannot be substantiated by the works themselves. Whether Faria e Sousa or any number of his compatriots, the choice to write in Spanish cannot be reduced to a singular cause. Shades of opportunism, strategem, necessity, and custom all color our understanding of this practice. When it comes to early modern Portuguese literature, it is a mistake to reject or favor authors based solely on the language of their writings.

Faria e Sousa as Literary Critic

Among the many genres that comprise Faria e Sousa's collected writings, literary criticism stands out more prominently than any other. This includes the introductory sections of his poetic masterpiece *Fuente de Aganipe* (1627); his critical editions of Camões's lyric poetry, *Rimas varias de Luis de Camoens, principe de los poetas heroicos, y Liricos de España* (1685); and his most celebrated work, *Lusiadas de Luis de Camoens, principe de los poetas de España* (1639). He completed the four-volume edition of more than two-thousand columns over the course of twenty-five years of intense study, writing, and revision. This includes a 1621 draft in Portuguese, a more extensive version in 1638 (by that time translated into Spanish), and the official publication of 1639 (Askins, "Inéditos" 220). His all-encompassing look at Camões's masterpiece cross-references at least five-hundred additional authors of world literature, with special emphasis on Virgil. In the opening paragraph of his introduction to the Imprensa Nacional-Casa da Moeda's 1972 commemorative edition of the work, Jorge de Sena describes the enormity of Faria e Sousa's undertaking and achievement, calling it "um dos mais extraordinários monumentos erguidos por alguém, devotadamente, a um poeta e a uma cultura" (9; "one of the most extraordinary monuments erected by someone, unconditionally, to a poet and a culture"). "Monumental," in any of its iterations, is actually one of the most repeated words put forward in written descriptions of what Faria e Sousa accomplished with this publication.[24]

In his autobiography, Faria e Sousa describes the meticulous process by which he completed the study:

> Empecé a leer a Homero con un cuadernillo blanco en la mesa y la pluma en la mano; como yo tenía en la memoria toda la *Lusíada*, luego [que] se me venía a los ojos cualquier lugar que de ella se parecía a alguno de los que iba leyendo en la *Ilíada* o *Ulisea*, éste copiaba en mi cuadernillo apuntando la estancia y el canto de la *Lusíada* con que se respondía, o por imitación o por concurrencia. De este modo me hube con cada uno y algunos a tres, porque de una es imposible cogerlo todo, ni aun de muchas; pero cogí mucho de todos, que por discurso de veinte años pasaron de quinientos libros, y así me hallé a lo menos con quinientos cuadernillos de notas sacadas con este trabajo, que jamás le tomó nadie en el mundo. (*Fortuna* 151)

This passage captures the persistent, all-encompassing effort of Faria e Sousa's critical work, including the initial memorization of Camões's poem, the intertextualization of the epic with the rest of Western literature, and the development of a research archive consisting of at least five hundred notebooks. Faria e Sousa explains that the major difference between his commentary and others is the long, concerted effort he dedicated to the poem: "Hablo con seguridad, i no sin respeto: porque yo no digo que lo obré por mayor entendimiento, ni sutileza, ni estudio, sino por mayor diligencia, i desvelo, i amor al credito de España por el ingenio, que Luis de Camoẽs le perpetuó con el suyo" (*Lusiadas*

14). In reference to a passage from vol. 4 of his commentary in which the author describes the pathetic state he was in following a half-century of tireless reading and study of *Os Lusíadas*, Asensio makes an acute observation: "Faria y Sousa recuerda al Caballero de la Triste Figura, tanto por su traza física como por su espléndida obsesión" ("Fortuna" 319).

While the magnitude of Faria e Sousa's commentary alone is remarkable, its superb erudition is also noteworthy. Sena acknowledges both of these qualities at the same time that he underscores its relevance to today's readers:

> os comentários de Faria e Sousa são mais relevantes hoje do que o eram quando ele os publicou, porque nos colocam em contacto com uma multidão de referências que se perderam da memória culta e dormem o seu sono na vastidão das bibliotecas e arquivos deste mundo. Não precisavam tanto os contemporâneos dele da sua erudição, quanto o precisamos todos nós. Mas ele não é só erudição: é também, na sua 'vesânia' camoniana, no seu culto esclarecido pelo grande poeta, um intérprete, um iluminador de numerosos passos, e um crítico com a plena consciência da magnitude complexa da obra máxima de Camões, como do espírito que neste havia. (55)

> Faria e Sousa's commentary is more relevant today than it was when he published it, because he puts us in contact with a multitude of references that were lost to the educated mind, sleeping away in the wide expanse of libraries and archives of this world. His contemporaries did not need his erudition as much as all of us do. But he is more than just erudition: he is also, in his mental frenzy for Camões, in his enlightened scholarship on the great poet, an interpreter, a bright light on a dark path and a critic with a clear understanding of the complex magnitude of Camões's greatest work, as well as the man himself.

Faria e Sousa did not arrive at such a comprehensive study by accident. One of the guiding principles of his commentary on *Os Lusíadas* was that his critical work had to ascend to the heights of the original, which for someone with incalculable esteem for Camões is a tall order. In the prologue of his commentary, he makes his purpose clear: "Digo, pues, que el comentó no ha de ser cascarón del comentado: sino que se ha de hazer tan uno aquél con éste, que éste no se pueda desear sin aquél" (*Lusiadas* 5). As this passage illustrates, Faria e Sousa does not want to see his work easily discarded; in fact, he would have it so highly regarded as to make his commentary inseparable from the original (and by extension, the commentator from the poet). In Lope de Vega's estimation, Faria e Sousa achieved this very thing. He describes the commentary as "un trabajo invencible," adding that "deste genero de estudios no logra nuestra lengua semejante escrito; ni de las estrañas ay otro que se le pueda justamente aventajar" ("Elogio al comentador" 2). Over the centuries, many critics and historians have echoed Lope's assessment of Faria e Sousa's work, confirming its place at the pinnacle of all critical commentaries.[25]

Regarding the impact of Faria e Sousa's study, Lope de Vega explains how the Portuguese critic's commentary changed public perception of Camoēs and his work: "No ay duda, que el Poema de Luis de Camoes tuvo siempre estimacion de grande: pero desde oy la tendra de grandissimo, con los Comentarios de Manuel de Faria i Sousa ("Elogio" 1).[26] He adds, "Todos le teniamos por mayor en las Rimas varias, i agora sin comparacion es mayor en este Poema, con lo que su Comentador descubre" ("Elogio" 3). According to the latter passage, Faria e Sousa's critical commentary illuminated Camōes's epic to such a degree that the reading public would never again see Portugal's most cherished poet in the same way. That Camōes's fame rests primarily on his epic and second on his lyric poetry is a testament to Faria e Sousa's influence. Lope extends his praise even further by comparing Faria e Sousa's critical undertaking to Camōes's epic: "Como Luis de Camoēs es Principe de los Poetas que escrivieron en idioma vulgar, lo es Manuel de Faria de los Comentadores en todas lenguas" ("Elogio" 1). The parallels between the Poet and his Commentator extend well beyond Lope's precise observation. The deep structure of each work reveals a similar sense of loyalty to and veneration for Portugal. This likeness is often lost in the many attempts to discredit the theoretical approach and other perceived errors in the commentary. Anecdotally, Lope concludes his "Elogio" with a friend's astute observation: "Que Luis de Camoēs avia nacido solo para escrivir esta Poesia, i Manuel de Faria para comentarla" (26). Before the actual commentary begins, however, Lope's name appears one last time. In a metafictional turn reminiscent of Cervantes, Lope has fun with one of the dedicatory poems, using four lines from *Os*

Lusíadas to praise Faria e Sousa in the name of Camões as if they had been written for his commentator in the first place.

One can ascertain the value of Faria e Sousa's commentary by the mere fact that it is one of the few early modern Portuguese-authored works in Spanish that survived the centuries. While many critics (including some of his contemporaries) have tried to dismiss the value of this work—basing their criticism primarily on superficial readings and character attacks—the disappearing act they have pulled on most Portuguese-authored works of the Dual Monarchy has not worked in this case. They have succeeded, however, in misrepresenting Faria e Sousa as a Castilianized Portuguese defector. It is clear that he lived many years and eventually died in Madrid, wrote most of his works in Spanish, and was a member of Madrid's Republic of Letters. These factors, however, do not mean that Faria e Sousa's glorification of Portugal was simply an act of self-fashioning. There is no textual or historical evidence to support the idea that he was marketing Portuguese exoticism and otherness for his own benefit. Never do his works directly glorify Spain, nor do his praises of Portugal read as an appeal for entry into the lettered elite of the empire. Instead, Faria e Sousa speaks of his native land in terms of differentiation, emphasizing how unique Portugal is in relation to Spain, sometimes expressing this distinctiveness in terms of superiority. Although there are some exceptions, Faria e Sousa and his nationalist contemporaries were not involved in a mudslinging campaign against Spain so much as a revalorizing movement, a crusade on behalf of the Portuguese nation.

From the outset of his master work, Faria e Sousa makes his allegiance to Portugal very clear. His patriotic agenda begins with the title: *Lusiadas de Luis de Camoens, principe de los poetas de España.*[27] Whereas the first part of the title quietly passes, what follows thereafter is striking. There is an important precedent for using the designation "prince" in reference to a poet. It appears on the Peninsula as early as 1555 in *Los doze libros de la Eneid de Vergilio, principe de los poetas latinos.* Thereafter, the Renaissance writer Garcilaso de la Vega received the same distinction among Castilian poets. In 1622, for example, Tomás Tamayo de Vargas titled his critical edition *Garcilasso de la Vega, natural de Toledo: Príncipe de los Poetas Castellanos,* only to be echoed four years later in Luis Brizeño's *Obras de Garcilasso de la Vega, Príncipe de los Poetas Castellanos.* While Virgil was given preeminence among authors who composed in Latin, Garcilaso assumed the same role in Spanish. By 1630, however, Luis de Góngora would enter the conversation of poetic preeminence through José Pellicer de Salas y Tovar's *Lecciones solemnes a las obras de don Luis de Gongora y Argote, Pindaro Andaluz, Principe de los Poetas Liricos de España.* As Laura Bass reveals in her compelling article "Poética, imperio y la idea de España en época de Olivares: las *Lusíadas comentadas* de Manuel de Faria e Sousa," Faria e Sousa was already thinking in terms of princification in his 1621 draft of the work (187–88). Rather than name Camões heir to a particular genre or kingdom of Spain, however, Faria e Sousa surpasses the scope of these previous works, increasing Camões's poetic reign to the entire Iberian Peninsula in the 1639 title of his commentary.[28] Bass further explains: "con su coronación de Camões como príncipe de los poetas de España, Faria e Sousa desplaza la cumbre de la poesía española desde Castilla hacia Portugal (y del castellano al portugués)" (195). While it is true that this attribution exalts his poet, as Hans Flasche points out, it also conveys Faria e Sousa's propensity to conceive of the world in Iberian terms: "Ao designar Camões como 'príncipe de los poetas de España,' Faria e Sousa fala a uma consciência ibérica que, pelo menos nele, se mantinha ainda viva" (12: "By designating Camões 'prince of the poets of Spain,' Faria e Sousa speaks to an Iberian consciousness that, at least in him, remained live").

Faria e Sousa seems well aware of the audacity surrounding the title of his work, although he considers it modest compared to the title he might have used. In section twenty-four of "Vida del poeta," one of the introductory sections of his commentary, he confidently affirms his position on the matter, extending the sphere of Camonian superiority even further: "A los que estuvieron congoxados con el titulo que en la fachada deste volumen dimos al Poeta, de Principe de los de España; no fuera mucho si dixeramos de todos los de Europa (que viene a ser de todo el mundo; pues solamente a ella cupo la suerte de las letras politicas, ingeniosas, i doctas) ya que el Poeta se aventajó a todos" (49–50). As is evident in this passage, Faria e Sousa esteems Camões above all others. "Mi gran Poeta," as he frequently describes Camões, embodies all of the scattered literary talent of the past: "España en solo Luis de Camões vio junta la grandeza de Homero, i Virgilio en lo Heroico:

la de Pindaro, i Oracio en lo Lirico: la de Menandro, i Plauto en lo Comico, con igualdad notable; apropriandose a si solo quanto consiguieron en diferentes edades, i sujetos los Griegos, i los Latinos; los Italianos, i los Españoles" (*Lusiadas de Luis de Camoens* 1.47). The divinization of Camões that occurs in this passage establishes him as none other than the Poetic Messiah. Just as the commentator argues that all literature before Camões points to his coming, he sees the best of his Iberian contemporaries as disciples of the Portuguese poet (Cisneros 2). Faria e Sousa's exaggerated description of Camões echoes his overall "tendencia patriótica" (Asensio, "Fortuna" 318) to hyperbolize Portuguese greatness in his commentary.

Faria e Sousa's title triggers a sense of competition characteristic of the baroque literary mentality. From Luis de Góngora's one-upping of Garcilaso de la Vega in his *carpe diem* sonnet "Mientras por competir con tu cabello" to Sor Juana's challenge of Padre Vieira's theology in *Carta Atenagórica*, the baroque overflows with examples of literary rivalry. In the case of Faria e Sousa's edition of Camões's national epic, the primary antecedent and rival to his work is Fernando Herrera's commentary on Garcilaso's *Obras* (1580). Herrera's critical work establishes Garcilaso as the father of Spanish poetry and initiates the "Príncipe" discussion, although he does not include the designation in the title of his work. In the opening pages of his *Anotaciones* Herrera refers to Garcilaso as "Príncipe de la poesía española" (fol. iv) and "Príncipe de los poetas castellanos" (fol. 8). As he clarifies, the scope of this designation extends to those writing in "el lenguaje español" (fol. 12). Faria e Sousa's editions of Camões's poetry constitute the first legitimate rival to Herrera's work on Garcilaso, and the Portuguese author seems well aware of it.[29] There is, in fact, a certain degree of tension or, to use Harold Bloom's useful expression, "anxiety of influence," in Faria e Sousa's attitude toward Herrera and Garcilaso: "Faria e Sousa recognizes in Garcilaso his condition as originator of a new poetic school, but at the same time he feels the need to repeat time and time again that his genius does not admit comparison with that of Camões" (Glaser, *Estudios* 11). While Faria e Sousa acknowledges Garcilaso's merit, he only grants the poet a fragment of Camões's greatness. Faria e Sousa's treatment of Herrera, on the other hand, not only withholds praise, but approaches hostility: "Tan afincado está su resentimiento contra

Herrera que inicia sus anotaciones a las *Rimas* de Camões haciendo objeto al andaluz de una furiosa arremetida. No ataca solamente su posición en determinadas cuestiones eruditas, sino que menosprecia la obra entera de su 'competidor'" (Glaser, *Estudios* 16). Faria e Sousa suggestively asks the reader, "en que se funda el titulo de Divino Herrera?" (*Rimas*, "Advertencias"), as if to question his worthiness of such a designation. The harshness of his assessment suggests that Faria e Sousa was speaking less as a literary critic than as a jealous bystander of the fame Herrera achieved for himself and the glory he brought upon his poet, Garcilaso de la Vega.

While the title of his commentary reflects the general literary climate of the Baroque, it also manifests Faria e Sousa's specific view of the Peninsula and his place therein. Faria e Sousa, after all, was born and lived the majority of his life in a "unified" Iberia. As much as this was a political unification, the artistic continuity between the Spanish and Portuguese was as proximate as it had ever been and, perhaps, ever would be. It makes sense, therefore, for Faria e Sousa to think in these terms. That is, framing his critical commentary in terms of the Iberian Peninsula fits a certain logic unique to annexation mentality. Clearly, an author as well read and metacritical as Faria e Sousa was aware of the differences between Spain and Portugal. Although it would be wrong to read in his appeal to a Peninsular space a distancing from his Portuguese origin, such a conception does suggest that some authors in the period identified themselves with more than one collectivity. Faria e Sousa and many of his Portuguese contemporaries affirm a belonging that links them specifically to Portugal, while at the same time acknowledging their participation in something of a larger scale. The most appropriate locus for the author and his work may very well be, then, the shared place between the Spanish and the Portuguese, what Ricardo Jorge calls an *intercultura* (xvi).

While the designation "Príncipe" certainly sets the tone for the entire commentary, the national fervor of the title page extends beyond the title itself. Gracing the bottom half of the page is the Portuguese coat of arms with its traditional five shields and seven castles. The coat of arms dates back as early as the twelfth century and is a fundamental symbol of Portuguese identity. Whether the author or the publisher is to be credited for this inclusion is unclear (that the coat of arms belongs on the title page of this most Portuguese of works cannot be doubted). One of the most consistent threads throughout Faria e Sousa's commentary is his fervor for Portugal. He weaves a variety of nationalist threads into a single discursive fabric that very much echoes the message of the work in question: *Os Lusíadas*. This fabric includes numerous references to history, geography, language, and religion. It is clear throughout the text that Faria e Sousa speaks not as a desperate outsider trying to reenter his beloved Portugal, but as a committed member of the Portuguese community working from beyond the linguistic and national borders of his native land in an effort to spread the glories of Portugal and her poet.

The opening sections of the commentary reaffirm the sentiment set forth on the title page. In the tenth section of "Advertencias para leerse," for example, Faria e Sousa states his motive for carrying out this work: "por la honra del Poeta i de la patria." In many other occasions he reiterates this same purpose for writing. It is as if Faria e Sousa is trying to match in his commentary the same glorification of Portugal that he sees Camões accomplish in *Os Lusíadas*: "no se hallará en todo este Poema digresión, episodio, ni otro adorno, que no sea, o que no toque acciones gloriosas de la patria" (6.42.97). While several scholars have criticized Faria e Sousa's overdependence on allegory in his reading of *Os Lusíadas*, one cannot discount the patriotic harmony between the text and the commentary: "Não esqueçamos também que a exaltação da Fé e do Império era, como para Camões, uma das intenções do comentário" (Flasche 22; "Let us not forget that the exaltation of Faith and Empire was, like in Camões's case, one of the intentions of the commentary"). In this regard, it can be said that Faria e Sousa masterfully echoes the national pride that underscores his reading of Camões's masterpiece. Faria e Sousa magnifies Camões's national epic by both reproducing it in Portuguese and offering a Spanish prose translation, thereby reaching a larger audience with both his annotations and Camões's original work. Making Camões's masterpiece accessible to a wider reading public is at the core of Faria e Sousa's decision to write his commentary in Spanish, at least according to the author: "Con averle comentado en Castellano, i con la traducion literal de las estancias, facilito a todos el entender esta lengua con poco estudio, mas de leer el Poeta, i el comento" (*Lusiadas* 1.13). In the sixth section of the "Advertencias para leerse con mas luz este libro" Faria e

Sousa makes a similar statement regarding his use of Spanish: "el intento en esta traduccion, assi sea, es para que quien no entiende el Portugues, entiende facil i llanamente lo que contiene cada estrofa." Aurelia Leyva sees Faria e Sousa's attention to language as a clear indication of his overall understanding of early modern Iberia: "En lo que atañe a Faria y Sousa, no se puede dudar de su pericia y sensibilidad de intérprete de *época* de la obra camoniana, al ofrecer una versión en prosa del poema, escrupulosamente atento a la traducción literal en castellano, convencido de la necesidad de favorecer la difusión del mismo" (207).

Benedict Anderson's idea concerning the nation as a simultaneously imagined cultural system is very helpful in describing Faria e Sousa's Portuguese-minded writings. In chapter two of *Imagined Communities*, Anderson describes the cultural roots from and against which nationalism comes into view (12). Herein he emphasizes the role of simultaneity in the development of the national imaginary, including the emerging voice of the collective self: we, us, our (32). This simultaneous expression of the nation is recurrent in early modern Portuguese literature, although less representative of the masses than the learned elite. It does, however, encompass Portugal in its entirety, not merely the exclusive voice of its cultural centers (although it is from these centers that the rest of Portugal is imagined). Faria e Sousa's commentary on *Os Lusíadas*, for one, is replete with examples of what Anderson terms a "world of plurals" (32). The frequency of the collective expression *nuestro*, for example, serves to imagine the "representative body" that constitutes the nation (32). While the recurrent theme of simultaneity is certainly fundamental in Portuguese annexation literature, this type of nation-building depends not only on the dissemination of the possessive adjective "our," but, more importantly, the collective recognition of what that adjective describes. "Our" tells us that "we" are; what follows indicates who/ what we are (at least according to that writer's construction). Faria e Sousa's works, as well as those of many of his Portuguese contemporaries, consistently make reference to our nation, our language, our sea, our loyalty, our valor, our poet (Camões), our religion, our history, our electness, and our preeminence. While the allusion to a broader community alone is a foundational aspect of the movement to which Faria e Sousa belongs, perhaps more significant is the fact that such authors were imagining Portugal in the same way. These collective expressions are embedded in the Spanish writings produced by the Portuguese during the Iberian Union.

Faria e Sousa repeatedly evokes this Portuguese collectivity in his commentary through expressions such as "nuestra nación" (e.g., 7.60.316), "nuestra patria" (e.g., 1.54.307), "nuestro Reyno" (e.g., 8.3.376), "nuestra lengua" (e.g., 2.1.373), "nuestro texto" (e.g., 3.125.169), and, most frequent of all, "nuestro Poeta" (of which there are hundreds of examples). These frequent references are key to our understanding of Faria e Sousa's nationalism in that they reveal the author's synonymous concept of self and national identity. Faria e Sousa does not see himself outside of the Portuguese national imaginary he works so deliberately to sustain. Therefore, when he discusses loyalty, bravery, electness, sea-mastery, or any other aspect of Portuguese essentialism, the writer speaks as an heir to this culture and not as an outsider looking in, as some would have it. As a result, Faria e Sousa speaks of the celebrated voyage chronicled in *Os Lusíadas* as if he were part of the fleet (the glory of Vasco da Gama's enterprise being the timeless inheritance of the Portuguese nation). This sentiment emerges in Faria e Sousa's response to a line from canto 7 in which da Gama speaks of the spreading fame of the Portuguese:

> Por este camino puede tener lugar el aver algunos estraños, envidiosos de la gloria Portuguesa, llamado locura a la acción deste viaje, teniendole por desigual a las fuerças humanas; i a la resolución, i osadia, prudentes: casi diziendo, que se huvieron como niños, dexandose llevar de un sonido que los incitava. I como las tales acciones dellos proceden de la sencillez, puede esta niñeria ser lustre de nuestra nación, que como sencilla siempre en obedecer a las vozes de la Iglesia Catolica. (7.60.316)[30]

This passage comes in response to a single verse of the poem that might otherwise pass without interest ("Ouvindo do rumor que lá responde / o eco" [7.60.8–9]). This simple example epitomizes the patriotic mileage that Faria e Sousa gets out of Camões's poem. The above selection is full of religious self-posturing and perspectivism. By introducing the dubious and envious voice of the other, Faria e Sousa is able to glorify the acts of his compatriots and elevate his nation.

In another passage Faria e Sousa begins by claiming Camões for the Portuguese people and then establishing the poet's words as a truth (better than fiction) to which all of the Portuguese subscribe: "[N]uestro Poeta se resolvió en no escrivir mentiras (porque no las huvo menester para hazer raro su Poema con sembrarlo de cosas peregrinas, hallandolas mayores en nuestras verdades, de las que en sus fabulas las inventaron Homero, i Virgil" (5.19.482). The "truths" Faria e Sousa verifies on behalf of the Portuguese differentiate the actual glories of Portugal from those invented by other nations and their respective poets. The commentator repeats this idea on at least four other occasions (5.4.450, 5.40.519, 5.86.619–20, 8.82.510), essentially affirming with each reiteration the superiority of Portuguese history over all other histories, real or imagined. The entire idea rests on the antithetical relationship between truth and fiction, which the author extends to Portugal and all other nations respectively.

Another nationalist trend found within Faria e Sousa's commentary is the repeated appeal to the primacy and singularity of the Portuguese. It is not enough to speak of Portugal's greatness. For this zealous baroque commentator, it is all about Portugal's superiority and uniqueness. Therefore, he is not content to merely mention the impossible deeds of his countrymen, but to elevate them to the status of "mayores imposibles" (3.492). He highlights Camões's ability to achieve this very effect, praising the poet for eulogizing the Portuguese through the mouth of Adamastor, the allegorical giant: "Mirad la industria del Poeta, haziendo que al mismo tiempo que el Gigante airado acusa la gente Portugesa la esté alabando de osada, i valerosa sobre todas las gentes del mundo, en mar, i en tierra, en paz, i en armas, i en todos exercicios heroycos: porque esta estancia, i la mitad de la siguiente, no es sino un elogio ilustrissimo de los Portugueses" (5.41.521). In another example, Faria e Sousa uses a verse from canto 4—"Este é o primeiro rei" (48.5; "This is the first king")—to launch into a discussion of some firsts that distinguish João I, and by extension, the Portuguese:

> No se le podia escapar al Poeta esta advertencia: porque es gran gloria ser primero en alguna cosa: i los Portugueses lo fueron en muchas. El Rey Don Juan fue primero deste nombre en Portugal, i primero en varias acciones, i una dellas, la desta

gloria e España, de passar las armas sobre los Moros en la propia
Africa, i vencerlos en ella, i tomarle felizmente la Ciudad de
Ceuta, plaça importantissima, no solo a la honra Portuguesa,
sino a bien comun de la Christiandad. (4.47.330)

Faria e Sousa accomplishes at least two important things in this
passage. On the one hand, he continues to outline the superlative
nature of Portugal. On the other, he contextualizes Portuguese
achievement within two important, and not unrelated, spaces:
Christendom and the Peninsula. The double-edged effectiveness
of this passage—allowing Portugal to stand alone and at the same
time recognizing the ways in which the Portuguese nation belongs
to other collectivities—did not go unnoticed by Faria e Sousa's
Spanish contemporaries.[31] Generally speaking, the author makes
it a point to draw attention to Portugal's singularity and the many
"Cosa[s] singular[es] sin duda en la gente Portuguesa" (7.2.214).

Nowhere does Faria e Sousa celebrate his nation's exceptionality
more than when he speaks of their unprecedented mastery of the
sea. Given the nature of the poem, the commentator has ample
opportunity to speak on this topic. In his introductory notes on
the poem, Faria e Sousa claims the sea for the Portuguese: "los dueños della son los Portugueses, que con esta de la India enseñaron
al mundo el gran navegar, que hasta entonces fue limitadissimo"
(1.1.109). When Camões speaks of "Mares nunca d'antes nave-
gados" (Lusiadas 1.1.3; "Oceans never before sailed") at the
outset of his epic, Faria e Sousa echoes with "los Portugueses son
los dueños desta acción" (1.1.144), adding a brief defense of his
poet's assertion as well: "De que lo fuesen no ay noticia, conforme
a muchos graves Autores: i los que la quisieren persuadir serán
vanamente enemigos del valor Portugues para quien el Autor de
todo se sirvió de guardar esta gloria" (1.1.144). As the poem pro-
gresses, Neptune, among other Greek gods of the sea, takes notice
of Portugal's maritime successes. The ocean prophet Proteus, for
example, tries to warn Neptune that the Portuguese are going to
usurp his power over the waters (Lusiadas 4.49).[32] Commenting
on this section of canto 4, Faria e Sousa adds, "los Portugueses
serán los Gigantes, que despojarán sin reparo a Neptuno de sus
Reynos marítimos" (4.49.332). During the course of the poem
Faria e Sousa notes the gradual humanization of the gods and
divinization of the Portuguese: "los Dioses vendran a ser humanos,

i los Portugueses a ser Dioses" (5.59.580). The Portuguese gain preeminence over the pagan gods through their metaphorical baptism performed at sea by God himself.

Another characteristic of Portuguese identity that Faria e Sousa promotes in his commentary is what I will refer to as the "David Principle" (taking its name from the well-known personage of the Old Testament). The idea is that an undersized Portugal, similar to David in his clash with Goliath (1 Sam. 17), manages to overcome all odds through God's divine assistance. Camões calls upon this biblical example in canto 3:

> Qual o membrudo e bárbaro Gigante,
> Do Rei Saul, com causa, tão temido,
> Vendo o Pastor inerme estar diante,
> Só de pedras e esforço apercibido,
> Com palabras soberbas, o arrogante,
> Despreza o fraco moço mal vestido,
> Que, rodeando a funda, o desengana
> Quanto mais pode a Fé que a força humana. (3.111)

> As when the robust and brutal giant,
> Whom King Saul judiciously feared,
> Seeing the harmles shepherd before him
> With stones as his only visible weapon,
> With proud, boastful words he insulted
> The slight youth, dressed in his rags,
> Who whirled the catapult, opening his eyes
> To the power of Faith, more potent than size.[33]

In concert with stanza 110, in which the poet speaks of the Christian's power as "fraco e pequeno," ("weak and small") Camões draws a clear parallel between David and the outnumbered Portuguese fleet. Of this particular stanza Faria e Sousa confesses, "No sè yo que nadie aya igualado tal comparacion, i tan bien explicada con grandeza de estilo, que no se puede exceder" (3.111.164). At the root of this trope is the dichotomy between quality and quantity, which Faria e Sousa seems to address in his commentary every time he is reminded of Portugal's inferior size:

> [E]ssa poca gente rara, poca, o pequeña, en quanto al numero,
> avia raridad de valor, en quanto al animo ... el poeta celebra
> aqui la poquedad porque con ella son los Portugueses raros en

> el mundo. ... [S]in atender a la poquedad de la gente, sino a su natural valor, con que se haze rara en parecerse a la palma que con el *mayor* peso se levanta mas. (3.34.49–50)

> Es assi que Portugal, no solo es una pequeña parte del mundo, sino de la Christiandad, siendo la parte della en el mundo arto pequeña. Pero el Poeta con industria pregona esta pequeñez de Portugal, en quanto a la cantidad, por subir de punto la calidad de la Religion, i de su valor. (7.2.214)

In each of these excerpts the commentator highlights the poet's ability to contrast the scarcity of their numbers with the abundance of their virtues, making it clear that quality matters more than quantity. In this there appears to be an implicit reference to other Old Testament stories in which the relative few, through God's help, overcome the multitudinous foe.[34]

Much of what Faria e Sousa has to say, explicitly or implicitly, in regards to the David Principle comes in response to the opening lines of canto 7, stanza 3: "Vos Portugueses poucos, quanto fortes / que o fraco poder vosso não pesais" (1–2; "You, Portuguese, as few as you are valiant / Make light of your slender forces"). In his commentary he pivots from a perceived weakness that Portugal and David share, to a mutual triumph:

> David, cuya flaqueza envistio con un Gigante, acompañado de un exercito poderoso: i la flaqueza de Portugueses ha envestido con el mundo todo. Para pintar valientemente estas valentias son confessadas aquellas flaquezas. Galano està el termino de que no pesan los Portugueses su poder, para decir que no reparan en ser pocos para envestir con muchos enemigos. (7.2.215)

This principle depends on a series of binary oppositions in which one side would seem the overwhelming favorite (e.g., small/large, few/many), except that the other has divine assistance. This rhetorical tug of war plays out time and again in Faria e Sousa's commentary:

> Vos Portugueses que sois pocos en numero, pero en valor inmensos, i que no meteis en balança, la pequeñez de esse número, sino la grandeza de essos coraçones: aumentando con el caudal de la vida, la ley divina, i vuestro nombre. (7.2.215)

> Encareció el valor de los Portugueses confessando el poco
> numero se su gente: agora con la misma industria encarece
> la Christiandad: pues viene a ser tanta en gente tan poca no
> sin misterio la eligió Dios, para cultura de la ley Evangelica,
> enviandola a partes tan remotas, usando della, como de sus
> Apostoles, i Discipulos, que siendo pocos hizieron mucho.
> (7.2.216)

Beyond his brilliant use of antithesis in both passages, Faria e
Sousa introduces another central aspect of the David Principle:
providentialism. To establish a similitude between David and
Portugal is to highlight the electness of the Portuguese nation.
Faria e Sousa wholeheartedly endorses this aspect of Portuguese
essentialism, advancing it, as I will analyze later on, throughout his
commentary. Additionally, the author establishes the similitude
between Portugal and Christ's apostles and disciples. The simile
comes on the heels of a statement referring to the Portuguese as a
chosen people sent to evangelize the world, grouping them with
those whom Christ commissions in the New Testament to take the
gospel message throughout the world.

Several other aspects of Portuguese identity emerge during the
course of Faria e Sousa's work. One such feature is the supremacy
of Portuguese valor. He states, "los Portugueses nacieron para
executar una acción de osadía, que otras naciones temieron ima-
ginar, y Luís de Camões para cantarlos con la mayor turba que
hasta agora se vio despues de Homero, i de Virgilio" (135).[35] Here
Camões, whose impact on the development of Portuguese identity
cannot be overestimated, is given credit as the most uniquely gifted
individual to recount the glories of the Portuguese. This passage
is particularly illuminating as it sets "nacieron" ("they were born")
and "naciones" ("nations") side-by-side, thus implicitly highlighting the etymological link between the two words and juxtaposing
Portuguese valor with the fear of other nations. As Faria e Sousa
later emphasizes, "entre las naciones del mundo, la Portuguesa no
cedió a alguna jamás en el valor militar" (4.15.260). He often uses
the term *nación* to introduce the virtues of the Portuguese people,
thus reflecting the synonymous relationship between *nación* and
gentes captured in Covarrubias's dictionary (see chapter 1). He
affirms, for example, that "portugueses son como el mar; muy
serenos en el sossiego, en la colera incomportables: ninguna nación

es tan suave en la paz; ninguna tan furiosa en la guerra" (4.6.245). On another occasion he states that humility "resplandece en la nación Portuguesa" (6.34.78). In reality, Faria e Sousa seems to take advantage of every opportunity available to exalt the land and people of Portugal. Further evidence of this appears in his various comments on Portuguese geography, history, religion, and language.

Explicit and implicit references to Portuguese geography by Camões often trigger an enthusiastic response from Faria e Sousa. A simple reference to the Iberian Peninsula by the poet (3.17.1), for example, conjures an exacting response from his commentator: "España se aventaja a todas las Provincias de Europa" (3.17.22). Subsequently, Camões designates the Peninsula the head of Europe—a privileged position when considering the New Testament equating of Christ and the head of the body/Church. Faria e Sousa considers this a perfect metaphor, stating that "muchos estranos confiesan la soberania de Portugal, en sitio, hermosura, fertilidad, valor, i Religión" (3.20.27). The author's zeal for Portugal leads him to take the metaphor one step further: "Notese la industria, con levantar aqui a España, para despues levantar más a Portugal, que es el fin que lleva. ... Exaltando la patria, con hazerla Corona de aquella cabeça (3.17.22–23). Faria e Sousa is consistent in his privileging of Portugal as he adjusts his geographic scope from the macro to the micro. A number of concentric circles lead the reader from Europe to Iberia, eventually arriving at the center: Portugal.

Faria e Sousa takes nearly every opportunity afforded by Camões's poem to launch into some form of praise for his homeland. A reference to Porto in the sixth canto—"Lá na leal cidade donde teve / Origem (como é fama) o nome eterno / De Portugal" (6.52.1–3; "In loyal Porto, the city [as is said] / From which Portugal derives her name")—complements the previous example regarding Iberia. In response to Camões's immortalization of the Portuguese name, Faria e Sousa states, "Es bonissimo el dezir eterno al nombre de Portugal, que por sus glorias parece inacabable: i por su antiguedad, casi que tiene principio con la restauración del mundo" (6.51.116). Faria e Sousa's esteem for his homeland is slightly bridled by "parece" and "casi," a rare instance of self-control on the part of the commentator. Although he hardly needs a reason to wax patriotic, these verses from *Os Lusíadas* stimulate the previous reflection and the following explanation:

> [S]iendo el Poeta docto en las cosas de la patria, no podía dudar desta en que conviene todos los Escritores; componiendose el nombre de Portugal, de *portu*, y *cale*, que todo es uno: porque esta ciudad se llamó primero Cale, quando estaba de la otra parte del rio, en frente del sitio en que agora está; i del nombre de Cale, i de estar situada en aquel puerto, el se llamava Puerto de Cale: i de ai el Reyno de Portugal. (6.51.116)

Here Faria e Sousa affirms a collective recognition of the etymology of Portugal. This is significant because a clear sense of origin is essential in the development of geographic nationalism. That is, in order for a people to take pride in their land (cities, rivers, mountains, etc.), they must share a sense of its founding and history. In addition to his commentary on Portugal, Faria e Sousa also traces the etymological evolution of the name Lusitânia (3.21.30, 8.3.376). These descriptions situate Portugal in a historical present that legitimizes its existence precisely when the same was growing weary of the constant effects of Castilianization.

If Portugal is the greatest nation in the world, as Faria e Sousa so often affirms, it would follow that its capital, Lisbon, would also receive preferential treatment. Faria e Sousa comes through with such a description, basing his conclusion on none other than Camões (3.57.1–2):

> [L]lama el Poeta a Lisboa Princesa de las Ciudades. Quieren algunos que Constantinopla, sea de las de Europa, la primera; Paris segunda; Lisboa tercera, en sitio, i numero de moradores. Si no se engañan (como yo creo arrimado a buenos testigos) quedará el Principado en Lisboa, que dize el Poeta, atendiendo, no a la grandeza por numero de gente, sino por la calidad della. (3.57.92)

This excerpt elevates Lisbon above all other cities by highlighting the quality/quantity dichotomy previously discussed. Elsewhere Faria e Sousa confirms the mythological origins of Lisbon, which include, among other fictionalized details, the founding of the city by Homer's Ulysses (8.3.379). In these descriptions of the Portuguese nation and its capital, Faria e Sousa's nationalist colors are on full display. It is not enough for Lisbon to be a great city; it has to be the greatest. Superlatives, in truth, find their way into almost every discussion of the Portuguese nation, with Faria e Sousa almost unfailingly crowning Portugal and her people the champions of all that is good. Building on the untouchable assertions of his national poet, Faria e Sousa reverts to the past in an effort to reconstruct a present imaginary through which the Portuguese nation can once again take shape and resume its long-standing autonomy.

The sixth paragraph of the "Advertencias" section at the beginning of Faria e Sousa's edition of *Os Lusíadas* presents one of the most significant aspects of nationalism. Speaking of the difficulty most Spanish-speakers have with the Portuguese language, Faria e Sousa discusses "la poca razón, o causa con que se les hace difícil nuestra lengua." In this section and throughout the commentary, language is treated as a fundamental aspect of identity, which agrees with José Mattoso's observation that "A maioria dos autores que têm tratado da identidade nacional atribui também uma grande importância ao fenómeno da língua" (7; "The majority of authors who have taken up national identity likewise attribute a great deal of importance to the phenomenon of language"). Although writing in Spanish and living in Madrid, Faria e Sousa still considered himself part of a community of Portuguese speakers.[36] "Nuestra lengua Portuguesa" (9.41.90) offers an important contrast to "their" language (the former Portuguese and the latter Spanish). Emphasizing this difference articulates an important opposition to the threats of linguistic assimilation. In a work of such magnitude, however, a few cursory comments about Portuguese does little to actually alleviate the linguistic threats bearing down on the language. As António Ferreira argued the century previous (see chapter two), one honors their native tongue by choosing it as a means of expression. For some, the choice by Faria e Sousa and his contemporaries to write in Spanish, regardless of the motivation, overshadows all other attempts by the authors to honor the Portuguese language. I reiterate this fact not as a point of resolution, but in order to problematize, once again, the decision to write in Spanish and, by extension, the essentialism of Portuguese identity. The point is not that Faria e Sousa was or was not "truly" Portuguese, but that the author never relinquished his native claim to Portugal. In his writings, he consistently constructs of/for himself a "pequena casa Lusitana" that Camões speaks of in his poem (*Lusiadas* 7.14.4; "small Lusitanian house").

Similar to the other nationalisms (geographic, religious, etc.) at work in his commentary, Faria e Sousa describes the Portuguese language in terms of superiority. Early in the first canto, Camões speaks of the similitude between Portuguese and Latin: "E na língua, na qual quando imagina, / Com pouca corrupção crê que é a Latina" (1.33.9–10: "In the language which an inventive mind / Could mistake for Latin, passably declined"). Commenting on these verses, Faria e Sousa, in the same way he claims the superiority of the Iberian Peninsula over the rest of Europe, elaborates on the finer points of his native tongue. He begins by explicating Camões's position: "Dize el Poeta que entre las otras razones porque Venus favorecia a los Portugueses agora, era por la lengua dellos, la qual se le parecia a la Latina con poca diferencia" (1.33.263). The commentary then turns into a theoretical linguistic discussion not unlike the many taking place in Europe at the time. First, Faria e Sousa establishes the criteria: "las cinco partes (mejor la Portuguesa) que deve tener una lengua para ser perfecta, que son copia, pronunciacion facil, brevedad; escrivir lo que habla, i al contrario; propiedad para todos estilos" (1.33.264). The parenthetical interjection in this excerpt is particularly revealing of the author's superlative attitude toward the Portuguese language. It can almost be read as a dramatic aside through which the commentator reveals his own perspective in the context of a more technical discussion. Having established the five points of a perfect language, Faria e Sousa concludes with two final statements concerning Portuguese: "en lo que toca a la dulçura, i gravedad, no ay estraño que no confiesse ventaja a la Portuguesa … hablar como escrive, ello es cierto, que la [Portuguesa] se aventaja a todas las lenguas" (1.33.264).

Other references to a national language appear throughout Faria e Sousa's text. For instance, he often provides both Spanish and Portuguese definitions in order to render Camões's text more intelligible for non-native speakers. Such references often sound something like the following: "Alcione es el Ave, que en Portugues llamamos Maçarico" (6.77.157). His consistent use of the first person plural to refer to the Portuguese language aligns the author with his native tongue and establishes his linguistic community of choice. Unlike the previous example, in which Portuguese and

Spanish use different words to say the same thing, there are a number of cases in which Faria e Sousa clarifies the divergent meaning of a word the two languages share: "Dizen algunos, que sobra aqui el amorosas, porque estando heridas de amor las Ninfas, luego estarian amorosas. Esso se llama no entender el Poeta. Amorosas estan aqui por blandas, suaves, dulces que el amoroso en nuestra lengua Portuguesa, se entiende a esto" (9.41.89–90). As in other passages, Faria e Sousa identifies himself with the Portuguese language, affirming, at the same time, the correctness of his reading of the poem.

Aware that his occasional movement between linguistic registers might be a cause for criticism, he explains: "se hallarán otros terminos que pueden parecer Lusitanismos: algunos serán por descuido, llamandome a ellos la naturaleza; i todavia otros son usados cuydadosamente, por parecerme bien el hazerlo assi" ("Advertencias" 4). The most important part of this description— at least for our present discussion—is his use of "naturaleza" to describe the accidental interference of Portuguese in his command of Spanish. Portuguese, by his admission, is his nature, while Spanish is a learned language and culture. One example of a word the commentator purposely leaves in Portuguese appears toward the end of the work. Faria e Sousa offers this in response to his choice to leave *mimoso* (9.83.2) in its original tongue: "Digolo con la palabra Portuguesa: porque pensar dezirlo con otra tan propia, es cosa vana; porque regalo, melindre, ternura, i todo lo semejante, no dà por los pies a mimo" (9.83.250). A polyglot like Faria e Sousa is certainly entitled to have his linguistic preferences, although he seems to take special pride in the inability of the Spanish language to produce a worthy translation of *mimoso*.

Similar to the religiosity inherent in the David Principle, a religious sense of nationhood also permeates Faria e Sousa's text. At the foundation of this form of nationalism is the belief that the Portuguese are God's elect, chosen and sent by Him to accomplish countless acts of greatness. In his preface to the commentary, Faria e Sousa establishes Christ as the true founder of Portugal and the Portuguese as His people:

> Heroes escogidos fueronlo de Christo los Portugueses.
> ("Argumento" 108)
> [D]el cielo fue enviada la gente Portuguesa para este descubrimiento. ("Argumento" 113)

> Progenie amada de Dios. El serlo la Portuguesa singular-
> mente, consta no solo de ser el propio Christo fundador
> de su Reyno… sino de muchos otros favores continuados.
> ("Argumento" 130–31)

Consistent with his use of superlatives to describe other forms of
nationalism, Faria e Sousa frequently refers to the Portuguese as
the most Catholic people in the world (9.76.217, 9.79.228). This
being the case, Lisbon might be considered, on account of its pure
practice of Catholicism, a Latin Church or a New Rome (6.7.12).

Faria e Sousa unequivocally claims the Portuguese as the
"mayor cultura de la ley Evangelica" (1.75.333), sustaining his
position with what he describes as the evangelizing power of the
Portuguese fleet: "empleado en redimir el mundo de vicios abomi-
nables, extinguiendolos; i de dar premio a las acciones heroycas,
para con el despertar los animos postrados a que se empleen en
ellas, con el exemplo de nuestros navegantes" (9.38.80). As the
commentator goes on to say in another passage, Catholicism is
such a part of the Portuguese that it seems to have originated with
them (9.42.91). This echoes a previous comment made in the
first volume of his work: "de ninguna cosa son los Portugueses
tan propios como della [Religion], ni ella mas propia de otras
naciones, que dellos. Creemos, que ninguna nos negara esta
gloria, a lo menos con justicia" (2.44.455). This final passage
offers two instances of simultaneity. His reference to "creemos"
reflects a sense of Portuguese collectivity on the one hand, while
on the other he interjects the indirect object pronoun "nos" with
the same basic effect. The inherent "we" essential in these words
evokes a national credo that defines the religiosity of Portugal and
their elect place among God's people.[37] These references to faith
speak of a present Portuguese identity at the same time that they
summon a historical legitimacy that reinforces the nation.

Lusiadas de Luis de Camoens, principe de los poetas de España
is one of the supreme works of early modern Iberia. It is not
Faria e Sousa's only important work of literary criticism, but it
is undoubtedly his best and most influential. Unfortunately,
however, it bears the distinction of a work frequently mentioned
but seldom consulted (Pierce 99; Hart 31). Both the author and
his monumental work are deserving of far more attention (Flasche
7; Marcos de Dios 41). Numerous studies over the past decade
would seem to indicate that the narrative on Faria e Sousa and

his masterpiece is changing for the better. What is more, many of these studies explore "the duality, ambivalence, and boundary crossings" within the commentary (Fouto and Weiss 4). A "nuançado contexto" (Sena 14; "nuanced context") such as the Dual Monarchy will always suffer when either/or approaches and other reductive readings rule the day. In my particular analysis of his commentary I have tried to establish a nationalist posture on the part of the author. Among the various markers of identity that punctuated his existence and his writings, Faria e Sousa asserted *portugalidade* as his native expression. This is who he "escolheu ser, em Espanha, e através do espanhol" (Sena 17; "chose to be, in Spain, and through Spanish"). Nowhere is this more evident than in his commentary.

Faria e Sousa as Historiographer

While his critical work on Camões was the crowning achievement of his literary life and one of the clearest expressions of *portugalidade* at the time, Faria e Sousa was also an active historiographer. The balance of his literary corpus, in actuality, tilts in favor of this genre. His knowledge of and interest in Portugal's past are made evident in his annotations on *Os Lusíadas*. What is more, both of his autobiographies—one in prose, the other in verse—capture the author's fascination with personal history. One could say that the author's historiography drifts between two primary subjects: the past, present, and future of the Portuguese nation; and his own personal legacy. History, as a genre, was particularly suited for projecting the names, places, and events associated with Portugal's glorious past onto the European landscape. John Stevens, the late seventeenth-century English translator of Faria e Sousa's historiography, does not consider the historian's Lusocentrism a problem: "Being a Portuguese, I cannot affirm him to be altogether impartial, for there is no Man whom the love of his Native Country does not a little sway, yet his can be no exception against him, because, if such, all History would be liable to the same censure" (Preface). Vázquez Cuesta takes things one step further, identifying history not merely as a place where nationalist sentiment inevitably appears, but as a preferred locus of patriotic expression: "El género preferido para servir de cauce al sentir patriótico que subterráneamente informaba buena parte de la literatura portuguesa de la época filipina es la Historia" ("Lengua" 646). Matthias Gloël's assessment of Portuguese historiography reads similarly: "lo que caracterizaría la mayor parte de la historiografía portuguesa de entonces: destacar la preeminencia portuguesa (o lusitana) sobre los demás territorios en general e ibéricos en particular" (34). What was it about history that made it such an effective vehicle of nationalist expression? For one, the cloak of authenticity that often accompanies the genre motivated many writers to aim high in their "official" rendering of the nation.

Overall, nation-minded historians cultivate a unique sense of the past. Their concept of history typically leads to the promotion of certain aspects of their national heritage and the silencing of others (both of which contribute to the creation of a foundational narrative). This ebb and flow of historical identity changes and develops according to the perspective of those in power. In the hands of nationalists, then, historical texts not only multiply but change. While the subjectivity of such efforts may be more readily apparent than other "pure" or "objective" histories, as Hayden White brilliantly outlines in his essay "The Historical Text as Literary Artifact" from *Tropics of Discourse* (1978), historiography cannot escape its literariness. The proximity of literature and history as systems of discourse was particularly close during the early modern period, when a single author tended to practice a variety of genres. In a point not too distant from White's, Benedict Anderson describes the imaginative writings of historico-national movements as a magic-act in which the historian turns chance into destiny (12). This occurs, as he later explains, because "nationalism thinks in terms of historical destinies" (149). Few, if any, words have enveloped the Portuguese imaginary over the centuries more than destiny in its various forms (*fado, destino, fortuna, sorte, providência; "fate, destiny, fortune, luck, providence"*). That Portuguese authors would continue to invoke the language of destiny during the annexation speaks to the longing they felt for an independent Portugal. Rather than change the historical frame to include the entire Peninsula as one might expect, Portuguese historians of the Dual Monarchy maintained a Lusocentric reading of the past.

To whatever degree we can speak of the collective inventiveness of history in general, we can certainly identify the specific creativity of nationalist historians to a much larger measure. The first author to look closely at Portuguese history from the perspective of a post-1580 Portugal was Fernão de Oliveira (1507–82). Previously, the author had published *Grammatica da linguagem portugueza* (1536; "*Grammar of the Portuguese Language*"), widely recognized as the first study dedicated to Portuguese grammar. Many of the nationalist ideas about language that circulate among Portuguese authors during the early modern period hearken back to this text. With this early work, Oliveira established himself as a prominent figure of sixteenth-century Portuguese culture. While *Grammatica* remains the work most commonly associated with Oliveira, *História de Portugal* (1580) may very well be just as significant as his earlier study.[38] Both works are foundational within their respective genres. Francisco Contente Domingues explains why Oliveira's historiographical work stands out: "é a primeira História de Portugal escrita depois de 1580, justificativa do direito do país a permanecer livre e independente—acusando portanto um discurso marcadamente anti-castelhano" (10; "it is the first History of Portugal written after 1580, a justification of the country's right to remain free and independent—presenting therefore a markedly anti-Castilian discourse"). According to Domingues, Oliveira was the first Portuguese historian to conceive of Portuguese history in light of the Dual Monarchy, which he openly opposed.[39]

Oliveira's conception of the past is directly informed by the political events surrounding the Iberian Unification. Hence, the author insists on Portugal's antiquity, its primacy and superiority above all other Peninsular kingdoms, and its right to autonomy (Franco 17). José Eduardo Franco describes *História* as a work whose fiery commitment to the reconstruction of Portugal's remote past is made possible by the political climate in which the aged author was writing (17). Unlike his younger compatriots or those eventually born during the Iberian Union, Oliveira had nothing to lose by coming forward with critical views of the annexation. The mythification of Portugal at the hands of the historian ennobles his homeland with a sacred past and a promising future. He creates a nation providentially destined to fulfill a divine mission (Franco 17–18). According to the author's characterization of Lusitânia, the annexation of Portugal places Spain in direct opposition to God's plan for Portugal. Oliveira exemplifies, therefore, the potential of historiography to operate as a vehicle for nationalist sentiment, "ao serviço de uma ideia, de uma posição e de um fim que é, em última análise, político-ideológico" (Franco 18; "at the service of an idea, a position, and a purpose that is, in the final analysis, politico-ideological"). The nationalization of history in Oliveira's work anticipated Portuguese annexation authors who would similarly make use of historiography to fashion an exalted past for their homeland that could justify an autonomous future.

While most nation theories concentrate on the modern era, the association of history with nationalism extends at least as far back as the early modern period. The nationalizing of history, in fact, is one of the most frequent brands of nationalism practiced by early modern Portuguese historiographers in the decades leading up to and following 1580. As we will see, Faria e Sousa transgresses the myth/history dichotomy Mattoso traces in the following passage:

> Até a um passado mais ou menos recente, conforme o grau de instrução dos sujeitos em causa, a memória colectiva apoiava-se frequentemente em mitos, alguns deles criados justamente para servirem de suporte da crença na perpetuidade, ou mesmo na sacralidade da Pátria. Tal foi a crença no milagre de Ourique, surgida no fim do século XIV ou princípio do seguinte e cuidadosamente cultivado pelas elites nacionalistas até meados do século XIX. (103)

> Until fairly recently, based on the level of education of those in question, collective memory was often supported by myths, some of which were created for the very purpose of sustaining belief in perpetuity, or in the sacredness of the *Pátria* itself. Such was the belief in the miracle at Ourique, which appeared at the end of the fourteenth or beginning of the fifteenth century and was carefully cultivated by nationalist elites until the middle of the nineteenth century.

Carolina Michaëlis de Vasconcelos, Teófilo Braga, Marcelino Menéndez Pelayo, and others accuse Faria e Sousa, for example, of authoring inaccurate history, not realizing that historical accuracy may not even be his aim, but rather the glorification of Portugal, the nationalizing of history. Such a project necessitates omissions on the one hand, and embellishments on the other. Hernani Cidade explains: "o sentimento da autonomia, com verdades apoiadas de mentiras, ia preparando a atmosfera, que o levaria a dinamizar-se no movimento revolucionário que no restituiu a independência" (105; "the feeling of autonomy, with truths supported by lies, gradually prepared the atmosphere, that would give life to the revolutionary movement that restored independence"). In Cidade's eyes, both truth and lies—history and fiction—contributed to the dynamic atmosphere that would once again render Portugal a sovereign nation. That is not to say that criticism of Faria e Sousa's historiography is unsubstantiated or that his work lacks historical merit. It would likewise be false to claim absolute self-awareness on the part of the author. Faria e Sousa's approach to historiography reflects both his background in literature and an unyielding commitment to his native Portugal. As Cidade describes, there was room within early modern historiography for both fact and fiction: "Assim a historiografia era género literário que confinava com a agiografia e com a epopeia. Não escluía a intervenção do sobrenatural—premissa que se estabeleceria como probabilíssima hipótese para toda a acção de certa transcendência política, social ou religiosa" (82; "So historiography was the literary genre that could include hagiography and epopee. It did not discount divine intervention—a premise that would be established as the go-to hypothesis for all actions of a certain political, social, or religious transcendence"). In the able hands of Faria e Sousa, Portuguese history becomes a story of providentialism, collective action and being, and hyperbolic accomplishment. Using his comprehensive knowledge of the Bible, the author portrays Portugal as an early modern equivalent of ancient Israel. While Faria e Sousa is certainly not a prophet by biblical standards, his storytelling and mythmaking qualify him as a prolific preacher of Portuguese nationalism.

Faria e Sousa's historical output takes on the history of Portugal to an unprecedented degree.[40] This includes, among other works, *Epítome de las historias portuguesas* (1628), *Imperio de la China* (1642), and the posthumously-published series *Asia portuguesa* (1666), *Europa portuguesa* (1678), and *Africa portuguesa* (1681), each edited by his son Pedro de Faria e Sousa. It is difficult to surmise to what extent, if at all, perceptions of Faria e Sousa might differ had he lived long enough to see his crowning historiographical works published. Had the fourth volume— *América portuguesa*—seen the light of day the author would have, at the very least, written himself into the colonial Brazilian canon, providing thereby a valuable antecedent to Sebastião Rocha Pita's *Historia da America Portuguesa* (1730).[41] Similar to other works by the author, he seems to have written his earliest drafts in Portuguese, only to translate them to Spanish as he worked on subsequent drafts.[42] Though the only extant copies of *Epítome* are in Spanish, for example, the widely-read work was originally composed by the author in Portuguese octaves and titled *Vida dos Reis Portugueses*. Given what Faria e Sousa says in the opening section of his prologue to *Epítome*, it seems likely that those works were also intended for Spanish translation. The majesty and grandeur of Portuguese, as he explains, makes it difficult for everyone but native speakers to understand, resulting in a text destined to be forgotten.

Epítome de las historias portuguesas is Faria e Sousa's most recognized contribution to Portuguese historiography and an important reference within seventeenth-century Iberian letters. Considering the dozens of times that António de Sousa de Macedo cites *Epítome* in his enthusiastic treatise *Flores de España, Excelencias de Portugal* (1631), Faria e Sousa's work must have been an instant success. Portugal's "credito i honor solamente ha motivado esta ponderación," as he explains in the prologue, only to close with "Yo no escrivo en la Patria, ni para ella. Sè que necessitan desto los estraños." Portugal, therefore, was his muse and not his audience. He understands his role in terms of evangelization; that his mission is to share the message of Portuguese greatness throughout the world. Eugenio Asensio will eventually describe this type of nationalist zeal in similar terms: "proselitismo nacionalista" ("España" 67). The dramatic, or perhaps, overdramatic style that characterizes *Epítome* is precisely what made the work a rich source from which playwrights and other writers could and did draw inspiration (see chapter 4). Fernando Bouza Álvarez's *Corre manuscrito* creates a picture of early modern Iberian texts that expands previously limited views of the written word. In the tireless writer Faria e Sousa, who would often spend his days and nights writing (sometimes with both hands), Bouza finds an individual whose reach, although great in its own right, extended far beyond his known published works: "En suma su amplia trayectoria como autor descansaba tanto sobre impresos como sobre manuscritos" (29). As impossible as it would be to measure the full impact of *Epítome* on other authors, the incalculable reach of his abundant production of manuscripts is even more difficult to comprehend.

Epítome de las historias portuguesas is exactly what its title promises: the embodiment of Portuguese history. This work comprises Faria e Sousa's attempt at a representative approach to Portugal's glorious past. Thus, *Epítome* is in part what his four-corner's work was to be in whole.[43] That his abstract is still hundreds of pages long is telling of the author's high regard for his homeland and its indispensable past. What would seem to be a fairly straightforward, albeit patriotic, work, however, was examined with caution by the Spanish Inquisition, appearing on the *Index of Prohibited Books* by 1632 as a work requiring expurgation (Asensio, "Autobiografía" 631). What was it about the text that alarmed the inquisitors? Whereas Faria e Sousa's Portuguese rivals tried to get his commentary on *Os Lusíadas* banned for what they deemed heretical content, such was not the case with *Epítome*, at least not in the religious sense.[44] It could very well be that a definitive answer may not be possible given our limited knowledge of the situation. I would only suggest that the work may have been targeted given its nationalist zeal, particularly the way in which it portrays past conflicts between Portugal and Castile. After all, any writing that destabilized the Empire, questioned the legitimacy of Spanish rule, or usurped the king's power also fell under the Inquisition's responsibility and could be dealt with accordingly. The anti-imperial nationalism evident in *Epítome* may have triggered the process that would eventually lead to the book's inclusion on the *Index*.

Two ideas seem to inform Faria e Sousa's approach to *Epítome*. On the one hand, he believes that no amount of paper is sufficient to capture Portuguese greatness in its entirety, and yet on the other, even a succinct consideration of the topic must be thorough enough so as to not diminish his homeland.[45] That is not to say that the author measured success solely by pages written—although there is some indication that he derived much self-worth from this very thing (see *Fortuna*). While the amount of Portuguese deeds was innumerable in the author's eyes, it was the quality of their heroics that exalted Portugal above all other nations. In other words, the point of *Epítome* is not to say everything, but to say enough so as to convince the reader of his implicit thesis: that no history can compare with that of Portugal. The challenge of his task, then, was to maintain a certain degree of brevity without diminishing Portuguese accomplishments.[46] In a number of instances the author reflects on the incomprehensibility of Portuguese history, a perception that does not make his task any easier. As he states, "si se detiene un rato el pensamiento a ponderarlo, antes parece sueño que discurso" (3.15.525). Faria e Sousa does not offer this comparison as an apology, but rather to reinforce his belief that Portuguese deeds are better than fiction even if they seem imagined. He cloaks Portuguese history with an air of mystery and intrigue as if it were supernatural.

While his fairy-tale approach to Portugal's past may seem to distance Faria e Sousa from the "unadulterated" practice of historiography, the author insists that, despite its fantastic nature, the Portuguese history that he writes is not fictional. He contends that no individual can imagine anything greater than that which the Portuguese actually accomplished: "Menos ai que creer en las fabulas de los libros vanos, que en las verdades de los hechos, i de los sujetos Portugueses" (3.15.525). In the specific case of Manuel I (1469–1521), he emphasizes the limitlessness of the deeds accomplished during his reign by stating that no amount of paper could record all of them (3.15.512). This captures the baroque spirit of Faria e Sousa's *Epítome* specifically, and his entire historical corpus in general. Just because all of the paper in the world would not be enough to record the entirety of Portugal's greatness, did not keep the author from trying. As he explains, most of his historiographical writings were not published because the market demanded shorter works: "en España un libro no ha de ser del tamaño que pide la materia sino de él de la voluntad de los compradores; y ésta es la razón de no imprimirse mis *Historias*, que son diez cuerpos de a 130 pliegos cada uno" (*Fortuna* 375). Overall, *Epítome* stands as a testament of the author's nationalist tendency to hyperbolize the past, divinize all things Portuguese, and promote a collective sense of identity.

In an attempt to validate his position regarding Portugal's past while maintaining some semblance of brevity, Faria e Sousa often uses overstatement, superlative, and exaggeration.[47] One example of this appears in the first line of his section on João II: "En el mas ilustre lugar de Europa (Lisboa), en el mas hermoso mes del año (quatro de Mayo), nacio uno de los mas excelentes Principes que vio la gente i el tiempo, don Juan hijo tercero i ultimo de sus Reyes don Alonso i doña Isabel" (3.14.495). The scope of this specific passage transcends the life of João II, providing the author with an occasion to exalt Lisbon and extend the importance of this event both temporally and geographically. While he structures his work according to the various Portuguese monarchs, Faria e Sousa's aim is not regal history per se, but Portugal altogether. During the course of the work, he actually uses royal lines to characterize the nation, always moving from the individual to the collective. Speaking of João I's conquest of Ceuta, for instance, the author weaves Afonso I and his son Sancho I into the history, ultimately extending the success and providentialism of this single victory to all Portuguese endeavors: "Que por divina dispensacion èl [Afonso] i su hijo don Sancho havian socorrido a sus [John I] vassallos en aquel conflito. No lo dude nadie, que las vitorias de los Portugueses todas son estupendas, todas imagen del poder de Dios" (3.2.363). As he often does throughout *Epítome*, Faria e Sousa synecdochically moves from part to whole in this passage in order to expand his praise to the Portuguese nation and not merely its royal power. What is more, he equates Portuguese history with divine will, thereby making his assertions irrefutable. In the following passage Faria e Sousa echoes the spirit of the previous citation, however in this case he uses an augmentative to accentuate the disparity in number between Castile and Portugal:

> Ivanse llegando los dos campos, desigualissimos en numero; salió del de Castilla un hermano de Nunalvarez a tentarle que se passasse de su parte. Mas viendo su constancia Diego Fernández Mariscal Castellano dixo: Alfin sois los mas honrados del mundo, o seais vencedores, o seais vencidos, porque si venceis siendo tan pocos y si os vencemos siendo tantos, toda la gloria y toda la fama es vuestra. (3.11.452)

Several details stand out in this reference. While there is room to speak of Portuguese essentialism and the strategic placing of praise in the mouth of a Castilian, I would instead draw the reader's attention to Faria e Sousa's measured view of the Portuguese. The primary focus of this excerpt is quantity, which he introduces with the augmentative "desigualissimos en numero." Numbers are an essential aspect of the Portuguese self-concept, with Portugal always making up for their quantitative deficit with their qualitative surplus. Faria e Sousa's historiographical works make this a fundamental aspect of Portuguese identity.

As in other works written by Faria e Sousa, the triumph of the Portuguese despite their "underdog" status is a constant theme within *Epítome* (see earlier discussion of the David Principle).

From Afonso I to Manuel I, Portugal always seems to defy the odds. Early on in the work, for example, he cites a speech given by Afonso before one of Portugal's many battles with the Arabs, wherein the prince calls attention to their sparse numbers and abundant value:

> Temeis por veros pocos? pues yo os asseguro que de lo propio tiembla toda essa Morisma: porque de la pequeñez del exercito infiere la grandeza de la gente. La diferencia no penseis que es poca: yo traigo compañeros, no vassallos; a vosotros os mueve el amor, la fuerça a ellos: ellos mas numerosos que justificados, nosotros con mas justicia que multitud; i es invencible tormenta la justicia. Si son las armas vuestras, de Christo es la causa. (3.2.352)

Faria e Sousa skillfully uses the figure of antithesis to structure this passage. In effect, a series of binary pairs characterizes the entire speech: us/them, few/many, love/obligation, right/wrong. At the root of each contrasting set is the basic division of quality and quantity. According to Faria e Sousa, the outstanding worth of the Portuguese comes from their Christian faith. Accordingly, the heavens open and Christ appears to the Portuguese soldiers right before the battle begins (3.2.353). Casting the Portuguese in this way allows the author to spin a potential negative (size) into a definite positive (value).

The leadership of Duarte Pacheco Pereira (c.1445–1533), one of the great heroes of Portuguese history, provides another example of the importance of scale in the Portuguese self-concept that Faria e Sousa constructs in his writings. In the following excerpt, Faria e Sousa highlights, in both certain and ambiguous terms, the improbability of Portugal's five-month defense of Kochi (India) as well as some of Pacheco's other successes:

> Duarte Pacheco, que, sin perdida de un solo Portugues desba-ratò muchas vezes muchas gentes, i con ochenta embistio todo el poder del Zamori, que conduziendo un campo de sesenta mil combatientes escandalizava el Reino de Cochin, i les hizo, que con perdida de muchos se retirassen vencidos en diferentes batallas navales, i terrestres, con admiracion de toda la Asia. (3.15.521–22)

Whether it is the lack of fatality on the Portuguese side, or the abundance of decadence on the other, Faria e Sousa emphasizes, and perhaps exaggerates, the quantitative details of Pacheco's military campaigns. In the specific case of Kochi, the author contrasts the relatively few Portuguese who miraculously prevailed against their numerous foes. He further emphasizes the victory by recounting the admiration they won throughout Asia.

In an effort to explain Portuguese successes in spite of their relatively small population, Faria e Sousa often evokes—sometimes implicitly, other times explicitly—passages from the Bible. The story of David and Goliath (1 Sam. 16–17), illustrates, for example, how David's intrinsic qualities—faith, courage, trust—allow him to overcome seemingly impossible odds—differences in age, size, weaponry, armor, and experience. This is precisely the type of parallel Faria e Sousa draws between David and Portugal: always outnumbered but never overpowered. According to the author, then, the Portuguese are God's chosen people, and, consequently, the odds are always in their favor (the very lesson illustrated in Judges 6–7). Overall, the biblical intertext that perhaps best reflects the author's view of the Portuguese nation appears in 2 Kings when the prophet Elisha offers direction to the king of Israel concerning the impending threats posed by Syria. His reassuring words to the king seem to inform Faria e Sousa's concept of Portuguese history: "Fear not: for they that be with us are more than they that be with them" (6.16). Not only does this verse reverse the disproportionateness of the situation, but also reinforces the distinction between *us* and *them*, one nation and another. Faria e Sousa borrows from this perspective in his *a posteriori* explanation of Portuguese success.

In a very revealing passage found in his discussion of Manuel's reign (1469–1521), Faria e Sousa situates Portugal's achievements within the broader context of the global landscape. Within his scope, however, he includes historical and fictitious figures, thereby demonstrating the supremacy of Portuguese among people both real and imagined:

> todos con poca gente desbaratando infinita feroz, armada, i belicosa, haziendo estipendiarios a sus Reyes, muchos Reinos, muchas Provincias, i aun la misma fortuna. Vana memoria es la que hazemos de los Argonautas, i de todas las osadias de los antiguos, mas dichosas que grandes, para encarecer las presentes: vana la de Hercules, la de Alcides, la de Teseo en las hazañas de la guerra; vanas las de Numa i de todas las togas en la paz. (3.15.524)

Here Faria e Sousa blurs the difference between the fictional and the historical so as to support his assertion that Portugal even surpasses the stuff of legends. The consistent use of *todos(as)* maintains the author's hyperbolic style, as does the contrastive use of *poca* and *infinita*. Another aspect of this passage that merits attention is the repetition of *vana*. The author would have the reader believe that any attempt to match Portuguese greatness is futile. He then upstages the three groups mentioned above—Argonauts (mariners); Hercules, Alcides, and Teseo (warriors); and Numa (kings)—by placing the Portuguese at the head of each category:

> Para los primeros son mayores los Portugueses; que en las aguas antes que hombres, fueron pezes. Para los segundos, un Viriato, un don Alonso Enriquez, un don Juan I i un Alonso V, un don Nunalvarez, un Alonso de Albuquerque, un Duarte Pacheco, un don Francisco i un don Lorenço de Almeida, un don Juan de Castro, un Nuño de Acuña, un don Pedro, i un don Duarte, i un don Juan de Meneses, un Lope Vaz de Sampayo, un Nuño Fernandez, un Lope Barriga, i unos infinitos son los verdaderos Hercules, Theseo, i Anteos en uno i otro Hemisferio, en uno i en otro elemento. Para los terceros, un don Sancho I, un don Dionis, un don Pedro, un don Christoval de Moura, un Lorenço Pirez de Tavora, la multitud me los confunde, i me empobrece. (3.15.524–25)

Here, as he does elsewhere, Faria e Sousa takes his argument to the extreme. It is not enough, for example, for the Portuguese to be superior at sea. Instead the author calls them fish, as if the ocean were their natural habitat. Upon completing an excessive list of seventeen Portuguese war heroes, Faria e Sousa boldly asserts that such figures continue *ad infinitum*, and that, unlike Hercules, Theseos, and Anteos, they are real and not imagined. Finally, he trumps the noble résumé of one Numa by presenting a number of Portuguese sovereigns, the multitude of which confounds his apt mind and capable hand.

While certainly a general digression from the topic at hand, the above citations echo the tone of Faria e Sousa's section on Manuel I. The author deifies the king to such a degree that his words become incapable of expressing Manuel's grandeur. To emphasize the king's godliness, Faria e Sousa mythologizes him as if he were actually Zeus, ruling over all other gods:

> Pronosticóle tambien la propiedad, i con tanta entrò reinando, que parecia haver arrebatado de las manos de los Dioses todos (permitase que lo digamos aora assi) el cetro de su govierno: al de las aguas, al de los vientos, al de la guerra: antes parecio que entrava a reinar sobre los elementos, que sobre la gente; i antes que sobre la suya sobre todas las estrañas. (3.15.511–12)

As his brief interjection suggests, Faria e Sousa's intent in this selection is not to promote pagan gods. It could be argued, rather, that the author sets up his argument in this way so as to emphasize the incomparable reach of Manuel's reign. It is the symbolic value of this paganism, therefore, that the author draws from as a means to an end. In other words, it is alright to make heretical references if it serves a Christian purpose. The rule of Manuel, God's chosen king, extended beyond humanity to include the elements (his kingdom comprised both land and sea, things at home and things abroad):

> Principe fue de toda España, jurado en Toledo, Emperador de todo el Oriente, i de todos los mares: i, al fin, despues de haver sucedido solo, a todas las venturas de los mas venturosos Monarcas, sucedio al Apostol santo Tomè, porque, haziendo bolar las vanderas cruzadas por toda la Asia enseñò la lei Evangelica, i plantò la firme en los coraçones de las gentes, i en los confines de la tierra; alcançò triunfos gloriosos. … El grande Imperio del Abexin, en la Etiopia. El Reino de Ormuz i Malaca el mas celebre Emporio de todo el Oriente: otros Reinos, otros Señorios, otras i otras naciones, tierras i climas, para cuya historia todo el papel es poco. (3.15.512)

Here Faria e Sousa gradually intensifies his praise of Manuel. The extent of his rule moves progressively from the Iberian Peninsula to the Orient to all of the oceans. He succeeds the rest of the Portuguese monarchs and, at the same time, picks up where St. Thomas left off in the holy apostleship, carrying the gospel across the globe, as Jesus had asked of his chosen servants (Matt. 28.19–20; Mark 16.15). Essentially, all the paper in the world is not sufficient to contain Manuel's accomplishments, another idea with a biblical counterpart: "And there are also many other things which Jesus did, the which, if they should be written every one, I suppose that even the world itself could not contain the books that should be written" (John 21.25).

The divinization of Portuguese history is one of the foundational aspects of Faria e Sousa's *Epítome* and a central feature of his literary corpus. As Javier Núñez Cáceres explains, "el nacionalismo de su obra ... revela su convicción en el destino mesiánico de Portugal" (261–62). In order to lift his nation to a more heavenly sphere and solidify its place in world history, the author aligns the main figures and events of Portugal's past with God's will. As a point of reference we might mention Faria e Sousa's contention that Christ himself founded the kingdom of Portugal (*Epítome* 3.17.548). With this in place it is easy to situate every other Portuguese accomplishment within the frame of providentialism. What results is the history of God's chosen people authored by God himself. As much as the author wanted recognition for his writings, Faria e Sousa's real purpose was to write in such a way so as to saturate the text with the presence of heaven.

Faria e Sousa's vision of the Portuguese nation, therefore, must include a people worthy of the divine favoritism he describes. This is evident in his depiction of the Egas Muniz (1080–1146). Faria e Sousa portrays this legendary figure as representative of all his fellow Portuguese: loyal, devout, obedient, self-sacrificing. The author showcases his ability to move from the micro (Egas) to the macro (Portugal) in the following selection:

> Era su ayo Egas Muniz, excelente Portugues que, afligido con tal defecto en una criatura que en lo restante de su proporcion y forma era bellissima, solicitò, devoto con Dios, el exercicio de los pies que la naturaleza le negava. Apareciole la Virgen Maria Señora nuestra. ... Desta manera, pues, va dando ya nuestro Reyno sus primeros passos con pies de Dios. (3.2.173)

The full version of the passage includes the "actual" words the Virgin spoke to Egas, including the instructions he would have to follow to bring healing to the handicapped feet of the infant Afonso. Thereafter Faria e Sousa moves metonymically from the feet of the prince to the divine inception of Portugal. The faith of Egas Muniz allowed him to receive such a visitation in the first place and also gave him the resolve to carry out the directions given by the Virgin. This mythical example lays bare the national consciousness of Faria e Sousa's historiography.

The theme of Portuguese electness appears frequently throughout *Epítome*, often serving as the author's rationale for his nation's success. A certain confidence underlines all Portuguese endeavors because, in Faria e Sousa's view, they had heavenly assistance. It is not uncommon, for example, to find passages like the following: "Quien duda dela vitoria que busca nuestra gente, si la haze el Cielo electora de un Rei, i pelean con èl ante sus ojos?" (3.2.354). Clearly Faria e Sousa is not fishing for an answer to this question. Of all instances worthy of mention for their divinizing character, however, the most significant has to be the author's account of Aljubarrota. This was the site of the well-known conflict between Portugal and Castile in 1385, which assured Portuguese independence and survived as a symbol of national pride. Among the Castilians, however, the memory was not so endearing.

This legendary clash did not intimidate Faria e Sousa as it had many of his contemporaries, who often skipped over this episode in their histories. While a seemingly sensitive matter requiring careful treatment, Faria e Sousa was not shy about expressing what "really" happened. Portugal's victory, he argues, cannot be attributed to the sun getting in the eyes of the Castilians or some other poor excuse, as some historians have suggested (3.11.453–54). The part of Faria e Sousa's account that I would like to emphasize is the aftermath:

> Admirando el Rei de Castilla la ruina prodigiosa de sus confianças, en tanta multitud con razon fundadas, si el Cielo con David desnudo tantos años antes no huviera assegurado que es suyo el vencer, puesto en huída pressurosa no parò hasta la villa de Santaren, de donde entrado en un navio diligente se puso en Sevilla, bien como otro Pompeyo llegando roto a Larissa, i desde alli por mar a Lesbos huyendo las armas vencedoras de Cesar en los campos de Farsalia. No halló el Rei en muchos tiempos consuelo equivalente a su tristeza, descubriendo su coraçon en lo exterior de un luto que truxo siete años: *No por ser vencido* (dezia èl), *antes por serlo de quien no lo esperava.* (3.11.454; italics in original)

Of all possible vantage points, Faria e Sousa's chooses to discuss Portugal's miraculous victory from the perspective of the Castilian king, who is awe-struck at the ruination of his armies given the circumstances that weighed so heavily in his favor. He marvels even more at what this loss could mean: that God favors Portugal, not Castile. As the significance of these realities sinks in, the king and what is left of his army run off with their tails between their legs. While the defeat was tremendous by any standards, it was the way that Castile fell that prompted the king's seven years of mourning. He was not prepared to cope with a defeat that rendered him and his kingdom a fallen Goliath.

In the same way that he weaves Portuguese electness and the David Principle into his historical writings, Faria e Sousa also reinforces the national collectivity by speaking on behalf of the nation. In the selection that follows, he frames everything within a collective *nuestro* that elevates the Portuguese nation as a whole and celebrates the specific region of Portugal where he was born and raised:

> Llorese la falta de la memoria de quantas hazañas serian obradas por los *nuestros* en el assedio i escala del mas ilustre propugnaculo de España. Pues si Enrique la ganò con el Rei su suegro, con sus vasallos solos dio muchas batallas grandes, con que adquirio varios lugares de entre Duero i Miño, Provincia a quien *nuestro* Reino deve sus glorias: porque en ella està la ciudad de o Porto que le dio nombre: en ella la villa de Guimaraens que le dio Rei: en ella la gente que le dio coronas: en ella edificios nobles de *nuestros* primeros Principes. (3.1.295; my emphasis)

If the communal voice marks the boundaries of the frame, the repeated use of "en ella" certainly situates Douro e Minho at the center of the picture. While Faria e Sousa's primary objective is the glorification of Portuguese history, he still takes advantage of the opportunity to emphasize the contributions of his native region to the greater identity of the nation. Considered in its entirety, it is clear from reading *Epítome* that the author identifies himself with Portugal. There is no attempt at an objectivity that would leave the author absent from the text. He is proudly there with the rest of his compatriots, even if their collective presence is only imagined within the text. Of course, no matter how much the author has to say in favor of Portuguese history, the reader is acutely aware that Faria e Sousa remains divided between an impossible, autonomous Portuguese identity, and the blended Iberian existence underlying early modernity.

One curious feature of the national imaginary that Faria e Sousa develops throughout the course of his work is that it is not merely a place of privilege for the rich, noble, and/or learned. In the Portugal that he imagines, everyone has a voice (provided that they are Christian):

> Mas reconociendolo todo, el ánimo Lusitano estuvo un poco dudoso: pero deshecha la suspensión, con la señal de acometer, dixo un Sacerdote al mismo punto: *Verbum caro*. Preguntaron unos rusticos que era lo que havia dicho, i respondioles otro: *Que les havia de costar caro*. Sea (replicaron) *enorabuena*: y arrojandose al peligro, hallando valerosa resistencia en los contrarios, casi suspendieron la corriente de la vitoria. (3.11.453; italics in original)

This citation is crucial, in that it highlights the courage of the commoner and gives him a voice in the discourse of the nation. These rural soldiers do not live outside of the national imaginary, but are active participants in its construction. Portuguese valor emerges from this passage as it does in many others from *Epítome*, with the important difference that the commoners provide the case study. My emphasis on Faria e Sousa's socio-economic openness to the nation should not be confused with a general open-door policy to the Portuguese. In his picture of what it means to be Portuguese, the author focuses more on affirming Portuguese essentialism than attempting to specify those who do not fit the profile. Hence, instead of directly telling Protestants or Muslims that they do not belong in Portugal—a view the author may or may not have espoused—he makes Catholicism a central feature of Portuguese nationness.

Faria e Sousa's nationalist vision of Portuguese history is consistent up to the death of King Sebastião. The king's tragic disappearance on the field of battle in Africa was followed by a crisis of succession that led to the annexation of Portugal by Felipe II in 1580. Faria e Sousa's treatment of these two royal lines is markedly different from his otherwise cohesive view of Portugal's glorious past. These two figures were very much a part of his present life, thus he could not speak about them with the same openness and confidence that he might have displayed with more temporally distant characters of Portuguese history (a technique often employed by early modern dramatists). Faria e Sousa appears trapped between two conflicting conceptions of the nation. His nationalism keeps him from abandoning his exalted view of Portuguese destiny altogether, while his realism fuels a present sadness that cannot help but see a nation in irreversible decline. While the former feeling prevails for most of the text, the latter imposes its will on Faria e Sousa's vision of Sebastião's death and Felipe's claim to the throne.

In speaking of the young king's passing he states the following: "podremos dezir, no sin dolor, que con la vida del Rei más dichoso se acabaron todas las verdaderas dichas, i glorias Lusitanas" (3.15.513). In this passage, Faria e Sousa figuratively speaks on behalf of the entire nation, which mourns the death of the king and the end of an era. The author is committed to the idea that something was lost with the king that will never be recovered. That does not mean that Faria e Sousa was ready to accept a provincial place on the Peninsula forevermore, only that as a historian and a native of Portugal he acknowledges the significance of this moment in Portuguese history. Even more revealing of his perspective of Sebastião's death is a passage toward the end of the book:

> [F]uimos vencidos en 4 de Agosto; infausto dia a Portugal, que en èl dexò teñida la arena Africana en sangre de tantas vidas, i la patria anegada en llanto de tantas muertes: lastimosas exequias del Reino muerto en tierra agena. Alli acabaron los triunfos lusitanos: murio el orgullo i brio, la pompa i fuerça, la riqueza i esperança, sirviendoles fatalmente de sepulcro aquellos campos, que en una hora cubrieron la vida i honra ganada en el discurso de tantos centenares de años. (3.17.551)

Faria e Sousa packs these lines with decadent language. In his view, the battle at Alcazar-Quibir (1578) marks the low point of Portuguese history. Hundreds of pages covering hundreds of years of history cannot overshadow the loss the author feels in describing this event. The subjectivity of this passage suggests a living affinity between Faria e Sousa and his native Portugal. Writing a little more than half a century after Sebastião's death, the event is still too recent for Portugal's wounded self-concept to heal, yet distant enough for the author to frame the domino effect it has had on the national imaginary. What made Sebastião's death so significant and the birth of *sebastianismo* thereafter so prevalent was what each symbolized for those who adapted either of the two stances. A lifeless king denoted a fallen empire, whereas an immortal king meant that Portugal could still realize its historical destiny.

In the same way that Faria e Sousa carefully avoids any reference to *sebastianismo* in *Epítome*, he also bites his tongue when it comes to discussing the Iberian Union. Some critics want to impose on the text a favorable view of the annexation on the part of the author. They contend that he articulates a clear, pro-Felipe agenda. Ciriaco Bustamante Pérez, for example, cannot reconcile what he sees as a patriotic view of the past and a sympathetic view of the present in the text (5). To begin to unpack this issue we must first recognize that "Faria e Sousa's attitude toward Philip II and his successors ... does not differ markedly from that of the majority of his compatriots" (Glaser, Introduction 12–13). The similitude between Faria e Sousa and his contemporaries discounts this issue as a legitimate marker of difference in their loyalty to Portugal. I use my words carefully because looking at *Epítome*, to say nothing of the sum of Faria e Sousa's works, blurs this very issue. *Epítome* offers a cursory view of Felipe II's right to the Portuguese throne and his subsequent rise to power. Faria e Sousa concludes his inquiry into the various claims to the throne by saying "Nunca lo sabrà nadie dezir cómo èl [Felipe II] lo supo executar" (3.18.561). In context, the tenor of this phrase is hardly one of undying allegiance and support. Faria e Sousa was impressed by the king's ability to orchestrate the annexation and it shows in his positive portrayal of Portugal's first Hapsburg king. Did Faria e Sousa tell the story of the Hapsburgs favorably out of preference or self-preservation? Although interesting, the answer to this question is in many ways inconsequential. Faria e Sousa's life and works debunk the either/or categorizations to which critical commentaries have reduced most Portuguese writers of the seventeenth century. He could have supported Hapsburg rule *and* wanted Portuguese autonomy. An individual of mixed polity can legitimately claim more than one identity. Both the man and his work, therefore, are best understood "dentro de las complejidades coordinadas culturales de una monarquía compuesta en la que ... las nociones de patria y nación eran más flexibles de lo que cabría suponer" (Bass 184). As is the case with so many of his other works, the balance of his love and loyalty in *Epítome* consistently tips in favor of Portugal.

The way I have approached Manuel de Faria e Sousa in this chapter is not limited to the works on which I have focused my attention. By this I mean to say that Faria e Sousa offers much more by way of historiography and literary criticism, not to mention thousands of poems. What is more, within many of these works he likewise makes *portugalidade*, and his allegiance to it, the centerpiece. Not to be missed is the fact that his initial fame as a writer came as a poet. In *Laurel de Apolo*, Lope celebrates Faria e Sousa as a poet-historian: "entre muchos científicos supuestos / eligen a Faría,/ que en historia y poesía / saben que no pudiera / darle mayor la lusitana esfera" (3.155–59). António de Sousa de Macedo's assessment is similar: "si en el verso es tan excelente, no lo es menos en la prosa" (*Flores* fol. 10). Although this chapter has had little to say about his poetry, several poems from Faria e Sousa's seven-volume masterpiece *Fuente de Aganipe* (many of which first appeared in *Divinas y humanas flores*) fit the scope of this study. Many of these poems highlight prominent figures of Portuguese history: Viriato, Inés de Castro, Nuno Álvares Pereira, Alfonso de Albuquerque, Camões, Sebastião, etc. If we are to believe Faria e Sousa's son, Pedro's defense of his father's life and work that appears in a letter to the reader at the beginning of *Asia portuguesa* (1666), the poems from *Fuente de Aganipe* that appear to trumpet Hapsburg rule are actually veiled criticisms of the crown and celebrations of the *Restauração* and João IV. While these issues relate specifically to Faria e Sousa's relationship to Spain and Portugal, poems of this kind are exceptional within his poetic corpus—still the most understudied of all his works.

In his literary criticism and historiography, Faria e Sousa frequently lays claim to his Portuguese roots, articulating a sense of nationalism that at once confirms and rejects the continuity of early modern Iberian identity. Any approach to Faria e Sousa that would ignore his Spanish or Portugueseness ignores a significant aspect of his person. There is no debating his Portuguese origin or the fact that he spent most of his life in Madrid, where he would turn out works about Portugal primarily in Spanish. The close reading of those works that I have put forward in this chapter reveals a man who self-identified as Portuguese and labored tirelessly to erect a monument in her name. He maintained a complicated relationship with his homeland throughout his life, ever-praising her in his writings, never to claim her again as home. The complexities of this association stand out most prominently when considered together with the disproportionate praise he received compared to that given:

Como historiador y crítico hizo conocer al mundo, más que ningún otro, la gloria literaria de su país, los hechos famosos y aventuras prodigiosas de sus naturales. A él, por escribir en castellano, más que a Camoens, Barros y Couto, debe quizá Portugal el ser conocido en el extranjero; servicio que no solamente no reconoció, sino que pagó con ingratitud. (García Peres 208)

These words by the Spanish bibliographer Domingo García Peres are especially striking given the date of their publication (1890). He might have followed the critical mass of the time and disparaged Faria e Sousa, but instead his entry offers a balanced assessment of the author. Faria e Sousa's erudition, writing ability, and work ethic promised a place among his literary heroes, but the Portuguese author has not been able to fully overcome the ways in which most authors of the Dual Monarchy were condemned thereafter; their heterogeneous existence distorted by the homogenous categories that would exclude them. Indeed, among the seventeenth-century Portuguese authors overlooked by modern scholarship, Faria e Sousa may very well be its primary victim (Glaser, *Estudios* 3). That which has served for so long as justification for his decentralized status, however, is slowly being discredited. Publications from the past decade alone attest to this critical shift. While there were always voices praising the author in one way or another over the years, it was the second half of the twentieth century that really ushered in a new age of Faria e Sousa criticism. Jorge de Sena's apt description synthesizes the complexity of this distinguished man of letters: "o Faria e Sousa que escolheu ser, em Espanha, e através do espanhol, um propagandista de Portugal e de Camões" (17; "the Faria e Sousa that he chose to be, in Spain, and through Spanish, a propagandist for Portugal and Camões"). The beginning and end of his existence, indeed the love of his life, was Portugal. The model he celebrated and zealously followed was none other than his poet, Luís de Camões. In a way that can only be understood within the unique time and place that was the Iberian Union, his pursuit of poet and *patria* led him from Portugal to Spain and from Portuguese to Spanish. Eleven years after his death, Faria e Sousa's body returned to the land that his heart never left. Portuguese by birth and by choice, Spanish by circumstance, he was neither one nor the other but an Iberian par excellence.

Chapter Four

Staging the Nation

Cordeiro, Azevedo, and the Portuguese *Comedia*

In the prologue of his first published play, the fifteen-year-old Portuguese dramatist Jacinto Cordeiro (1606–46) makes his purpose for writing clear: "tenho de eternizar grandezas de minha patria" (*La entrada*; "I must immortalize the greatnesses of my homeland").[1] At the root of his drama lies a commitment to immortalize Portugal. The young playwright maintained this position during the course of his literary career, dedicating many of his *comedias* to the praise of the Portuguese nation. Cordeiro, however, was not alone among his contemporaries. While not all Portuguese playwrights employed their literary genius in favor of Portugal, many of them situated their works within their native borders and made frequent reference to Portuguese-related themes and history in their plays. Within the latter category, for example, we discover one of Cordeiro's female contemporaries, Ângela de Azevedo (1600?–60?), whose three *comedias* reflect a similar place-based approach to theater.[2] A consistent effort to stage the nation is apparent in the works of Azevedo and Cordeiro as well as many of their compatriots. Altogether, these plays affirm the past, present, and future worth of their native Portugal, and highlight the important contribution of Portuguese dramatists to the *comedia* tradition.

Considered within their context, it is not surprising to find early modern dramatists paying tribute to their respective nations. Such patriotic imaginings, in fact, were frequent among the most well-known authors of the era, not to mention their sixteenth-century predecessors (see chapter two). Early modern Iberian theater is particularly inviting for those reading the period and the genre with an eye on national consciousness. Two main waves define sixteenth- and seventeenth-century dramatizations of Spain and Portugal. The first—which I partially addressed in chapter two—includes Gil Vicente and the school of playwrights that preceded the Iberian Union. It is difficult to overestimate Vicente's influence on Golden Age Theater in general, and the outpouring of early seventeenth-century interest in Portuguese-themed drama in particular. The second wave—what we might appropriately call a tidal wave—consists of Lope de Vega and the *comedia nueva*. The role of Portugal and the Portuguese in this second group, a topic traditionally overlooked, is the focus of the present chapter. Lope and the new school that he founded produced numerous nationally-motivated *comedias*, many of which are specifically related to Portugal. Spanish and Portuguese dramatists had looked to Portugal for artistic inspiration in the past, but during the second half of the Dual Monarchy, the Portuguese nation had become a legitimate dramatic impetus, feeding the frenzy that was Spanish Golden Age Theater. Despite the relatively scarce attention their works have received, many Portuguese playwrights rode the popular wave of the *comedia nueva* with their Spanish contemporaries and took advantage of the medium to affirm their own national identity at a time when the Spanish empire had culturally subsumed Portugal. The *comedias* of Cordeiro and Azevedo move freely across linguistic, literary, and cultural boundaries, manifesting their connections to Spain at the same moment that they affirm their *portugalidade*.

The ubiquitous cross-dressing characters of the *comedia* are a useful point of reference for understanding Portuguese playwrights like Cordeiro and Azevedo (and Portuguese authors of the time in general). These characters (e.g., Rosaura from *La vida es sueño*) alter their appearance in order to obtain some stated objective: revenge, autonomy, proof of fidelity, love interests, insider information, etc. When Portuguese authors dress their writings in Spanish they accomplish something analogous. As I have illustrated elsewhere, Portuguese authors often explain that the choice to write in Spanish is based on their desire to reach a broader audience with their demonstrations and celebrations of *portugalidade*. While their motives are more complex than this single reason, their writings tell us that this is one of their main objectives. In Azevedo's *El muerto disimulado*, it is understood that Clarindo must become Clara (a rare case of male cross-dressing in the *comedia*) in order to obtain the desired outcome: to confirm that his lover (Jacinta) has remained faithful and to kill his traitor-friend (Don Alvaro). Likewise, the Portuguese must write in Spanish in order to realize their various purposes for writing. Writing in Spanish does not mean that they are not Portuguese, just like dressing as Clara does not make Clarindo any less himself. It is an enhancement of their existing role; not Portuguese then Spanish, but Portuguese and Spanish.

Literary historians often consider the seventeenth century a decadent period of Portuguese letters.[3] They point to the cultural Castilianization of Portugal—intensified, but not caused, by the 1580 annexation—as the major cause for this collapse. Perhaps most astonishing, especially when considered in comparison to their Spanish contemporaries, is the decline of the theater. After all, Portugal boasts one of the greatest Iberian dramatists of the sixteenth century in Gil Vicente, not to mention Luís de Camões and especially António Ferreira's dramatic contributions. Critics often point to Francisco Manuel de Melo's *Auto do fidalgo aprendiz* (1665) as one of only a few bright spots in seventeenth-century Portuguese drama. His farce builds on both Portuguese and Spanish dramatic technique—Vicente's frequent use of satire, social critique, and the *redondilha*, on the one hand, and the division of the work in three *jornadas*, cloak and dagger scenes, and stock characters, on the other. The mother-daughter relationship within the play, however, departs from standard *comedia nueva* practice. The *comedia* generally lacks mothers altogether, to say nothing of the self-determined, power-driven Isabel who drives Manuel de Melo's play. The brevity (1065 lines) of the work, among other aspects, keeps it from measuring up to *comedia* standards. It might be best, therefore, to think of *O fidalgo aprendiz* as a mix of Vicente and Lope; a hybrid that reflects the century-and-a-half of Peninsular theater preceding its composition. The play deserves the praise and recognition that literary critics and historians have bestowed upon it, but not to the exclusion of Portuguese-authored drama in Spanish. Taking into consideration the vast body of Portuguese *comedias* written in Spanish—which may number as high as three hundred[4]—drastically alters the perception of the literary, and more specifically, the dramatic production of Portuguese authors during the seventeenth century, leading to the inevitable conclusion that there *is* such a thing as a Portuguese *comedia*.[5]

In addition to the three primary motifs—religion, love, honor—identified by Margaret Wilson during the mid-twentieth century (*Spanish* 42), critics have spent decades establishing and defining categories for organizing the thousands of *comedias* written during the Golden Age. There are, of course, familiar designations such as cloak and dagger, wife-murder, honor, and historical. David Castillejo's *Guía de ochocientas comedias del Siglo de Oro* (2002) goes even further, dividing Lope's *comedias*, for example, into sixty-seven different groupings (96–110). One group of texts that represents an important *comedia* sub-genre not recognized in Castillejo's guide are the various Portuguese-themed plays, which may number anywhere from the twenties (modest estimate) up to the fifties. Castillejo's work puts forward the category "*La historia de España*" in his section on Lope, but it is apparent that works related to Portugal, the New World, and other relevant spaces do not necessarily belong. With *El otro siglo de oro: cuarenta dramaturgos recuperados* (2007), Castillejo gets at some of what was missing in his earlier study, but its panoramic scope remains too broad for the Portuguese to see the kind of sustained treatment that their dramatic output warrants.[6] A similar trend runs through *comedia* criticism in general. Often overlooked, and certainly understudied, are the many Portuguese-themed *comedias* authored by both Spanish and Portuguese dramatists.

Just as Portuguese playwrights of the seventeenth century had a clear predecessor in Gil Vicente and his nation-minded theater, Spanish dramatists writing about Portugal during the Golden Age could look to Bartolomé de Torres Naharro for inspiration. Torres Naharro, in fact, may have been the first Spanish dramatist to take up Portuguese themes in his plays. He penned at least two works that speak to the developing sense of national consciousness in Iberia at the time, especially as it pertains to the Portuguese. His polyglot play *Tinelaria* (1517), for example, not only incorporates Spanish, Portuguese, Catalan, French, and Italian characters, but also has them speak their respective languages and embody, with a certain degree of essentialism, their respective nationalities. Most of the play takes place during a meal at the servants' eating quarters of some great palace. The setting and dialogue are very picaresque. For the most part, the work revolves around the conversation taking place between the various characters at meal-time. One of the more entertaining exchanges in the play occurs between Francisco (Castilian), Mathía (Sevilian), and an unnamed Portuguese man:

> FRANCISCO. ¡Gran Castilla!
>   Que si saca su cuadrilla
>   no hay, par Dios, quien se le acueste.
> MATHIA. Que solamente Sevilla
>   puede sacar una hueste.

PORTUGUES. Eu vos fundo	I am with you on that
e vos concedo o segundo,	and I will concede the second point,
que Sevella he muyto boa;	that Seville is great;
mais Sevella e tudo o mundo	but Seville and all of the world
he merda para Lisboa. (1.60–69)	is shit compared to Lisbon.

While the conversation begins with talk of the military strength of various Peninsular regions, the Portuguese servant takes advantage of the occasion to make a general comment about Lisbon's superiority above all other cities in the world. Some of the other characters add their voice to the discussion, but none of them challenge what the Portuguese has said nor make such an audacious claim of their own. That said, his comment about Lisbon pales in comparison to what he later says about the relationship between God and Portugal: "Naun zumbés, / que Judas foi cordovés / e muyto ben se vos prova; / e Deus foi portogués / de meu da Rua Nova" (2.110–14; "Do not make a fuss, / Judas was Cordoban / look into it if you want; / and God was Portuguese / from the middle of Rua Nova"). God, according to the Portugués, is so Portuguese that one can trace his roots to Lisbon's early modern equivalent to Main Street—*Rua Nova*—the heart of Lisbon, and, by extension, the Portuguese nation.[7] In these verses, Torres Naharro captures Portugal's elevated self-concept; an attitude he may have picked up from his Peninsular contemporary, Gil Vicente, whose *Templo d'Apolo* also asserts God's Portuguese origin (see chapter 2). The influence of his Portuguese contemporary is particularly evident in Torres Naharro's *Comedia Trofea*, a likely spinoff of Vicente's *Auto da fama* (Figueiredo, "Prefácio" 37). Such references in the work of Torres Naharro become commonplace by the seventeenth century among other Peninsular dramatists who attempt to characterize Portugal and the Portuguese.

Vicente, Torres Naharro, and other sixteenth-century Iberian authors influenced Lope and the new school of theater that he founded during the first decades of the Dual Monarchy, especially in terms of the historico-national dramas that they would produce. By the time he published the *Arte nuevo de hacer comedias en este tiempo* (1609), his treatise on the fundamental characteristics of the *comedia nueva*, Lope had polished his dramatic technique significantly (483 plays written up to that point, by his count). His Spanish and Portuguese contemporaries were soon to follow, as the public theater quickly became a popular Peninsular pastime for all members of society. As they did with other literary genres, Portuguese authors took advantage of their proficiency in Spanish to participate in the widespread popularity of the *comedia*. Whereas a work in Spanish had audiences throughout Iberia, plays in Portuguese could only be staged for limited audiences in Portugal. That they had to be written in Spanish, however, did not mean that they had to be written about Spain. In fact, for some Portuguese dramatists, the opposite was true. The *comedias* of Ângela de Azevedo and Jacinto Cordeiro, for example, constitute a deliberate attempt to stage the Portuguese nation. They perform *portugalidade* by invoking Portuguese history, language, geography, and other key features. Many Spanish playwrights also dedicated entire works to Portugal, but the glorification and immortalization of Lusitânia that naturally occurs in Azevedo and Cordeiro's plays distinguishes them from their Peninsular contemporaries.

Although the Portuguese were writing in Spanish and actively participating in the same *comedia* trends as their contemporaries in Spain, and the Spanish were busily writing dozens of Portuguese-themed plays, the two groups are not one in the same. Not unlike the point Jorge Luis Borges makes in "Pierre Menard, autor del *Quijote*," there is a qualitative difference between Spanish and Portuguese playwrights saying/doing virtually the same thing (in this case, dramatizing the Portuguese nation). The layers of signification in the work of the Portuguese differ from that of their Spanish contemporaries, if not for any other reason than because the Portuguese write from within a category of belonging and self-identification that does not pertain to the Spanish. They highlight this claim in a variety of ways, the most obvious being the repeated use of *we* and *our*. Traditionally, the Portuguese are left out of critical conversations related to the *comedia*. Separating them from the Spanish allows me to examine their general participation in Golden Age Theater as well as their unique contribution to nationally conscious theater. I speak of nationality fully aware that the Iberian Union (1580–1640) held Portugal under provincial status for most of the first half of the seventeenth century. Thus, I am not speaking of nationality in terms of political autonomy, but rather as a native claim to history, place, and culture (as detailed in chapter one). That is to say, anyone can praise Portugal, but not anyone can state from the outset that their purpose is to immortalize the greatness of their *patria* as Cordeiro, for instance, does in the prologue to *La entrada del Rey en Portugal*.

When Portuguese authors write about Portugal, they cast a collectivity to which they claim affiliation, whereas the Spanish remain distant from their subject matter when it relates to Portugal. Even when Spanish playwrights focus on their own national identity (e.g., *Fuenteovejuna, Numancia, Las mocedades del Cid*), it is not presented with the same cohesiveness as works focused on Portugal. This is due, in large part, to the relative stability of the Portuguese imaginary at this time, particularly when one considers, as a point of contrast, the emerging, yet disjointed concept of Spanish identity.[8] While some may argue with this effort to distinguish the two dominant Iberian personalities, what is beyond question is the increased emphasis Spanish and Portuguese dramatists of the seventeenth century placed on the nation. From the early nationalist template established by Gil Vicente, to the numerous nation-themed *comedias* of the Golden Age appearing throughout the Peninsula, the nation frequently dominates early modern Iberian theater. While Portugal may have dropped off in many ways during the decades of the annexation, its presence on the stage was never more widespread nor important than at this time. My purpose is not to list every dramatist and work related to the nation, but to trace the general development of this topic in Peninsular drama during the late sixteenth and early seventeenth centuries, with special emphasis given to the representations of Lusitânia found in the works of Cordeiro and Azevedo. Of all the literary genres that Portuguese authors took advantage of in order to spread the glories of their homeland, theater was the most common and the most effective way to communicate their sense of *portugalidade*.

A wave of *comedias* dealing with Portuguese history and themes appeared throughout the Peninsula during the Golden

Age. Portugal was in vogue, acting as a muse for virtually every major playwright of the day. Many scholars have studied this phenomenon as it relates to specific authors such as Lope, Tirso, and Calderón.[9] These studies suggest that many of the *comedias* dealing with Portugal were written specifically for a Portuguese audience. In general, interest in Portugal can be attributed to the increased cross-cultural exchange between Spain and Portugal ushered in by the annexation, not to mention the influential work of sixteenth-century authors such as Vicente. It is worth noting that from 1580 to 1610 few Spanish authors took interest in their longtime Peninsular neighbor. The final decades of the annexation, however, saw both an outpouring of Portuguese-themed *comedias* and an increased interest in Lisbon as a destination for theater companies from Madrid (Rennert 194; Vázquez Cuesta, "Lengua" 634). The concentration of Portuguese-themed works during the second half of the annexation coincides with both the rise in popularity of the *comedia* in general, as well as the active participation of the Portuguese in Peninsular culture. Many Portuguese authors, in fact, stimulated interest in their native land by publishing works that celebrate Portuguese history and culture. The influence of Portuguese authors writing in Spanish, therefore, is incalculable. It includes those who directly read, heard, or interacted with their writings in some other way, as well as those who went on to produce poetry, plays, history, and other texts inspired by what they read from the Portuguese.

Faria e Sousa's *Epítome de las historias portuguesas* is one example of a Portuguese-authored work that had a real impact on the production of Portuguese-themed *comedias* among Spanish playwrights.[10] As scholars have long pointed out, *Epítome* served as the source for at least two *comedias* written during the Golden Age—Tirso's *Las quinas de Portugal* and Calderón's *El príncipe constante*.[11] Tirso and Calderón not only reproduced the historical facts laid out in *Epítome*, but also captured the patriotic zeal of the work. Faria e Sousa's influence on Calderón and Tirso only hints at the potential influence he had as a writer in his day. These and numerous other Spanish *comedias* include Portuguese characters, take place partially or entirely in Portugal, are related to Portuguese history, and contain other references to Portugal. Among Lope's works alone, we find *La tragedia del Rey D. Sebastián*, *El duque de Viseo*, *El más galán portugués*, and *El Brasil restituido*, among others. Glaser describes this early seventeenth-century phenomenon as follows: "Los comediógrafos españoles hallaron una importante fuente de inspiración dramática en diversos temas de la tradición y de la historia lusitana; sea el trágico amor de Inés de Castro o la lucha contra los holandeses en Brasil" (Introducción viii–ix). In some instances, a single figure from Portuguese history inspired a series of dramatic works. This was certainly the case with Inés de Castro and King Sebastião. As José Ares Montes observes, what these works lack in historical fidelity, they make up for in theatricality: "No importa que la fidelidad histórica se disluya en la inventiva poética; la historia de Portugal está ahí, vista con admiración y cantada con entusiasmo, así como elogiado en extremo la belleza de las portuguesas y el valor, generosidad y fidelidad de los portugueses" ("Portugal" 15). With very few exceptions, critics call attention to the goodwill demonstrated by Spanish dramatists toward the Portuguese in their *comedias*.[12] This is partially due to the fact that they were writing for Portuguese audiences, but there is more to it. Portugal's rich folkloric tradition and high output of works about Portugal in Spanish made it an easy source from which early modern dramatists could draw. Portuguese history and themes offered a degree of familiarity and novelty that both playwrights and audiences from across the Peninsula could appreciate. That a Lusocentric playwright like Cordeiro was praised throughout the Peninsula, is proof enough that Portuguese-themed plays were not merely intended for Portuguese audiences. Based on his success, in fact, one may ascertain that the Spanish did not feel threatened by such pro-Portuguese texts.

No Spanish playwright got more dramatic mileage out of Portugal than Tirso de Molina. From the well-known description of Lisbon in *El burlador de Sevilla* to his treatment of the mythical founding of Portugal in *Las quinas de Portugal* to the entertaining switches between Spanish and Portuguese in *El amor médico*, Tirso had an in-depth knowledge of the very features of the Portuguese nation so frequently cited by authors during the Iberian Union. Overall, he penned at least seven predominantly Portuguese *comedias*[13] and another eight with Portuguese characters and frequent references to Portugal (Ares Montes, "Portugal" 16). As Edwin S. Morby points out, "the peak of enthusiasm" among Tirso's Portuguese-themed works has to be *Las quinas*, the author's last *comedia*. The play recounts the legendary feats of Afonso Henriques and the founding of Portugal. What is more, it imagines the same national identity cast by Tirso's Portuguese contemporaries: invincibility (478, 675), valor and fidelity (528, 755–57, 1125–26, 1569, 2042, 2404), the David Principle (723–30, 854, 890, 1083–97), and providentialism (1743–49, 1840–41, 1890–1985, 2030–33).[14] While Faria e Sousa's historiographical work ensured the survival of such foundational myths, it was in the pages of the *comedias* written by Tirso de Molina and his contemporaries and on the stages their works were performed, that such conceptions of the Portuguese nation took root and produced fruit throughout the Peninsula.

Although *Las quinas* is based on Faria e Sousa's *Epítome*, there is at least one important difference between how one author speaks of the events surrounding Portugal's famed beginning and the other. For Tirso, speaking of the *quinas* is a matter of description, whereas for Faria e Sousa it is, in a collective sense, self-description. The distinction is subtle, yet significant. It is a "we" instead of a "they," an "our" rather than a "their." Understanding this difference is particularly important when it comes to reading the variety of Portuguese-themed *comedias* written by both Spanish and Portuguese dramatists during the Golden Age. Portugal is typically at the heart of such works. Together, they invoke the rhetoric of *portugalidade* and lead readers through a tour of Portuguese history and geography. Among many Portuguese playwrights, however, there seems to be more at stake. The way they speak of the Portuguese nation is a difference of degree, not kind. Their plays both exalt and pledge allegiance to Lusitânia. They are at once art and ideology. Sustaining such a pro-Portuguese agenda during the Iberian Unification constituted a speech-act of real import. Beginning with the early work of Simão Machado, and then moving on to Jacinto Cordeiro and Ângela de Azevedo, I hope to trace the rhetoric of nationhood within the Portuguese *comedia*, including the various times at which they articulate a native claim to their homeland and subscribe to a national collectivity.

Simão Machado (1570–1640) was one of the first Portuguese playwrights to experiment with the dramatic innovations coming out of the late sixteenth century from a nation-based perspective. Having lived during the dawn of the annexation, the turn of the century, and well into the 1600s, Machado provides a meaning-ful bridge between Vicente, Torres Naharro, Camões, and other sixteenth-century dramatists, and the many seventeenth-century Spanish and Portuguese playwrights writing with the nation in mind. *Comédia do Cerco de Dio* and *Comédia da Pastora Alfea* were likely written during the 1590s, although not originally published until 1601 (Ares Montes, "Portugal" 13). Another edition of his plays, bearing the same title as the 1601 version but with the addition of several *entremeses* attributed to Lope and Francisco de Quevedo, was published in Lisbon in 1631 with the name *Comedias portuguesas. Feitas Pello Excelente Poeta, Simão Machado.* Similar to some of the sixteenth-century dramatists discussed in chapter two, as well as Torres Naharro, Machado consistently alternates between Portuguese and Spanish throughout his two *comedias*. Machado's *Comédia do Cerco de Dio* bears the mark of a Portuguese apologist who, at the occasional expense of his Castilian neighbors, uses his polyglot works to exalt Portugal. The two verses found in the third to last stanza of *Cerco de Dio* capture the spirit of Machado's literary devotion to his homeland: "Louvay sempre os Portugueses, / Pois são vossos naturais" (fol. 56; "Always praise the Portuguese, / for they are your people").

Similar to many of his Iberian predecessors, Machado uses language as a mode of characterization in *Cerco de Dio*, sugges-tively assigning Spanish to the lowliest characters in the work. In response to his alternating and subversive use of the two languages, Vázquez Cuesta asks, "¿será demasiada suspicacia atribuir a encubierta mala fe nacionalista el hecho de que ponga el autor hablando castellano precisamente a aquellos personajes que constituyen en la pieza los enemigos de los protagonistas portugueses: moros e indios?" ("Lengua" 635). It is not out of the question to think that Machado would play with language in this way, especially in light of Vicente and Camões's previous efforts to characterize the Spanish accordingly. From beginning to end, Machado's *Cerco de Dio* answers Vázquez Cuesta's question. The two lines of stage directions that anticipate the initial verses of the play set things in motion: "Entrão Mouros e Christãos, pele-jando, e dizem os Mouros: Arma, mueran estos locos, / Mueran soberbios Christianos" (1.1–2; "Moors and Christians enter, fighting, and the Moors say …"). The switch from Portuguese to Spanish, from the Christian playwright Simão Machado to the

Moorish enemies, is significant. This characterization identifies the Moors with the Spanish through a linguistic common ground (a potentially subversive insinuation). After all, this play was written only a hundred years after Granada fell and the centuries-old Spanish *Reconquista* came to an end. In the late sixteenth, and well into the seventeenth century, struggles against Islam persisted on the Peninsula. Thus, by grouping the Moors and the Spanish under one linguistic banner, Machado casts an unseemly insult. Spanish remains the means of communication for all Moors throughout the play. Nevertheless, several others, including the king, speak Spanish. Does speaking Spanish ennoble the Moors, disgrace the king, or neither of the two? The Portuguese, after all, took great pride in their loyalty. It would seem out of character, then, for Machado to in some way dethrone the king. Interpreting the function of language switches in Machado's plays, therefore, may seem fairly straightforward as it pertains to the Moors, but highly inconclusive in the case of the king.

During the time of the Portuguese annexation, one would expect to find patriotic statements in favor of an autonomous Portugal. While many would expect Portuguese to be the *lingua franca* for such manifestations, Machado and many of his contemporaries appropriated Spanish as a means of dissemination. An example of this appears at the beginning of *Cerco de Dio*, when a Moorish solider reflects on the puzzling military success of the Portuguese given their relative smallness as a nation: "es posible que tan pocos / resistan a tantas manos" (1.4–5). Traditionally, the Portuguese take great pride in being able to defend their sovereignty despite being outnumbered by the opposition (e.g., Aljubarrota). A parallel passage appears later in the play, as Rao, a Moor and main character in Machado's work, makes specific mention of the military prowess of Portugal, "nunca vencida en la guerra" (fol. 16). While it may seem ironic for Machado to include such statements in his text while Portugal remains annexed, this reference to the glorious past could also be read as an attempt to inspire his fellow Portuguese to action. This seems very possible, considering Claude-Henri Frèches's contention that Machado likely participated in the intellectual movement of resistance to Spanish dominance (21). Just as Machado, many of these intellectuals published works that collectively remember Portugal as she once was and as she might once again be.

It is evident that Machado felt uneasy about the cultural Castilianization (and other foreign influences) taking over the Peninsula, particularly in his native Portugal. In *Comedia da Pastora Alfea*—a work not as overtly Portuguese as *Cerco de Dio*— the author reflects on the changes occurring on Portugal's literary landscape as a result of the annexation and other related factors. It contains, for example, many explicit and implicit references to the socio-historical climate in which Machado composed his works. To some extent, one could say that *Pastora Alfea* predicts the complete shift in Portuguese theater from the Portuguese and polyglot texts of the sixteenth century, to the near saturation of the national theater by the Spanish language in the seventeenth. The work reads as a haphazard mix of characters, eleven of which speak in Portuguese, eight in Spanish, and two in Italian. Between the first and second parts of the play, Machado inserts an intriguing *dicho*[15] on the state of Portuguese culture and society, decrying the assimilation of foreign (especially Castilian) influences at the expense of Portugal's own identity. It relates the story of an artist who is commissioned to paint the nations of the world, distinguishing each one by his dress. While the Castilian, French, and Italian all wear their customary attire, the Portuguese is depicted with fabric in hand. Asked why the Portuguese figure appears this way, the artist complains of the difficulty of portraying Portugal since one never knows what to expect one day to the next from the ever-changing Portuguese:

Velos eis disse a Francesa,	He said you see them à la French,
Despois disse a Castelhana,	After he said à la Castilian,
Oje andão a Valoneza,	Today they are à la Walloon
A amanhã a Sevilhana,	Tomorrow à la Sevilian
E ja nunca a Portuguesa. (fol. 78)	And never ever à la Portuguese.

The artist goes on to say that the choice to represent the Portuguese holding material was better than the alternative: painting him with thirty different outfits (the suggestion here being that Portuguese vanity is boundless).

Having drawn a clear picture of the problem, the satirical *dicho* moves away from the painting proper to a much larger stage: the condition of the arts in Portugal at the turn of the century. What follows is a complaint that the Portuguese public has become constant in their shiftiness and incessant in bad-mouthing (79).

Two verses from the antepenultimate stanza capture the spirit of lament akin to this liminal text: "e do vosso natural / Nada vos parece bem" (79; "when it comes to your own people / Nothing seems good to you"). It is not difficult to sense the anxiety of the artist in these verses. The text unequivocally states that an author committed to the cultivation of Portuguese language and aesthetics will not survive among his own people, which, given the limited readership for works in Portuguese, is his only audience. The message is not unlike the longstanding proverb of biblical origin: *In patria natus non est propheta vocatus.*[16] The closing verses of the *dicho* emphasize the point even further, criticizing the fact that Portuguese authors have to write in Spanish in order to gain favor in their own country:

Vendo quão mal aceitais,	Seeing how poorly you receive,
As obras dos naturais,	The works of your own people,
Fiz esta em lingoa estrangeira,	I wrote this one in a foreign tongue,
Por ver se desta maneira	To see if in this way
Como a elles tratais.	You treat us as you do them.
Fiome no Castelhano,	I have confidence in Castilian,
Fiome em ser novidade,	I have confidence in my novelty,
Se nua e noutra me engano,	If in both cases I am mistaken,
Vos Portugal eu o pano,	You, Portugal, will cut me,
Cortay a vossa vontade. (fol. 79)	The fabric, according to your will.

The last two verses complete the dramatic scene that Machado paints from the outset. Rather than the painter being analogous to the early modern Portuguese artist, Machado associates the painter with the Portuguese public (presumably the reading public [cultural consumers]). Accordingly, the artist is the fabric, fashioned according to popular demand. This, of course, turns previous criticism upside down, as most literary critics and cultural historians primarily hold the artists accountable for the Castilianization of Portuguese letters.

Machado's plays present a fascinating blend of past and present, native and foreign, Portuguese and Spanish, problematizing both sides by bringing them together on the same stage. *Cerco de Dio* fits in well with the current of nationally-determined drama of the sixteenth century. *Pastora Alfea* focuses on the nation in a different way, predicting the complete saturation of the Portuguese stage by Spanish language and dramatic technique. Rather than reading both works as a contradiction or a problem to be solved—the one praising, the other criticizing the nation—I see them as forming a bridge between sixteenth- and seventeenth-century Iberian Theater. While he looks at early modern Iberia from a Portuguese perspective, his preoccupations, his influences, and his audience are Peninsular. There are times, however, when the dramatist reminds the reader that he is indeed Portuguese, and that at different times, his works are keenly directed to his compatriots. Machado believes that Portugal merits praise in general, but is particularly insistent that the Portuguese esteem that which is Portuguese once again: "Louvay sempre os Portugueses, / Pois são vossos naturais" (*Cerco* 56; "Always praise the Portuguese, / for they are your people").

Despite the bleak picture of Portuguese letters painted in *Pastora Alfea* and António Ferreira's earlier warnings and threats against those who would abandon their native tongue to cultivate another (see chapter two), seventeenth-century Portuguese theater became precisely what many sixteenth-century Portuguese authors had feared: an extension of Castilian culture. It is erroneous, however, to argue that since these plays were mostly written in Spanish, that they are somehow not Portuguese. Such a perspective would be a modern imposition that does not fairly consider the nuances of language and identity at the time. In effect, many playwrights utilized their Spanish proficiency to celebrate Portuguese identity both before and after the Restoration of 1640. They accepted their context for what it was, and wrote in praise of Portugal anyway. In other words, they did the best with what they had. Annexation literature was peripheral to and strongly influenced by the Castilian center, but that should not keep us from acknowledging its valuable contribution to early modern Iberian letters. Rather than blame Portuguese playwrights for the Castilianization of the national theater, García Peres points to the unique impact of the annexation on the stage: "Lástima que Machado y otros ingenios portugueses careciesen de un teatro público en que pudiesen, como los dramáticos castellanos, lucir las galas de su ingenio. A ésta, y no á otra circunstancia, se debe el que nuestra literatura dramática no corresponda en importancia á su hermana la castellana" (339). García Peres is right to suggest that the conditions in Portugal kept artists from achieving the success that their literary ability promised. He perhaps overstates the point, however, in claiming that were it not for the absence of a public theater, the Portuguese would rival the accomplishments of their Spanish contemporaries. One would be hard-pressed to find any national theater tradition to match what Spanish playwrights achieved during the Golden Age. The way García Peres constructs his argument, positioning the Portuguese against the Spanish, is refreshing, even if a bit misguided. It is encouraging to find someone trying to make sense of the general lack of dramatic works in the Portuguese language during the seventeenth century, but he oversimplifies the issue when he attributes the disparity between Spanish and Portuguese artistic production to the Dual Monarchy because the matter is much more complex and also because the categories "Spanish" and "Portuguese," at least in literature, are not nearly as stable and distinct as he makes them out to be.

Many Portuguese dramatists of the annexation period continued along the same patriotic lines that Vicente established during the first half of the sixteenth century, and Machado carried into the seventeenth. As Machado's works describe, the stakes of literature, language, and politics had changed as a result of the annexation. A close reading of Ângela de Azevedo and Jacinto Cordeiro's *comedias* reveals the uniqueness and variety of Portuguese-authored attempts to stage the nation in the seventeenth century. Both authors dramatize Portugal's rich folkloric tradition, incorporate Portuguese history, and weave other national themes into their plays (e.g., Lisbon's grandeur, *saudade*, qualitative supremacy). While Cordeiro reads much more overtly Portuguese than Azevedo, the female dramatist is also upfront about her affection for Portugal. Cordeiro takes broad, unmistakable strokes, announcing, before the work even begins, that the reader can expect a glorified rendering of the fatherland. Azevedo, on the other hand, exerts her *portugalidade* in subtle ways, inserting herself between the lines, brilliantly locked in the tropes she employs. Cordeiro was one of the most successful Portuguese dramatists of the Golden Age. Azevedo's works, if staged at all, were performed for small, most likely female audiences. Ultimately, both playwrights embody the Portuguese nation in distinct, yet complementary ways.

From an early age, Jacinto Cordeiro had a clear sense of what he wanted to accomplish as a dramatist. In the prologue to his first *comedia*, *La entrada del Rey en Portugal* (1621), published when he was only fifteen years old, the budding playwright reveals the purpose of this particular work as well as the aim of his entire literary corpus. A typographical error on the cover page, however, reflects the patriotic underpinnings of the work before Cordeiro can even announce his stated purpose. While almost certainly accidental, the Lisbon publication reads *La entrada del Rey em Portugal*. Leaving the preposition "em" ("into") in Portuguese serves as the first gesture of a symbolic striptease that will eventually leave the true Portuguese character of the work completely exposed to its readers. Turning a few pages, the prologue reveals Cordeiro's inspiration for writing: "tenho de eternizar grandezas de minha Patria" ("I must immortalize the greatness of my homeland"). At least two things stand out from this statement. First is the author's choice to write the prologue in his native tongue rather than in Spanish, the language of the *comedia*. This is important in that it demonstrates a prevailing commitment to Portugal. Spanish was not only the language of prestige on the Peninsula at this time, but, on top of that, Portuguese dramatists had little hope of staging works in their native tongue. Where Cordeiro does have a choice—the prologue—he revealingly opts for Portuguese. What is also significant about his stated purpose is that it distinguishes *his* motivations from the many Spanish dramatists who also took up Portuguese history and themes in their works. That is not to say that Lope, Tirso, Vélez de Guevara, Calderón, and others did not care for Portugal, only that their intentions were not as Lusocentric, nor as personal, as Cordeiro's ("minha Patria"). It is also possible that Cordeiro wants to draw a distinction between himself and those of his compatriots who seem to have forgotten Portugal altogether.

Hence, from the beginning of his literary career, Cordeiro seems to have had a sense of what he wanted to accomplish in his works. That they would be staged throughout Iberia, only adds an exclamation point to his nationalist intentions since the theater is "el más poderoso *mass media* de la época" (Vázquez Cuesta, "Lengua" 634). The significance of the aforementioned title goes far beyond the apparent editing mistake previously mentioned. Felipe III's visit to Portugal in 1619 inspired an outpouring of literary works, including Violante do Céu's *Comedia de S. Engracia*, which had the honor of being performed for the visiting king. A number of other works, including Cordeiro's *comedia*, specifically discuss, at least in the title, the king's celebrated visit to Portugal. This includes, most notably, Francisco Rodrigues Lobo's *La jornada que la Magestad Catholica del Rey Felipe III hizo al reino de Portugal, y el triunfo y pompa con que le recibió la insigne ciudad de Lisboa* (1623). Similar to other works commemorating this event, this text pays poetic tribute to the king. While the title of Cordeiro's play may suggest that, like his Portuguese contemporaries, the author also intends to heap praise on Felipe III, the king is only peripherally situated on the stage, a side note to the real protagonist: Portugal.

One of the first overt attempts to glorify Portugal is the author's consideration of Lisbon, "una Ciudad tan gallarda, / donde tantas alegrias, / tantas fiestas, tantas danças, / tantos fuegos, tantas luzes, / tantas invenciones varias, / tan graves actos de amor / se hazen" (fol. 3). This hyperbolic description of Lisbon was a common practice among nationally inclined writers of the time—not to mention many Spanish authors (Ares Montes, "Poetas" 16)—and continues throughout Cordeiro's play (fol. 4, 14). While Ares Montes's contention that authors glorified Lisbon with hopes of persuading the king to make it the capital of the Dual Monarchy seems reasonable, it would be inaccurate to reduce the outpouring of praise to this single motive. Much of the Portuguese elite that supported the annexation in the first place felt that the Hapsburg capital would eventually move from Madrid to Lisbon. This kind of zeal, however, faded over the decades, leaving the capital "sozinha e quase viúva" (Bouza, *Portugal* 22; "alone and almost widowed").[17] By 1619, Portugal was beginning to pull away from the empire. It seems more likely—not to mention more in line with the actual *comedia*—to read the title of Cordeiro's work satirically, since it has little to do with Felipe III. Rather than give voice to the minority elite, it seems much more probable that Cordeiro's praise of Lisbon follows after Camões's tastes. In *Os Lusíadas*, for example, Camões offers this description of Lisbon: "E tu, nobre Lisboa, que no mundo / facilmente das outras és princesa" (3.57.1–2; "And thou, noble Lisbon, in the world / easily princess of all others"). This apostrophe complements another well-known selection from the sixth canto in which Camões describes Bacchus's anger over the divine favoring of the Portuguese and their esteemed capital: "Via estar todo o Céu determinado / De fazer de Lisboa nova Roma; / Não no pode estorvar, que destinado / Está doutro Poder que tudo doma" (6.7.1–4; "All of Heaven determined / to make of Lisbon a new Rome; / Which cannot be hindered, destined / as it is by the Almighty"). The providentialism of this passage and the overall praise of Lisbon in this and other works of the sixteenth and seventeenth centuries extends the meaning of Cordeiro's characterization of Lisbon well beyond the self-fashioning that Ares Montes suggests.

The staging of the Portuguese nation in Cordeiro's play, however, includes more than singing the glories of the capital city. The work attempts to define the Portuguese identity by stressing a number of essential characteristics. This includes "la lealtad Lusitana" (fol. 3, 6), "el amor Portugues" (fol. 3, 6), the David versus Goliath self-conception (fol. 4), "gran valor" (fol. 6), and their unyielding obedience (fol. 14), just to name a few. Cordeiro also consistently suggests that Portugal is the envy of the world (fol. 3, 10) and "sin igual" (fol. 10, 11). In fact, in comparison to other great civilizations, he states that "la Lusitana grandeza, / ... ha dexado atras a quantos / se hizieron en Roma ò Grecia" (fol. 14). Perhaps the most significant comparison comes, however, toward the end of the play when one of his characters, upon discovering improprieties between a Castilian and his sister, contrasts moral conduct in Portugal with that of Castile: "En Portugal / no tratan essa baxeza / que alla llaneza llamais" (fol. 38). Here Cordeiro recalls the competitive spirit of early modern Iberian literature at the same time that he intensifies the rivalry by bringing up national loyalties.

As if these references were not enough to reveal the Portuguese character of his *comedia*, Cordeiro stages a competition among three of the male characters of the play in which each tries to outperform the others in his poetic rendering of Portuguese history, drawing inspiration from a number of arches inscribed with Portugal's past deeds. What is particularly surprising about this contest is that it comprises more than eight hundred lines, which ends up covering most of the second act. This excess—another trademark of the time—does not enhance the work artistically, but accomplishes a great deal ideologically. While his work only flirts with the aesthetic potential of the *comedia nueva*, it is fully

engaged with the nationalist agenda put forward in the prologue. As the reader might expect, Cordeiro concludes the work
by echoing the "thesis statement" of the prologue in the final
verses: "Y aqui senado se acaban / los triumphos de Portugal, / y el
dichoso en las desdichas / nuestras faltas perdonad" (fol. 39). The
Portuguese playwright once again reiterates that this work is not
about Felipe III nor the Spanish empire, but an opportunity to
stage the glories of Portugal.

La entrada del Rey serves as the perfect gateway into Cordeiro's
literary corpus. The prologues of *Seis Comedias famosas* (1630)
and *Segunda parte de las Comedias* (1634), for example, announce
a similar teleology to that put forward in his first *comedia*, and are
also written in Portuguese. Whether by direct praise or by the fame
generated from the artistic merit of his plays, Cordeiro's purpose
remains centered on the eternal glory of Portugal. The fact that his
basic purpose for writing remains unaltered throughout his career
reveals a certain degree of substance to the prologue from his first
play, which Ares Montes superficially groups with other opportu-
nistic texts from the time. By this I do not mean to suggest that
the fifteen-year-old had everything mapped out at such a young
age. Clearly there was more to his work than what the dramatist
states from the outset. Within a decade, however, Cordeiro was
back saying essentially the same thing. In the prologue to the
Segunda parte, he justifies his nationalist focus by stating that
Portuguese deeds "excedem o credito humano ... excedem a todas
as monarquias do mundo" ("exceed human belief ... they exceed
all worldly dominions"). This passage, as many others like it
from the sixteenth and seventeenth centuries, underlines the preeminence of Portugal. Camões and his many seventeenth-century
disciples, including Cordeiro, offer a clear and consistent answer
to the question posed in *Os Lusíadas* concerning the worth of
Portugal in relation to the rest of the world: "E julgareis qual he
mais excelente, / Se ser do mundo Rey, se de tal gente?" (1.10.7–
8; "And you will judge which is better, / being King of the world,
or of such people?"). Still another example of Lusocentrism
within Cordeiro's writings from the same time period is his *Elogio
a Poetas Lusitanos* (1631), a poem he published a year after Lope's
Laurel de Apolo in order to correct Lope's omission of so many
(nearly fifty!) gifted Portuguese authors from his work (including
Violante do Céu).[18]

Cordeiro's *Los doze de Inglaterra* stresses national identity in ways similar to *La entrada del Rey*, but also includes a number of creative innovations. This *comedia* relates a well-known story of Portuguese folklore also celebrated in *Os Lusíadas*, the truth of which is inconsequential to the desire to create history that coincides with his idea of *portugalidade*. Benedict Anderson describes this creative historiography as a magic-act in which chance becomes destiny (12). As he explains, this occurs because "nationalism thinks in terms of historical destinies" (149). In the first scene of Act 1, Cordeiro sets up the frame of the traditional story: twelve Portuguese knights are obliged by their honor to travel to England to challenge the twelve infamous English knights whose disrespect for women demands a noble response, which England is apparently unable to provide. While eleven travel by sea, one of the twelve goes by land, rescuing the Almirante de Francia on his way.

In a passage similar to the hyperbolic description of Lisbon from *La entrada del Rey en Portugal*, Cordeiro describes the worth of these twelve Portuguese knights: "cavalleros tan supremos, / tan valientes, y arrogantes, / tan esforçados, tan buenos" (fol. 61). Cordeiro doubles the rhetorical value of this statement by later heaping his praise on Don Alvaro Vaz de Almada, the one knight who travels by land. That is to say, in the same way that Don Alvaro represents in part what the twelve are as a whole, so do the twelve reflect in part what the Portuguese embody as a people. Toward the end of his opening monologue, he explains that "sólo un Portugués" is enough to accomplish almost anything (fol. 61). Later he surpasses this original position with an even more audacious suggestion: "Que es conmigo loco Ingles, / por los Evangelios Santos, / que basta para otros tantos / la mitad de un Portugués" (fol. 63). Here Cordeiro exaggerates the strength of the constantly outnumbered Portuguese, claiming that half of one Portuguese knight is enough to take on several others. The constant references to just one or half of a Portuguese knight are important in that they synecdochically reflect all of Portugal, a strategy that remains in force through the end of the *comedia*. By the end of Act 1, "Los Leones Portugueses" have defeated the English, restored honor to the women, and begun their return home (fol. 64).

At the beginning of the second act, Costa, the well-named *gracioso* of the play, appears with his master Don Alvaro and one of the other twelve Portuguese knights who has joined them for the journey to Portugal. This includes a promised visit to the Almirante, whom he had previously rescued from a near-death situation. Following Don Alvaro's statement that little can be known by one who does not read, Costa nostalgically remembers a *donato* who once invited him to his bookstore, which, fortunately for the illiterate lackey, ended up being a *bodega*. To end his comic story, Costa makes use of Portuguese: "E falando em conclusão / em nossa lingoa verdades, / inda tenho saudades / do vinho, do frade não" (fol. 65; "To tell you the truth, / and using our language, / I still long for the wine, / but not for the friar"). This brilliant moment of metatheater highlights Cordeiro's symbolic invoking of the collective self—"nossa lingoa" ("our language")— not to mention a reference to the nationally meaningful and uniquely Portuguese word *saudade* (see chapter one). In the first instance, Cordeiro paints the "world of plurals" that reinforces the national imaginary (Anderson 32). References to *us, our,* and *we* are an important step in the simultaneous conception of the national self. *Saudade* is particularly relevant in this call to the collective because it is not merely a word in Portuguese like the rest of the passage—although this shift from Spanish to Portuguese is significant—but an untranslatable Portuguese word. *Saudade* was no stranger to annexation literature, appearing in the works of virtually every Portuguese author of the time, including each of the major writers included in this study.

The rest of *Los doze de Inglaterra* reads like many other *comedias de enredos*. There are letters, balconies, tokens, love interests, jealousy, cases of honor, a near duel, and most of the other ingredients Lope outlines in the *Arte nuevo*. Cordeiro, however, continues to mix occasional references to his native Portugal with the rest of the work, always finding some way to exalt his homeland. In comparison to *La entrada del Rey*, this *comedia* is a much better reflection of Cordeiro's artistic talent. The storyline, characterization, *enredos*, and resolution are carefully crafted in a way that complements the nationalist undertones of the work. Thus, while *La entrada del Rey en Portugal* is more of an attempt at the *comedia* by a young Portuguese nationalist trying to find his way, *Los doze de Inglaterra* represents the work of a seasoned dramatist who has successfully married his art with his ideology. Cordeiro's ability to raise the quality of his dramaturgy without compromising his nationalist message brought him success throughout the Peninsula and the favor of his compatriots following the Restoration of 1640. In fact, the Chamber of Commerce of Coimbra actually commissioned the performance of one of Jacinto Cordeiro's plays in celebration of this historical moment (Ares Montes, "Portugal" 13). It seems clear, then, that the nationalism apparent in Cordeiro's *comedias* now, was similarly received by audiences then. Why else would his works have been staged in celebration of the return of Portuguese sovereignty, unless the Portuguese likewise saw in the dramatist the very nationalist imprint I have been describing? Indeed, Cordeiro's dramatizations of the Portuguese nation may have been more effective at promoting *portugalidade* than any other seventeenth-century Portuguese author. *La entrada del Rey* and *Los doze de Inglaterra* are not the only *comedias* that demonstrate Cordeiro's "overt Portuguese pride" either (Cruz-Ortiz 21). Between his two works on Duarte Pacheco and the many appearances of Inés de Castro in other plays, it is clear that Portugal's past was alive and well in Cordeiro's present (21).

Given the widespread acclaim his works received, how is it that Cordeiro remains in obscurity? As is the case with Portuguese annexation literature in general, Cordeiro does not deserve the critical cold shoulder he has faced during the past centuries. In Jaime Cruz-Ortiz's assessment, Cordeiro's "corpus measures up well to that of the seventeenth century's secondary playwrights" (16). He was not prolific compared to the Spanish giants of the time (e.g., Lope, Tirso, Calderón, etc.), but his contribution to the Portuguese *comedia* was significant. Vázquez Cuesta captures the problem perfectly: "sólo por el hecho de ser portugués de nacimiento y de corazón se explica la poca atención que Jacinto Cordeiro—autor que por su opción lingüística no puede ser incluido en las historias de la literatura portuguesa" ("Lengua" 637). I agree with her assessment of Cordeiro's Portuguese nature, but I do not believe that we have to continue recycling the false idea that national canons have to maintain linguistic purity, especially when doing so is anachronistic. If language is not the holy grail of national identity, as modern nation theories tend to agree, why do some scholars continue to defend their respective canons on the basis of linguistic purism? Similar to most of his Portuguese contemporaries who also dressed their works in the Spanish language, "Cordeiro has been considered not Spanish enough for one and not Portuguese enough for the other" (Cruz-Ortiz 15). Being Portuguese, however, does not justify the relegation of annexation literature to the periphery of Spanish letters, just as the choice to write in Spanish should not keep the Portuguese from reading and appreciating these authors and their important role in early modern Iberian culture.

As much as Cordeiro stands out as a prominent fixture of seventeenth-century Iberian theater, he was not the only Portuguese dramatist having success throughout the Peninsula. Others such as Violante do Céu, Manuel Galhegos, and Pedro Salgado also come to mind. The most widely published Portuguese playwright of the era, however, was Juan Matos Fragoso (1610–89), who published dozens of works individually and in collaboration with many of the most prominent Spanish dramatists of the period, including Juan Pérez de Montalván, Agustín Moreto, and Luis Vélez de Guevara. If seventeenth-century Portuguese drama were a coin, Matos Fragoso would represent one side and Cordeiro the other, with the former taking advantage of his Spanish proficiency for self-promotion and personal achievement, and the latter using it primarily to exalt Portugal. That is not to say that it can only be one way or the other, only that the two authors generally fall into those two categories.

Although not as recognized as the other Portuguese authors of this study, Ângela de Azevedo demonstrates a commitment to Portugal in her plays not unlike Cordeiro's unyielding love for his homeland. Her background is largely unknown, with only three surviving *comedias* comprising her literary corpus: *El muerto disimulado, La margarita del Tajo que dió nombre á Santarén,* and *Dicha y desdicha del juego y devoción de la Virgen.* The biographical information available celebrates Azevedo for her discretion and talent, recognizing her relationship with Isabel de Borbón, to whom she was a lady-in-waiting (García Peres 7). The general absence of information on the playwright limits our understanding of Azevedo, at least in comparison to her more well-known Spanish and Portuguese contemporaries. Her writings, nonetheless, paint a clearer picture of the dramatist than critics have previously acknowledged.

Since Teresa Scott Soufas's publication of Azevedo's *comedias* in *Women's Acts: Plays by Women Dramatists of Spain's Golden Age* (1997), most critical studies related to the author have concentrated on the construction and performance of gender within her plays. Christopher Gascón's observation that "Azevedo's female characters are anything but one-dimensional," however, could just as easily be used to describe the dramatist herself (125). Of the multiple layers that define Azevedo and her works, her native connection to Portugal is certainly one of the most prominent, although her nationality has received relatively little critical attention.[19] Soufas's text, in fact, blurs this very issue by lumping Azevedo together with her Spanish contemporaries under the banner of *Spain's* Golden Age (an issue to which I will return at the end of the chapter). While it is clear that Azevedo and many of her Portuguese contemporaries contributed to the Spanish Golden Age in meaningful ways, it is a mistake to ignore the fascinating markers of identity and origin that many Portuguese-authored works— especially *comedias*—contain. Not nearly as overt as Cordeiro, Azevedo writes her *portugalidade* in between the lines of her plays.

That Azevedo, Cordeiro, and their Portuguese contemporaries wrote *comedias* in Spanish does not diminish the importance of their native claim to Lusitânia. If anything, writing in the language of the dominant culture highlights the complexities of early modern identity by problematizing emerging categories of nationhood. Azevedo, as many other Portuguese annexation authors, affirms her *portugalidade* at the very moment she evidences her Spanishness. Rather than see this as grounds to ignore her works (as many have reasoned when it comes to Portuguese annexation literature), or even as a problem to be solved, I embrace the complexities surrounding the dramatist and her works, arguing that while the author clearly transmits her love for and loyalty to Portugal—staging the nation much like her Portuguese predecessors—she is more than a Portuguese playwright. Similar to the cross-dressing of Lisarda and Clarindo in *El muerto disimulado*, and the self-determination of Irene in *La margarita del Tajo*, Azevedo's crossings between Spain and Portugal, Spanish and Portuguese, underscore the heterogeneity of Iberian culture at this time, highlighting the dramatist's multiculturalism.

From geography to language to religion, Azevedo's *comedias* have a strong Portuguese presence, giving the author a stage upon which to celebrate Lusitânia. Each of Azevedo's plays, for example, takes place in a specific part of Portugal, namely Porto (*Dicha y desdicha*), Lisbon (*El muerto disimulado*), and Santarém (*La margarita del Tajo*). This is particularly significant considering the common *comedia* practice of situating all or part of a work in a foreign land. This often occurs in historical *comedias* such as Lope's *El nuevo mundo descubierto por Cristóbal Colón* and *El Brasil restituido*, Zárate's *La conquista de México*, Tirso's *Las quinas de Portugal*, and Vélez de Guevara's *Reinar después de morir*. This practice was not limited to historical works, however. Lope situates *El castigo sin venganza* in Italy, Tirso sets a number of his works in Portugal (e.g., *Averígüelo Vargas* and *El vergonzoso en palacio*), and, in perhaps the most well-known case, Calderón places *La vida es sueño* in Poland. Azevedo builds on this same convention (sending her characters abroad), but instead of situating her piece in some unknown foreign destination, she elects the heart and soul of her native soil. After all, Porto and Lisbon represent the centers, past and present, of Portugal and its cultural development. If the author was not in a position to return to Portugal, she might as well send her characters there. The choice of Porto is especially significant since Portugal derives its own name from this ancient city (Mattoso 59). As Bárbara Mujica observes, "El hecho de que situara sus tres obras existentes en Portugal a pesar de vivir muchos años en la corte española es un testimonio del cariño que siempre sintió por su país natal" (232). Azevedo's zeal for her homeland, however, only begins with the cities in which they take place. In her *comedias* she also evokes Portugal's maritime tradition, shipwreck motif, religious folklore, language, and many other characteristics of her native land. All of these elements combine to advance one cohesive message: *"eu sou portuguesa"* ("I am Portuguese").

Azevedo's *comedias* are clearly encoded with her affinity for Portugal. One of the best examples of this occurs in *El muerto disimulado*. In the opening scene, Jacinta tells her servant, Dorotea, of the extreme sorrow she feels as a result of the passing of her lover, Clarindo. Shortly thereafter, Lisarda, Clarindo's sister, appears in Lisbon dressed as a man and ready to avenge her brother's death. Lisarda's slapstick sidekick, Papagayo, immediately speaks of his affection for Lisbon upon entering the city:

> PAPAGAYO. Ya en Lisboa estás y este
> el tercero es de Palacio,
> tropiezo hermoso de Thetis,
> rica adoración del Tajo.

LISARDA. ¡Gallarda plaza por cierto!
PAPAGAYO. Todo en Lisboa es gallardo,
pues no ha visto cosa boa,
según lo afirma el adagio,
el que no ha visto Lisboa. (1.545–54)

Azevedo introduces these two characters to the play with these lines of praise for Lisbon. While positive references to Lisbon were also prevalent among Spanish authors (e.g., Torres Naharro's *Tinelaria*), it signifies differently when coming from a Portuguese author. Anyone could potentially make use of this same aphorism, but not every dramatist has seen or esteems Lisbon to the same degree that Azevedo apparently does. She highlights her native claim to Lisbon by alternating between Spanish and Portuguese—*boa*, or good, being the Portuguese equivalent of the Spanish *buena*—a linguistic move that has a doubling effect on Lisbon's (Lis*boa*'s) goodness. Given that the Portuguese prided themselves so much on their capital city, this patriotic gesture should come as no surprise to readers. Azevedo's other plays also contain references to the geography of her homeland, including a number of cities, rivers, and other significant places.

Dicha y desdicha takes place in Porto (1.1026, 1160), the location of Portugal's most important waterway (the Douro). The play, in fact, develops around a number of themes related to the ocean. Toward the end of the first act, Tijera and Don Fadrique appear for the first time, having returned to Portugal after ten years of commercial success in India. Their joyous return, however, went awry, as a storm nearly cost them their lives. Between India, where they were, and Porto, where they are now, Azevedo succeeds in situating her work within Portuguese spaces. What is more, she links one of the most important issues of the play—economic status—to the sea. *Os Lusíadas* establishes the maritime spirit of the Portuguese and their deep connection to the ocean, to say nothing of the seemingly endless literary references to the Portuguese and their connection to the sea.[20] In contrast to analogous situations in other Spanish *comedias*, the two characters are returning from colonies in India, originally founded by the Portuguese, not the Spanish colonies in the West Indies. The shipwreck theme flourished in Portuguese literature during the early modern period, inspiring a subgenre that would find its greatest expression in *A história trágico-marítima* published in 1735–36

(Williams 48). Azevedo attributes the possession of wealth among the two *galanes*, Don Fadrique and Felisardo, to their respective maritime ventures. Like so many of his countrymen, both real and fictitious, Don Fadrique has made his fortunes at sea, although Azevedo omits the details of his adventures abroad. His trip to the East Indies, together with Don Felisardo's failure to reach the Portuguese colony, set up one of the primary conflicts of the play.

The initial exchange between Tijera and Fadrique sets the fearful *gracioso* in opposition to the fearless *galán*. In Tijera's opinion, man belongs on land, not at sea, to which Fadrique retorts that both land and sea present a variety of dangers. Tijera, however, is not convinced:

> Pues si en la tierra hay desgracias,
> ¿qué será en la mar, señor,
> donde hay corsarios, piratas,
> sustos, naufragios, zozobras;
> y si acaso de bonanza
> un día un cristiano tiene,
> al punto se le preparan
> a millares las tormentas,
> a montones las borrascas,
> y a veces un huracán
> cuando menos de la casta
> del que nos iba poniendo
> en la postrera jornada;
> en términos de no vernos
> ésta de la Lusitania
> bella ciudad, dulce fin,
> que es del Duero y nuestra patria? (1.941–57)

In this passage, Tijera doubts that the advantages of being at sea outweigh the threats, especially when the land left behind is Lusitânia (fittingly rhymed with *patria*). By referring to Portugal in this way, Azevedo is able to evoke her native land's antiquity. There is much more at play in these lines, however, than the mere response of a *gracioso* to his master. Fadrique, in fact, epitomizes the maritime spirit of the Portuguese—the same courage that led them to initially take on the dangers that Tijera describes—and tame the waves of the sea for their benefit and glory. While, for Tijera, Portugal ends where the ocean begins, for Fadrique the land and the sea are one ("ya sea por mar o por tierra" [1.940]). In the end, Fadrique credits the Virgin Mary with their successes (1.992). Tijera echoes his praise, explaining that she calmed the sea in their behalf. This entire conversation hearkens to a number of national discourses already established within Portuguese literature. Later in the play, in fact Azevedo attributes Portuguese successes on the sea to Mary, stating "es María del mar luciente estrella" (2.1514). That is, the Virgin is the guiding light of the Portuguese. This verse echoes Azevedo's many literary compatriots who likewise viewed Portuguese triumphs abroad in terms of providentialism. Between the divine favor they receive, the importance of the sea, and the invocation of Lusitânia, Azevedo saturates this scene with *portugalidade*.

While *Dicha y desdicha* borrows primarily from historical and literary themes in its depiction of Portugal, *La margarita del Tajo* takes a slightly different approach. As Soufas explains, this work captures Azevedo's connection to Portugal's rich folkloric tradition through the dramatization of Saint Irene, a well-known figure within Portuguese hagiography and balladry (2). In *Europa portuguesa* (1679), for example, Manuel de Faria e Sousa dedicates several pages to the telling of Irene's legendary story (1.3.19.351–54). Because Faria e Sousa's work was likely published after Azevedo's death, his text could not have served as a direct source for Azevedo's play. The *comedia*, nonetheless, echoes Faria e Sousa's description quite thoroughly, incorporating nearly every geographical reference mentioned in the legend: Nabantia (Tomar) where Saint Irene was born, the Nabão River in which her body was discarded, the Tagus River in which her body was discovered, and the city Scalabis (now Santarém), where the Nabão and the Tagus meet.[21] Reference to the Tagus, especially in the title of the play, stands out because both Spain and Portugal share and esteem the river. Making a Portuguese saint the *margarita*, or pearl, of the Tagus consecrates the river for Portugal, not Spain, even though the river begins and finds its greatest extension in Spain. Faria e Sousa hints at these very ideas in his discussion of Irene: "Assi tiene esta Santa en Portugal el mas ilustre, el más pomposo Entierro del Mundo: pues uno de los mayores Rios es su Tumulo: una de las mayores Villas su Epitafio. Una de las más principales aguas la esconde; una de la más ilustres Poblaciones la publica" (1.3.19.354). Whether claiming the river for Saint Irene, extending Portugal's dominion to the sea, or exalting Lisbon, Azevedo finds many different ways to publish ("publica") the supremacy of Portugal.

Whereas most annexation authors typically express the nationalist aim of their works—in the case that there is one—at the beginning of the text, Azevedo, whose *comedias* do not include the standard introductory sections, closes *La margarita del Tajo* by laying out, in no uncertain terms, the purpose of her writing. As previously mentioned, *La margarita del Tajo* dramatizes the legendary story of Saint Irene and her martyrdom. Rather than ending the play with the conventional request that her "audience" forgive the flaws in her work, Azevedo states that it does not matter what they think, because it was not written for them:

> Así el poeta la acaba,
> y advierte que para ella,
> ni pide perdón ni víctor,
> sea mala o sea buena;
> pues no la escribió, Senado,
> en gracia o lisonja vuestra,
> sino por la devoción
> de la santa portuguesa. (3.4185–92)

The explicit claim in these verses is devotion to the *Portuguese* saint. Both the hagiographic figure and her Portuguese identity are meaningful, although my present interest rests upon the latter. The way she ends her play is revealing as to the character of this and other works by the playwright. All of the religious, linguistic, and geographic connections to her country make Azevedo's play a celebration of Portugal. What is more, her disregard for her audience is in open defiance of Lope and his insistence in the *Arte nuevo* that the bottom line of dramaturgy is to please the audience. Some might argue that Azevedo exhibits little concern for her audience because she had none, but that does not take away from the national consciousness of these final verses, nor the defiant spirit they exhibit. The author draws a line between the Spanish audience and the Portuguese saint, making it clear where she sides on the matter. While she does not express the teleology of her other *comedias* as explicitly, there are clear indications in each of her works that one of the playwright's principal objectives is to celebrate Portugal—the land that she left, but which apparently never left her.

One of the most fascinating elements of *portugalidade* that Azevedo incorporates into her plays is the occasional use of the Portuguese language. Compared to some of Tirso's *comedias* (e.g., *El amor médico*), Azevedo's use of Portuguese in her plays is quite minimal. Decoding Azevedo's alternation between Spanish and Portuguese, however, reveals a conscious attempt to elevate her native tongue and, by extension, her native land. The playwright wastes no time introducing Portuguese in *La margarita del Tajo*. Etcétera, Britaldo's cleverly named *gracioso*, switches to Portuguese to emphasize that he has heard enough of his master's "letanías, / digresiones y progresos, / hipérboles, elogios / y otros encareci-mientos" (1.429–32). With rhetorical flourish, he asks, "¿Posible es que para un hombre / decir que se siente preso / de amor, sean menester / circunstancias ni rodeos / si no decir claramente / con un portugués despejo / 'Querolhe bem, acabouse?'(I really love her, that is all)" (1.445–51). The way the Portuguese enters the dialogue—with that native air ("portugués despejo")—may indicate that the character did not feel that Spanish could express what this character needed. These lines may also reflect what communication was like for the Portuguese who lived in a predominantly Spanish-speaking world (something to the effect of "where I come from we say"). For the *gracioso*, Portuguese possesses a clarity ("claramente") and simplicity that, for whatever reason, surpasses what he might have said in Spanish. Azevedo makes no effort to explain how it is that Etcétera knows Portuguese, making it that much easier to associate the lines with the author herself.

Not unlike Faria e Sousa, Azevedo introduces untranslatable Portuguese words and expressions into her works. The finest example of this appears in Act 1 of *El muerto disimulado*, where Azevedo introduces *saudade* to her Spanish-speaking audience.[22] Although Spanish language dictionaries have, for centuries, recognized the importance of this word in Portuguese and the absence of an equivalent in Spanish, the word has never been adopted, even if a number of Spanish American authors have incorporated it in their works.[23] Numerous writers have offered their definition of *saudade* over the centuries (see Botelho and Braz Teixeira), including a number of Portuguese authors preceding Azevedo (see chapter one). Perhaps the most relevant definition comes from Azevedo's contemporary Francisco Manuel de Melo. In *Epanáforas Amorosas*, Manuel de Melo describes the unparalleled nature of *saudade*:

> [L]hes toca mais aos Portugueses, que a outra nação do mundo,
> o darle conta desta generosa paixão, a quem sòmente nós
> sabemos o nome, chamando-lhe: *Saudade* ... Florece entre os
> Portugueses a saudade, por duas causas, mais certas em nós,
> que em outra gente do mundo ... Amor e ausência, saõ os
> pais da saudade; e como nosso natural, é entre as mais nações,
> conhecido por amoroso, e nossas dilatadas viagens ocasionam as
> maiores ausências; de aí vem, que donde se acha muito amor e
> ausência larga, as saudades sejam mais certas. (224–25)

> It is the duty of the Portuguese, more than any other nation in
> the world, to account for this generous passion, of which only
> we know the name, calling it: *Saudade* ... Saudade flourishes
> among the Portuguese, for two reasons, both of which find
> their truest expression in us ... Love and absence give life to
> saudade; and as one of our own, it is found among most nations
> and affectionately known, our extensive travels create the great-
> est absences; from there it originates, saudades never more
> certain than where you find abundant love and long absences.

In this passage, Manuel de Melo establishes a collective sense of
Portuguese identity through his repeated use of the subject pronoun "nós" ("us") and the possessive adjective "nosso" ("our").
He describes *saudade* as a sensation felt by many different nations
yet articulated exclusively by the Portuguese. The word is charged
with identity and history. Manuel de Melo goes on to link *saudade*
to love and absence, contending that the two conditions culminate among the Portuguese (which would explain why they have a
word to describe the feeling resulting from an intense combination
of the two). The idea that *saudade* communicates something that
most of humanity feels, but only the Portuguese can adequately
express, repeats itself throughout Portuguese literary history.
Consequently, the use of the word in literature should not be
overlooked nor underestimated. It is one of the easiest and most
effective ways to communicate *portugalidade*.

In *El muerto disimulado* Azevedo makes no attempt to replace
saudade with an inadequate Spanish equivalent, but instead
proudly inserts the word right in the middle of the text. Similar
to Lisarda and Papagayo in the earlier example, Azevedo does not
let the first scene go by without characterizing Jacinta in some
uniquely Portuguese way. Speaking of the deep sense of loss she

feels in the absence of her lover, Jacinta makes repeated mention of *saudade*, multiplying its presence through the use of polyptoton:[24]

> Con esto nos despedimos
> si él saudoso, yo más saudosa;
> que es cierto, que a quien se queda,
> más las saudades ahogan. (1.353–56)

The appearance of this term is highlighted by Azevedo's own self-referential explanation of its unintelligibility for her Spanish-speaking audiences:

> No repares en la frase,
> que de ausencia este síntoma
> solamente se declara,
> cuando en Portugués se nombra. (1.357–60)

Echoing the previous passage from Manuel de Melo, Azevedo defines *saudade* as a symptom of absence. As Mercedes Maroto Camino explains, "Azevedo, recalling her own geographical and linguistic displacement, emphasizes that only the word *saudade* can describe accurately the feelings of the protagonist" (316). However, Jacinta should not need to explain the meaning of *saudade* to Dorotea, a fellow native of Portugal. Therefore, one can only assume that she is speaking to her Spanish audience. This metatheatrical scene underscores Azevedo's consciousness of the untranslatability of *saudade* and her own identification with Portugal. The reader cannot help but step back and read *saudade* beyond its immediate function in the work. *Saudade*, in other words, is not merely the symptom of two separated lovers (Jacinta and Clarindo), but also the byproduct of a people (the Portuguese) and the devotion they feel for their homeland (Portugal). Azevedo and her compatriots are distanced from the self-actualized Portugal of yesteryear, leaving them in a condition that can only ("solamente") find proper expression in Portuguese.

Despite the examples previously cited, reading Azevedo's *portugalidade* is not without its challenges. Azevedo's audience, for example, was much different than, say, Cordeiro's. It is unclear what her motivations were for writing in the first place. In *La margarita del Tajo*, Azevedo explains that she writes in praise of the Portuguese saint, but it is not clear whether she was purely self-driven in her writing or whether she was commissioned by another (presumably Isabel) to do so. If she was commissioned, did Azevedo choose the content of her works, or was she specifically asked to write about her homeland? That is to say, the greater market forces that impacted Faria e Sousa, Cordeiro, and others, probably did not have a direct influence on Azevedo. The dramatist, nonetheless, may have been well aware of the strong current of Portuguese-themed *comedias* being written during the first decades of the seventeenth century. Not having to meet the expectations of a large and diverse audience, it could be said that Azevedo's *comedias* are more organic than those of her contemporaries. Whatever else critics are able to uncover will surely complement the Portuguese reading of Azevedo's plays that I have, in part, conducted in this chapter and elsewhere.[25] As so many other Portuguese expatriates writing during the annexation, Azevedo did not leave Portugal behind, but, instead, praised her homeland by staging the nation.

While there is certainly nothing wrong with the Spanish rendering, Ángela de Acevedo, the dramatist and her works remain incomplete until we acknowledge the Portuguese-born Ângela de Azevedo. Orthographically and critically it may appear to be but a small detail, yet it shifts the way we read the dramatist and her *comedias*. One of the most fundamental aspects of her three plays is Portugal, which the dramatist consistently emphasizes in her works, even though none of them are as overtly Portuguese as Cordeiro's *comedias* or perhaps even Lope's *El más galán portugués* or Tirso's *Las quinas*. Azevedo's stagings of the Portuguese nation are more subtle, and, perhaps, more natural. That is, the dramatist did not have to turn to historiographical works or other source material because Portugal was a native part of her persona (her life was her source material). The framing of her *comedias* relies heavily on Portuguese culture. Her plays show a preference for Portuguese themes and an insistence on remembering and honoring the identity of her homeland. Her approach to staging the nation hearkens back to many of her Portuguese predecessors and links the dramatist with the current of Portuguese annexation writers who also made Portugal the focus of their writings in Spanish. Fortunately for Azevedo and the field of Golden Age Theater, her works were rediscovered in the 1990s and integrated thereafter into the *comedia* tradition. In this process of incorporation and celebration of another female dramatist, however, it would be a mistake to overlook Azevedo's native claim to Portugal; a reality that enlightens our understanding of the dramatist, her works, and the time in which she was writing.

Seventeenth-century Portuguese literature is clearly not the "wasteland" that some have made it out to be (Haberly 50). The decadence of this time is in the eye of the beholder, who, in the past, has often failed to give them more than a superficial consideration. That they remain, for the most part, on the periphery of the Spanish and Portuguese literary canons does not reflect poorly on them, but on us, the gatekeepers. That Ângela de Azevedo's *comedias* have been recovered is a great start, and hopefully a prologue of things to come in the field. Jacinto Cordeiro, for one, merits much more critical attention. Jaime Cruz-Ortiz's critical edition of *El juramento ante Dios, y lealtad contra el amor* (2014) is a step in the right direction. That Cordeiro was considered one of the best of his time should be enough to lead critics to at least look at his works now (Vázquez Cuesta, "Lengua" 637). His Portuguese origin and nationalism do not justify his neglect by *comedia* scholars, nor should his widespread use of Spanish marginalize him in the Portuguese literary canon. Cordeiro and Azevedo both masterfully dramatize *portugalidade* in their *comedias*. They call attention to the significance of *saudade*, hearken to their national poet (Camões), and invoke Portuguese history and folklore. They also pay tribute to their homeland in less conspicuous ways: situating their works in Portugal, reinforcing Portuguese essentialism, and occasionally introducing words or verses in their native tongue. All of these gestures combine to form an intelligible rhetoric of nationhood. While they are not saying exactly the same things about Portugal, their voices harmonize in singing the glories of their homeland. That is the magic of Portuguese annexation literature: that so many writers at this time could produce a coherent national discourse.

Not all Portuguese theater of the seventeenth century is of high artistic and ideological value; just as obvious is the fact that there are treasures among Portuguese dramatists waiting to be discovered. Not only will they enhance our overall understanding of and admiration for early modern theater in general, as well as the development of nationally conscious theater in particular, but will also correct a mistake that Hispanists and Lusists have perpetuated for centuries. At issue, then, is not whether we can speak of Portuguese theater during the seventeenth century or not; clearly we can. By improving their visibility we can come to appreciate their overall contribution to the comedia tradition and their unique efforts to stage the Portuguese nation during the Dual Monarchy. In the very least, studying these works can expand our understanding of Portuguese-themed *comedias* by the Spanish. During the sixteenth and seventeenth centuries, Spanish and Portuguese dramatists assured that Portugal would occupy a permanent place on the Iberian stage. Gil Vicente made an art form out of staging the nation, providing his fellow Peninsularists with a pattern for dramatizing nationally relevant themes. The performance of Portuguese identity on the early modern stage helped preserve and promote Portugal before, during, and after the period of annexation. While it remains to be seen whether Cordeiro and his Portuguese contemporaries successfully immortalized the greatness of Portugal or not, four centuries later we are still finding reasons to read their works and understand what they uniquely contribute to our understanding of language, literature, identity, and politics, both then and now.

Chapter Five

Anticipating and Remembering the Restoration
Sousa de Macedo, Violante do Céu, and Manuel de Melo

Six decades was more than enough time for the Portuguese aristocracy to discover that they wanted out of the Dual Monarchy their predecessors had helped to orchestrate in 1580. With the Spanish Empire overwhelmed in 1640 by a variety of conflicts inside and outside of Iberia, the Portuguese successfully applied an exit strategy in December of that same year that would see João II, Duque de Bragança, become João IV de Portugal, *o Restaurador* (John IV of Portugal, the Restorer). The name by which this event would be christened by the Portuguese forevermore was the *Restauração da Independência*. It would take twenty-eight years, however, for Spain to officially recognize Portuguese sovereignty again. Notwithstanding these major political changes and the conflicts that they occasioned, Spanish remained the primary language of expression for Portuguese authors. The most oft-cited example of this phenomenon is João IV's own *Defensa de la musica moderna* (1650), which should give pause to anyone who would think to incriminate Portuguese authors for continuing to write and publish in Spanish following the Restoration. Spanish did not become the literary language of prestige among the Portuguese in 1580, hence it stands to reason that the Portuguese would continue to write in Spanish after the Iberian Union. It would be decades, in fact, before the early modern preference for Spanish finally came to an end.

Although the *Restauração* did not result in an immediate turn away from the Spanish language, the rhetoric of nationhood that had filled the pages of many Portuguese-authored texts from 1580 to 1640 intensified thereafter. Many of the authors that published important works leading up to the Restoration played a decisive role in the preservation of Portuguese sovereignty thereafter. The literature written during the post-Restoration period, echoes the nationalist sentiment originating with Portugal's sixteenth-century literary giants and proudly carried forward by Portuguese authors during the Dual Monarchy. Some continued writing as they had before, celebrating *portugalidade* in all its past, present, and future glory. Others penned works specifically commemorating the Restoration. Still others, as Vázquez Cuesta points out, employed their literary skills in defense of Portuguese independence, which was by no means secure: "Una abundante literatura político-jurídica se encarga de difundir dentro y fuera del país las razones que justificaban la existencia del Portugal Restaurado a fin de conseguir su transformación de régimen de hecho en régimen de derecho y propiciar su reconocimiento por otros países" ("Lengua" 670). Regardless of genre, the majority of Portuguese-authored texts were still written in Spanish and not Portuguese. However, from one work to the next—and sometimes within the same text—authors moved between Spanish and Portuguese with greater frequency, increasingly more willing to hang up their Spanish costumes.

Just as sixteenth-century authors such as Gil Vicente, Luís de Camões, and António Ferreira constitute one bookend of this study (see chapter two), the post-Restoration literary movement championed by António de Sousa de Macedo, Violante do Céu (1607–93), Francisco Manuel de Melo, and others, represents the other. Sousa de Macedo, one of the most active defenders of Portuguese independence following the Restoration, carries the distinction of being Portugal's first journalist and one of its most important ambassadors from 1640 to 1668. The poet-dramatist Violante do Céu stands out as one of Portugal's greatest literary talents of the time, as well as the nation's first prolific female writer. Traditionally, Manuel de Melo is the most celebrated Portuguese writer of the baroque, excelling in poetry, drama, literary criticism, philosophy, and history, not to mention the author of a large number of letters. Whether in Portuguese or Spanish, many of the works penned by Sousa de Macedo, Violante do Céu, and Manuel de Melo sustain the rhetoric of nationhood crafted so masterfully by their compatriots both past and present. In many of the works published by these authors and their Portuguese contemporaries following the Restoration, however, something else takes place. Whereas so many Lusocentric works written during the sixteenth and early seventeenth centuries celebrate Portugal's rich past, in the 1640s the focus becomes the nation's renewed present. It is this particular shift that this chapter highlights.

Most of the authors who actively wrote during this new era had given signs of their patriotic potential leading up to 1640. António de Sousa de Macedo's *Flores de España, Excelencias de Portugal* (1631), for example, may very well be the culminating expression of Portuguese literature dedicated to the praise of Lusitânia during the Iberian Union, considering that it offers readers a comprehensive assessment of all things Portuguese. Within its pages he celebrates many of the same aspects of *portugalidade* that I have highlighted in previous chapters. What the twenty-five-year-old accomplished in this work is nothing short of a perfect arrangement of Portuguese excellences (which one might also describe as embellishments). The heavily-referenced work enlists all of the best Portuguese writers from the early modern period in a single cause: the glorification of the *patria*. Given the nature of Hernani Cidade's early twentieth-century study, it is not surprising that Sousa de Macedo's treatise receives significant attention in *A literatura autonomista sob os Filipes* (*Autonomous Literature under the Philips*). As the Portuguese critic points out, "Jamais se escreveu livro assim túmido de desmedido orgulho nacionalista, sobretudo em condições mais contra-indicadas" (130; "A book so enflamed with nationalist pride was never written, especially under such counter-indicative circumstances"). Vázquez Cuesta, in her synopsis of early modern Portuguese literature, offers a similar description: "bate el récord en atribuir a su patria méritos y prioridades, tanto materiales como espirituales, que la colocan no ya por encima de los demás reinos de la Península sino del mundo" ("Lengua" 646). She appears keenly aware of the work's acquaintance with hyperbole and acknowledges Sousa de Macedo's attempt to establish Portugal as the pinnacle of all that is good. Despite these statements and others, *Excelencias de Portugal*—the shortened version of the title preferred by its author—is often mentioned but scarcely analyzed with any degree of critical depth.

In the same way that the title is revealing of the content that follows, so do the prefatory sections foreshadow the pro-Portuguese agenda. The first prefatory section after the Licenças is a letter "Al Rey Nuestro Señor" in which the author justifies his outright exaltation of Portugal by proposing that any praise of

Portugal only serves to glorify Spain and her king, since Portugal is merely one of the empire's many adornments. In the context of the entire work, however, this rationale comes across as somewhat disingenuous. Even when he describes the king as the "mayor excelencia del Reyno," he clarifies that this is due to his Portuguese ancestry, reasoning that "es quasi impossible de claros progenitores dexar de nacer ilustres hijos." Beyond his specific words to the king, there is no textual evidence to support the idea that Sousa de Macedo is, in actuality, elevating Spain in his praise of Portugal. Essentially the author dangles the possibility of synecdoche before the king, only to discard the trope once the work commences.[1] The subsequent prefatory section—Sousa de Macedo's dedication to the Kingdom of Portugal—presents the author's true object of praise. The heading reads, "Al Reyno de Portugal... muy alto, y poderosissimo reyno, soberana Monarchia." It is easy to overlook Sousa de Macedo's mention of sovereignty here, as it comes on the heels of his praise of Portugal's exalted and powerful status, but this claim should not be missed. Introducing the question of autonomy so early in the text (as well as the context), I would argue, is indicative of the Restorationist disposition of many Portuguese authors at this time.

In his dedication to Portugal, Sousa de Macedo confesses his unworthiness to relate the accomplishments of his homeland, seeing that they are so exceptional. He explains that the great rulers of antiquity employed the finest literary talent of their day (e.g., Homer, Virgil) to dress their deeds with elegance and majesty. Sousa de Macedo, in contrast, reverses the relationship between the artist and his object of interest (in this case Portugal). Instead of giving the author the credit for his representation of the past, Sousa de Macedo argues that Portuguese history, by virtue of its grandeur, honors and ennobles the humblest of pens. The artist, therefore, does not make Portugal, but Portugal the artist. This conception of the artist/object relation coincides directly with Faria e Sousa's contention that the greatest of fictions cannot compare with Portuguese reality (see chapter three). Sousa de Macedo concludes his words to the Kingdom of Portugal by offering a brief explanation of his choice to write in Spanish rather than Portuguese: "Y perdonad si dexada la excelente lengua Portuguesa escrivo en la Castellana, porque como mi intento es pregonaros por el mundo todo, he usado desta por mas universal, y porque tambien los Portugueses saben estas excelencias, y assi para ellos no es menester escrivirlas" (*Flores de España, Excelencias de Portugal*). Here the author reiterates one of the guiding premises of my entire study: that Portuguese authors wanting to make the glorious past of Portugal known to a broader audience, chose Spanish as a means of expression. As is the case with many of his compatriots of the same era, he identified himself as Portuguese, seeing Spanish as a way to express his *portugalidade* more effectively.

Sousa de Macedo focuses his final prefatory section on the reader. Since the king is not likely to read his work and his countrymen supposedly know everything he has to say—reinforcing the idea of a shared vision of Portugal—the author takes aim at the many individuals throughout Europe who may not know much about his fatherland. As he explains to the reader, this treatise comes in response to his desire to "hazer algun servicio a mi patria." In his entry on *patria*, Covarrubias affirms the word's Latin base and defines it as the "tierra donde uno ha nacido" (857). What the lexicographer does not clarify, however, is the extension of the land in question. It could refer to the town or village one comes from, but may also designate a larger community. In Sousa de Macedo's case, it is evident that *patria* is not Spain, Iberia, or even Sousa de Macedo's birthplace, Porto, but Portugal. His work constitutes a conscious effort to recover Portugal from the threat of oblivion that it faced half a century after becoming part of the Spanish Empire: "No le bastan a un Reyno para ser famoso heroicas virtudes de sus naturales si le faltan escritos que las publiquen, porque la memoria de aquellas con el tiempo (como todo) se acaba, y estos hazen con que viva eternamente libre de las leyes del olvido" (*Flores de España*). In order to complete the arduous task of condensing Portuguese greatness into a relatively brief work, the author explains that his preparation included reading as many works about Portugal as possible, giving special attention to non-native voices so as to authenticate the perspectives of his countrymen, who might be suspected of partiality. His encyclopedic use of references to substantiate his claims seems to suggest that Sousa de Macedo is out to prove Portugal's superiority, not merely call attention to her merits. With that the author closes the preface to his work. Each of the dedications that follow have something to say about the social, political, and historical moment in which Sousa de Macedo penned his work. Altogether they acknowledge Portugal's provincial place in Iberia, her relative obscurity in the world, and her self-awareness as a unique community.

At the end of the prefatory sections is a table of contents that further prepares readers for the nationally-charged rhetoric that is to follow. Each of the twenty-four chapters of *Flores de España* highlights some unique aspect of Portuguese excellence, including the "buen clima del Reyno de Portugal" (chapter 1), "la fidelidad de los Portugueses" (chapter 13), and "lo mucho que Portugal ha sido siempre estimado de Dios" (chapter 24), to mention only a few. It is as if Sousa de Macedo had taken all of the aspects of *portugalidade* that other annexation authors mention in part, and wrote a chapter on each one. Sousa de Macedo maintains, for example, that Portugal is geographically superior to other nations of the world (a common declaration among annexation authors attempting to resituate the Portuguese nation in the physical world). Overall, his argument develops in the following way: Europe is the best of the four parts of the world, the Iberian Peninsula is the best part of Europe, and Portugal is "el primer lugar entre todas las tierras" (fol. 3–4). He extends his praise further by identifying God as the author of Portugal's superiority: "está Portugal puesto en tal sitio, y parte del mundo, que queda como cabeça de todo el, que parece, que previendo Dios en la creación del mundo las grandes excelencias que este Reyno avia de tener, le quiso hazer cabeça del mundo, y dar al mundo tal cabeça" (5). As Jean-Frédéric Schaub observes, "La presentación de Portugal como cabeza no es una metáfora inocente y no puede ser tenida por puramente geográfica" (29). Such providential claims are a common feature of nationalist rhetoric. As is so often the case among seventeenth-century Portuguese writers, Sousa de Macedo's inspiration for this claim comes from the following verses from *Os Lusíadas*: "Eis aqui, quase cume da cabeça / En Europa toda, o Reyno Lusitano" (3.20.1–2; "Behold here, almost the apex of the head / In all of Europe, the Lusitanian Kingdom"). Rather than a people, these passages from Sousa de Macedo and Camões emphasize the geographic superiority of the Portuguese nation.

One aspect of Portuguese geography one would expect Sousa de Macedo to address is the preeminence of Lisbon. Whereas many annexation authors remain fairly general in their glorification of Lisbon, likening the greatness of the city to the quality of its inhabitants, Sousa de Macedo lists many specific reasons for exalting the Portuguese capital above all other cities:

> Basta tener por cabeça la ciudad de Lisboa la mas grandiosa del mundo, y en que mas bienes de naturaleza, y fortuna concurren: por la sanidad, y templança de los ayres, por la fertilidad, y amenidad de los campos, en que todo el invierno ay flores, por la grandeza del pueblo, por la magestad de los edificios, por la hermosura, y comodidad del puerto capacissimo, y seguro, por el comercio, y trato de las mercaderias del Oriente, y Occidente, y de todas las partes del mundo, por la riqueza de los ciudadanos, por la frequencia de tantas naciones que a ella concurren, que parece un mundo abreviado. (fol. 25)

In all of his descriptions of the Portuguese nation and its capital, Sousa de Macedo exemplifies the kind of widespread simultaneity found in Portuguese annexation literature. The work also foregrounds his epic poem *Ulisippo* (1640), which breathes new life into the mythical beginnings of Lisbon: "la leyenda de la fundación de Lisboa por Ulises da pretexto al autor para inventar una complicada trama argumental con mezcla de Mitología y Cristianismo en la que no falta la visión profética de las hazañas llevadas a cabo por la aristocracia lusa a través de los siglos" (Vázquez Cuesta, "Lengua" 644). Building on the epic assertions of his national poet regarding Iberia, Portugal, and Lisbon, Sousa de Macedo reverts to the past in an effort to reconstruct a present imaginary through which the Portuguese nation can once again take shape and resume its longstanding sovereignty.

In *Flores de España*, Sousa de Macedo literally leaves no stone unturned when it comes to his affection for his native soil. What makes this, in many ways, the single most important expression of nationally conscious annexation literature, is the fact that the young Sousa de Macedo shows complete mastery of the canon. That is, he cites the authors treated in this study and many others, both within and without Portugal, brilliantly gathering all of the best descriptions of *portugalidade* into one single narrative. As an exclamation point to his hyperbolic account of the Portuguese nation, the author concludes by taking up a question put forward in *Os Lusíadas*:

> Aquí se infiere la respuesta a la question, si es mejor ser Rey de
> todo el mundo sin Portugal, ô de solo Portugal sin mas cosa
> alguna del mundo? La qual excitó el gran Camões, quando
> hablando con el Rey Don Sebastian le dixo en sus *Lusíadas*: "E
> julgareis qual he mais excelente, / Se ser do mundo Rey, se de
> tal gente?" (1.10.7–8). Y podemos responder que mejor es ser
> Rey de Portugal solamente. (fol. 236)

The effort to celebrate Portugal's exalted status is on full display in
this passage. Sousa de Macedo adds his voice to that of Camões—
an obvious appeal to authority—in concluding that it is better to
govern Portugal alone, than all the rest of the world combined. The
strategy that sees him invoke the name of Camões is characteristic
of the Portuguese authors this study highlights, yet as William
John Freitas observes, it takes on renewed significance in the years
leading up to and following the Restoration: "when it became
apparent that the dual monarchy had evolved into an ill-disguised
form of annexation, Camoens' name served as a watchword for
plotters seeking to restore national independence" (177). Overall,
Flores de España documents the self-sufficiency and supremacy of
Portugal and can be read as an argument for Portuguese autonomy.
The work, therefore, anticipates the Restoration of 1640 as well as
the many defenses of Portuguese sovereignty that were written in
the decades that followed. Sousa de Macedo, in fact, would be
active in composing many such works including *Lusitania liberata
ab injusto Castellanorum dominio* (1645; "Lusitania Liberated
from Unjust Castilian Rule"). If *Flores de España* is on one end
of the subversive title spectrum, *Lusitania liberata* is on the other.
The title alone is full of useful information for the reader. That it is
in Latin gives the work the tone of authority generally reserved for
legal and religious texts. The title also invokes Portugal's antiquity
and origins by using the name Lusitânia. Finally, it describes the
Restoration as a liberation from Castilian injustice, which gets at
the issue of justification regarding the Iberian Union in the first
place. Over the remaining years of his life Sousa de Macedo would
continue to dress his works in the three primary languages of publication on the Iberian Peninsula during the seventeenth century
(i.e., Spanish, Portuguese, Latin), ever celebrating and defending
the excellences of his native land.

In addition to Sousa de Macedo and Camões, it is interesting
to consider exactly who we are to read into the first person plural

"podemos" used in the long passage from *Flores de España* on the previous page. Undoubtedly, the collectivity cast by "podemos" would include the immediate precursors and contemporaries that fill the pages of this study, of whom Sousa de Macedo makes frequent mention in *Flores de España*. In the section titled "De las mujeres y otras portuguesas," Sousa de Macedo names one such compatriot: "Violante del Cielo, monja en el Monasterio de la Rosa en Lisboa, con el grande ingenio con que haze comedias, y otras admitibles obras en verso va dando a Portugal nuevas alabanças" (fol. 70). In another work of great erudition, *Eva y Ave* (1676), he continues: "en las lenguas Portuguesa, y Castellana Soror Violante del Cielo ... con admirable espiritu ilustró su patria, y acreditó el ingenio de las mugeres" (fol. 85). In both instances, Sousa de Macedo focuses on the relationship between Violante do Céu and Portugal. While a relatively understudied aspect of her poetry, scholars have given some attention to the political character of Sor Violante do Céu's works in the past. Nieves Baranda, for instance, focuses on this topic in her article "Violante do Céu y los avatares políticos de la Restauração." In it she explores the *poemas panegíricos* of Sor Violante's literary corpus, with particular emphasis on the silences within the text that, in her estimation, reflect circumstances that undermine politically-charged readings of Sor Violante's poetry. Overall, Baranda makes a strong case for an apolitical approach to the relatively few poems that can even be considered politically-minded at all. In a broader sense, her work walks back any criticism that would quickly enlist Sor Violante in the army of Portuguese writers actively defending Portugal's liberation from the so-called Babylonian Captivity.

While not a defining characteristic of her entire poetic corpus, some of Violante do Céu's poems are punctuated by many of the same ideas that characterize Restoration texts in general, including references to liberation, tyranny, a Christological view of João IV, divine approbation, and the decadent state of Portugal under Hapsburg rule. José Maria da Costa e Silva dedicates nearly forty pages of his *Ensaio biographico-critico* to her poetry, including some consideration of her political leanings. He posits that "Soror Violante do Ceo abraçou com todo o enthusiasmo a gloriosa revolução de 1640" (8:72; "Soror Violante do Ceo embraced with complete enthusiasm the glorious revolution of 1640"), which he primarily supports by citing several sections of her poem "Sylva a

El-Rei D. João IV" (8:73–74). Overall, this poem casts Spain as a tyrant from which Portugal has been divinely liberated. In the same way that the Portuguese had read divine favor into all of their previous achievements, God, according to much post-Restoration literature, was once again at the helm of Portuguese triumph. This providential view of 1640 reignited the story of Portugal's divine destiny. Justifications for the Restoration appeared in a range of Portuguese texts, from legal defenses such as António de Sousa de Macedo's *Lusitania liberata* (1641), to dramatic representations such as Manuel de Araujo de Castro's *comedia*, *La mayor hazaña de Portugal* (1645).

The three sonnets by Sor Violante that follow demonstrate that even though they are not characteristic of her entire literary corpus, they still evidence her patriotic feelings for Portugal, her king, and the *Restauração*. The two sonnets addressed to the newly crowned João IV, in particular, clearly communicate her favorable view of an independent Portugal. They express a theme commonly found within the body of Portuguese texts produced after the Restoration, namely the relationship between God's will and Portugal's reclaimed autonomy:

"A el-Rei D. João IV"
Que logras Portugal? Hum rei perfeito:
Quem o constituio? Sacra piedade:
Que alcançaste como elle? A liberdade:
Que liberdade tens? Serlhe sujeito:
Que tens na sujeição? Honra, e proveito:
Que he o novo Rey? Quasi deidade:
Que ostenta nas acções? Felicidade,
E que tem de feliz? Ser por Deos feito.
Que eras antes delle? Hum labyrinto,
Que te julgas agora? Hum firmamento,
Temes alguém? Não temo a mesma Parca
Sentes alguma pena? Huma só sinto.
Qual he? Não ser hum mundo, ou não ser cento,
Para ser mais capaz de tal Monarca.

"To King John IV"[2]
What gained you Portugal? A king's perfection.
Who constituted him? Pure piety.
What was obtained through him? My liberty.
What liberties are yours? Be in subjection.
What's yours by this subjection? Honor and gain.

Who's this new king? Almost divinity.
What do his actions bring? Felicity.
What brings him joy? That God chose him to reign.
What were you like before? A labyrinth.
What are you now with him? A firmament.
Who do you fear? Not Fate nor anything.
And do you feel some sorrow? Only one.
Which is? I'm not a hundred worlds or sun
That I could prove more worthy of this King.

Although she was one of Luis de Góngora's many Portuguese followers, the first of the two sonnets dedicated to the king is far from the obscurity frequently associated with *culteranismo*. Here the aim is clarity, as if hers was the responsibility to write the "Frequently Asked Questions" section of the *Restauração* website. In order to communicate her Restorationist message, Sor Violante makes use of the figure of *hypophora*: "asking questions and immediately answering them" (Lanham 87). Through this series of questions and answers, Sor Violante elevates the king ("Um rei perfeito") by attributing the Restoration to deity ("Sacra piedade"). The second quatrain essentially restates the ideas put forward in the first. The freedom gained is happily surrendered to a king divinely constituted. Spanish efforts to reappropriate Portugal, therefore, stand in contrast to God, himself, who orchestrated Portugal's liberation in the first place ("Ser por Deos feito"). Portugal's confused state ("um labyrinto") under Hapsburg rule, has given way to the heavenly influence of a Portuguese king ("um firmamento"). Accordingly, divine order has been restored. The use of *hypophora* intensifies the patriotic ideals that Sor Violante spells out in her sonnet. The Spanish empire does not need to be present in name for the poet's message to be self-evident; if God orchestrated Portugal's liberation, then it goes without saying that whoever challenges the Restoration stands in opposition to God.

While not as flashy, her other sonnet dedicated to D. João reinforces one of the primary ideas contained in "A el-Rei D. João IV," namely the deification of the king:

"Ao Mesmo Senhor Dom João IV"
Hum só pezar, Senhor, sente a vontade
Neste excesso da gloria Portugueza
E he não poder comvosco huma fineza
Deixar de parecer commodidade.

Quem se vos rende, alcança liberdade,
Quem vos adora, ostenta subtileza,
Servirvos muito he denotar grandeza,
Morrer por vós buscar eternidade.
Tudo finezas são, mas de tal modo
Commodidades só parecem, quantas
Finezas ha, na paga que dais nellas;
E assim de todas o remedio todo
He fazermos por vós finezas tantas,
Que talvez o pareça alguma dellas.

"To the Same Lord John IV"
One single sorrow, Lord, grieves the will
During this outpouring of Portuguese glory
And that is failing to keep Thy grace
from seeming a convenience.
Who submits to Thee, attains liberty,
Who worships Thee, exhibits discretion,
Great service to Thee is akin to greatness,
To die on Thy account salvation.
It is all grace, but in such a way that
Convenience is all it seems, so much
grace there is, paid by Thee in full;
And thus with so many the cure-all
Is to change through Thine abundance,
That maybe then we can return a kindness.

The message here is much more subtle than the call and response of "Que logras Portugal?" but no less effective. Similar to the previous poem, the poetic voice expresses a longing to be worthy of the newly crowned king, whose very presence extends grace to those around him. The sonnet's conflict resides in the poetic self, here representing all Portuguese people, because she cannot possibly give anything to Portugal and her king to rival what she has received from them; in other words it's about the impossibility of reciprocity. As in the previous sonnet, here the effort seems to be the exaltation of João IV, thus lending legitimacy to his reign and Portugal's independence.

Both of Sor Violante's sonnets to the king are in Portuguese. Just as Portugal has removed the yoke of Spanish rule, so has the poet cast aside the Spanish language in these patriotic sonnets. Portuguese authors of the seventeenth century were acutely aware of the consequences and significance surrounding language decisions. Not all of Sor Violante's pro-Portuguese texts, however, appeared after the Restoration nor were they all in Portuguese. While it can be difficult to assign specific years to many of her writings, her sonnet in celebration of António de Sousa de Macedo's *Flores de España, Excelencias de Portugal*, was almost certainly written before the Restoration. It reads as a poem you would expect to find in the dedicatory pages of the work itself. Its praise of Sousa de Macedo's work, in fact, surpasses the five poems that do appear in the work, including a sonnet penned by a young Francisco Manuel de Melo. That Sor Violante would dedicate a sonnet to Sousa de Macedo should not be interpreted as merely a return of favor, since many were her admirers to whom she never dedicated a poem (at least that we know of). The choice to celebrate Sousa de Macedo and his patriotic work, therefore, tells us something of her own *portugalidade*, if not also her esteem of Sousa de Macedo:

> "A António de Sousa de Macedo"
> *Em lovour do seu livro das Excellencias de Portugal*
> Quando de Portugal las excelencias
> Explicas singular, sabio describes,
> Com la misma excelencia, com que escribes,
> Buelves las descripciones evidencias.
> Los tropos, los conceptos, las sentencias,
> Con que a sublime lauro te apercibes,
> Las excelencias son, con que prohíbes
> Al Asia con Europa competencias.
> Oh feliz Portugal, pues juntamente
> Adquiere por tu causa mil vitorias,
> Y mil vezes por ti queda excelente:
> Una por ser assunto a tus historias,
> Otra por ser de ti patria eminente,
> Y muchas, porque vive en tus memorias.

In these lines Sor Violante establishes a reciprocal relationship between the excellences of Portugal that Sousa de Macedo celebrates in his work, and the excellence of the author himself. With singular skill, he captures the grandeur of this singular place. In his capable hands, descriptions become proof and a thousand victories plus a thousand excellences seem but a few. Sor Violante was called out by Sousa de Macedo and she called back. Hers was among hundreds of names in *Flores de España*, but in writing this poem to Sousa de Macedo she confirms her place within his text and the Portuguese imaginary.

Few if any of those cited in Sousa de Macedo's *Flores de España* would have been younger than the author. At least one exception to this is Francisco Manuel de Melo, who is responsible for one of the dedicatory sonnets at the beginning of the work (the only time his name comes up). He was only twenty three at the time with a long career of arms and letters ahead of him. Given the opportunity to choose only one of Manuel de Melo's many note-worthy texts in an effort to capture the essence of his nationalism, my choice unmistakably leads to his *Historia de los movimientos y separación y guerra de Cataluña* (1645), one of the few works of Portuguese authorship to be included in the canon of early modern Spanish literature. From basically the time of Portugal's liberation to his death nearly twenty years later, Manuel de Melo diligently advanced the national cause through his writings, often fueling resistance to Spain by emphasizing the empire's deca-dence. Overall, his works help preserve Portugal's independence during the volatile years following the Restoration by maintain-ing the nationalist discourse established during the annexation. In *Historia*, Manuel de Melo undermines Spanish credibility by repeatedly describing the various failures and weaknesses of the Spanish forces in their battles against Catalonia. The content of the book was controversial enough that Manuel de Melo originally published it under the pseudonym Clemente Libertino (Manuel de Melo, *Hospital* 102). In one of his later publications, he explains the significance of this fictitious name:

> *Clemente Libertino*, porque, a não ter o nome que tenho, esse houvera de ser o meu nome, sendo *Clemente* o santo titular do meu nascimento, o qual estimo pelo mais estimado horóscopo a ascendente; *Libertino*, porque já sabeis que era entre os romanos o nome dos filhos dos escravos libertos. Assim, acudindo à liberdade que já gozava minha pátria, fiz dele brasão e apelido. (*Hospital* 102)

> *Clemente Libertino*, because, if I did not have the name I do, that would have been my name, *Clemente* being the patron saint of my birth date, a fact that I esteem as much as the most esteemed ancestral horoscope; *Libertino*, because as you know among the Romans it was the name of the sons of freed slaves.

> Thus, in turning to the freedom that my homeland already enjoyed, I found my crest and my name.

Manuel de Melo chooses his pen name not simply for the sake of anonymity, but to reinforce his personal identity and the character of his homeland, celebrating their recent liberation. As he explains, Manuel de Melo had originally been appointed by the Spanish Court to write an account of all the war-related events. He explains that the mandate was to reveal things as they happened, not as hate or love would paint them (92). In *Hospital das letras* (1657), Manuel de Melo refers to *Historia* as "um livro tão verdadeiro" (90; "a most true book"), echoing the disciplinary insistence of truth claims that so often accompanied the writing of history (e.g., Bernal Díaz's *Historia verdadera de la conquista de la Nueva España*), and which Cervantes brilliantly parodies in *Don Quijote*.

In his account, Manuel de Melo criticizes the empire "no tanto con lo que dice," as Joan Estruch Tobella explains, "sino más bien con lo que calla o sugiere" (23). In other words, he lets the events of the war speak for themselves. In the third book, for instance, he reports on the success ratio of the Spanish army, adding some sharp adjectives to ensure a subversive tone: "Castilla, soberbia y miserable, no logra un *pequeño* triunfo sin *largas* opresiones" (*Historia* 201; my italics). It is interesting to note how Manuel de Melo inverts the categories that Portuguese authors of the annexation so often used to exalt Portugal. What was a qualitative advantage in the face of a quantitative disadvantage with the Portuguese, becomes a quantitative advantage and a qualitative disadvantage with the Spanish. In other words, no empire, no matter how great in size, can prosper against God's will. He emphasizes this at the end of the first book, offering a cutting view of Spain's attempts to colonize and Castilianize:

> Éstos son aquellos hombres (caso digno de gran ponderación) que fueron tan famosos y temidos en el mundo, los que avasallaron príncipes, los que dominaron naciones, los que conquistaron provincias, los que dieron leyes a la mayor parte de Europa, los que reconoció por señores todo el Nuevo Mundo. Éstos son los mesmos castellanos, hijos, herederos y decendientes de estotros, y éstos son aquellos que por oculta providencia de Dios son agora tratados de tal suerte dentro de su mesma patria, por

> manos de hombres viles, en cuya memoria puede tomar ejem-
> plo la nación más soberbia triunfante. Y nosotros, viéndoles en
> tal estado, podremos advertir que *el cielo, ofendido de sus excesos,*
> *ordenó* que ellos mesmos diesen ocasión a su castigo convir-
> tiéndose con facilidad el escándalo de escarmiento. (*Historia*
> 1.104.126; italics in original)

This significant passage divides into two main parts: Spain then
(late fifteenth to late sixteenth century), including several of
their past accomplishments; and Spain now (late sixteenth to
mid-seventeenth century). He begins by characterizing Spain
in terms of fame and fear. Due to their immense successes and
power, Spain intimidated the rest of Europe. One after another,
Manuel de Melo lists Spain's glorious accomplishments of the past,
emphasizing each one with the repetition of "los que," "aquellos,"
and "éstos." Their ascension culminates with "hijos, herederos y
decendientes de estotros." *Estotros* literally means "these others,"
referring to Spain as the Others rather than the superior self the
throne considered itself to be.

All of this, however, comes crashing down, triggered by a
revolutionary "agora." Manuel de Melo sets them up only to
violently pull them down (although, as he suggests in the passage
quoted above, Spain is responsible for its own fall). In comparison
to Spain before, Manuel de Melo now portrays them in terms of
mockery, divine punishment, and a fallen Empire. In other words,
Manuel de Melo calls upon the familiar medieval motif *ubi sunt*,
challenging readers to find the all-powerful Spanish. As Manuel
de Melo explains, Spain is nothing more than a memory, power-
less to change the course of its descent. He closes his criticism by
contending that their downfall was divinely mandated: "el cielo,
ofendido de sus excesos, ordenó." Nothing could be more subversive than to propose that God has withdrawn his support of
Spain, especially considering the Count-Duke of Olivares's claim
that "God is Spanish" (Brown and Elliott 190). This observation
derives not only from Manuel de Melo's own eyes, but from the
collective sight of all ("nosotros").

Manuel de Melo maintains this degenerative view of the
Spanish Empire throughout *Historia*, ending in very much
the same way that he began: "se abre y cierra con episodios
que ejemplifican la derrota y humillación del poderío español"
(Estruch 37). As Manuel de Melo explains, it all fell apart on the

battlefield of Monjuic: "había llegado ya aquella última hora que la divina Providencia decretara para castigo, no sólo del ejército, más de toda la monarquía de España, cuyas ruinas allí se declararon" (5.134.381). Just as his text ends, so does the Spanish empire. As Manuel de Melo explains, it was not just an unlucky day of war, but God himself was now against the Spanish. Their losses at Monjuic reflected their other previous failures—namely Portugal's return to independence—and would also serve to foreshadow greater Spanish losses in the future. Manuel de Melo would continue to write throughout his life, often reaffirming Portugal's individuality and autonomy and Spain's decadence with each subsequent publication.

What had fueled the writings of Portuguese-minded authors during the Iberian Union did not disappear in 1640 following the Restoration. Camões was still there as was *Os Lusíadas*. *Saudade* continued to make its way into Portuguese-authored works, whether in Spanish or Portuguese. More than ever the Portuguese were inspired to write for and about their *patria*. Attempts to fold Portugal's liberation into the larger narrative of Portuguese identity were underway almost immediately. The *Restauração*, then, became a new marker of *portugalidade*. By the mid-seventeenth century, the Spanish language was still in heavy use among the Portuguese. It was a phenomenon that gained momentum during the Dual Monarchy but began well before. The Spanish language did not stop being important politically, artistically, and economically from one day to the next. As a language of literary expression, however, the cultivation of Spanish by Portuguese authors had reached its apex. The end of the Iberian Union would see the beginning of the end of Portuguese-authored works in Spanish. The body of works coming off Iberian presses during those years put forward a cohesive view of Portugal and *portugalidade*, which for the better part of two centuries was communicated as much in Spanish as it was in Portuguese. For centuries this was seen as contradictory. A Portuguese writer in a Spanish costume, however, is only a contradiction for those unwilling to the give the texts and contexts of early modern Iberia a serious reading.

Conclusion

In Praise of the In-Between

Reimagining Early Modern Iberian Literature

In 2015 the Fundación Biblioteca Virtual Miguel de Cervantes (BVMC) launched *Literatura hispano-portuguesa*, a Web portal directed by José Miguel Martínez Torrejón. The stated objective of the portal appears on the main page: "Aspiramos a dar mayor difusión a un corpus que se extiende por todos los géneros literarios y que con frecuencia ha caído en el limbo de historiadores e investigadores debido a la configuración nacionalista de la historia de la literatura, en que un determinado territorio nacional o estatal queda asociado a la cultura de una lengua" (*Literatura*). This brief description captures some of the primary characteristics of the present study. For one, the intention was to make this topic-driven and not genre-focused. I was always most interested in the ubiquitous expression of *portugalidade* among male and female Portuguese writers of all genres. Similar to the Portuguese authors of the Dual Monarchy who hoped to extend the reach of their works by writing in Spanish, I hope that this book will bring greater attention to a group that, on the whole, has been overlooked by almost everyone but their contemporaries.

The hyphen between *hispano* and *portuguesa* in the title of the BVMC portal captures the essence of this book. A hyphenated word brings together two separate concepts that together mean something that neither could alone, which is how I view the relationship between early modern Spain and Portugal. Ultimately, something significant is lost when it is only ever one or the other; or worse, when Iberia is reduced to a sum of two. Iberia is more than a duality of language, canon, and identity because Spain will always be a plurality (i.e., las Españas). This is precisely what Joan Ramon Resina describes in his preface and introduction to the essays comprising *Iberian Modalities: A Relational Approach to the Study of Culture in the Iberian Peninsula*

(2013): "The innovative idea behind Iberian studies as a discipline is its intrinsic relationality and its reorganization of monolingual fields based on nation-states and their postcolonial extensions into a Peninsular plurality of cultures and languages pre-existing and coexisting with the official cultures of the state" (vii). *Being Portuguese in Spanish* is concerned with the give and take between Spain (the official, centralized version coming out of Madrid) and Portugal. Other approaches to early modern Iberian literature might favor other peripheral nationalisms; such is the promise and opportunity of Iberian Studies within this and other contexts.

The revaluation of Portuguese-authored works written in Spanish during the Dual Monarchy has been underway since the second half of the twentieth century. That said, as Tobias Brandenberger observes, "this phenomenon has not yet received the attention it is due" ("Literature" 600). Nevertheless, the extensive work advanced by critical giants of the mid-to-late twentieth century such as Edward Glaser, Eugenio Asensio, José Ares Montes, and Pilar Vázquez Cuesta, to only name a few, has put twenty-first century scholars in the enviable position of resuming the work they initiated. Upon reading the scholarship they put forward on the subject, it is not uncommon to find some kind of implicit (and sometimes explicit) invitation to challenge, develop, and/or broaden their conclusions. Eugenio Asensio's question, for example, is as relevant today as it was then: "¿Habrá un historiador que trate de salvar para Portugal algunas de sus más nobles figuras tachadas de filipinismo?" ("España" 109). Jüri Talvet puts forward a similar question: "where are the philosophically minded writers and literary-cultural scholars of our days, capable of transcending a limited national perspective and trying to establish a dialogue between 'own' and 'other'?" (88). Given the unprecedented access to the texts produced on the Iberian Peninsula during the sixteenth and seventeenth centuries as well as the heightened interest in Iberian Studies, it is hard to imagine a better time to explore the cultural cross-pollination that defined early modern Iberia.[1]

It is difficult to find any Portuguese author more suited for this study than Manuel de Faria e Sousa. He offers readers a seemingly endless amount of nation-minded writings to work with, including several different genres. From his early writings to his posthumous publications, one can follow Faria e Sousa as he works through the benefits and challenges of being a Portuguese writer during the annexation. His works capture both the clarity and complexity of annexation literature: clear in its stated purposes, complex—linguistically, culturally, etc.—in the carrying out of these objectives. I believe that my analysis in chapter three substantiates the author's love for his homeland at the same time that it exposes some of the shortcomings of such a perspective. Accompanying Faria e Sousa's frequent expressions of nationalism is an identity-driven anxiety. He is not sure who he is within the early modern Peninsular world, nor the place of his *patria* therein. He seems confident in Portugal's yesterdays, unsure of its todays, and hopeful that tomorrow will combine the glories of the past with the promise of the future. This is apparent in his commentaries on Camões's writings, his volumes of historiography, and in his poetry. He nationalizes each genre in such a way that allows them to converge at a single point: the glorification of the Portuguese nation.

While Faria e Sousa is perhaps the most important author of this body of nationally-conscious works and a pioneer of comparative Iberian Studies himself, the most effective genre for spreading the glories of Portugal—drama—was not one that he pursued during his career. Instead, his contemporaries, including Jacinto Cordeiro and Ângela de Azevedo, composed *comedias* featuring Portuguese history and identity. These works were not limited to the literate elite, but performed for the masses, making them an early form of mass media. Cordeiro and Azevedo constructed works based on key figures and events from Portuguese history and also found frequent occasion to reinforce the brand of Portuguese identity circulating in the works of the time. If Faria e Sousa's patriotic gaze was fixed primarily upon Camões, Cordeiro and Azevedo seemed to look to Gil Vicente for their inspiration. After all, the father of Portuguese theater had masterfully allegorized and exalted his *patria* in *Lusitânia*, *Fama*, and other dramatic texts. While neither Cordeiro nor Azevedo rely so heavily on allegory, their commitment to Portugal is comparable to Vicente's (the former articulating his nationalism much more overtly than the latter). The underlying character of their *comedias*, however, is Portuguese.

At the cultural crossroads of early modern Iberia, somewhere in-between Spain and Portugal, you will find Manuel de Faria e

Sousa, Ângela de Azevedo, Jacinto Cordeiro, António de Sousa de Macedo, Sor Violante do Céu, Francisco Manuel de Melo, and many others acting out *portugalidade* in Spanish. In the words of Edward Glaser, they are unquestionably "Portuguese in matter and thought" ("On Portuguese" 125). Rather than reject these authors due to their in-between status as many scholars have done over the centuries, this instead was the criteria by which I selected the authors who would occupy these pages. Although their works pledge allegiance to Portugal, they also invite readers to contemplate a Peninsular heritage that may never have been more pronounced than during the sixteenth and seventeenth centuries. This study, however, was always more about an idea than any specific authors. I have sketched an approach to these writers rooted in the theatricality of national identity; how many who took that stage ended up simultaneously inventing and performing *portugalidade*. I have tried to highlight some of the ways in which their performances overlap: in their appeal to Camões and *Os Lusíadas*, their exaltation of the *patria*, and their identification of and with a Portuguese collective, among other examples. That they did all of this in a Spanish costume simply adds another layer to the performativity of national identity.

While this study addresses a number of issues related to early modern Iberian culture, namely the interaction of language, literature, politics, and identity, many questions remain unanswered. How, for example, did the rest of the Peninsula interpret the *portugalidade* so common in annexation literature? Did the dominant culture feel threatened by the national consciousness of the Portuguese? With so many celebrated *comedias* about Portuguese greatness it does not appear to have been a significant issue, but further research could prove otherwise. In shedding new light on such an important thread of Portuguese annexation literature, I have not been able to consider, at length, other Peninsular perspectives. Lope de Vega—considering his relationship with Faria e Sousa—and many of the other Spanish dramatists who actively engaged Portugal as a literary topic, provide some insight as to how others throughout Iberia perceived the Portuguese (at least among the educated elite). I would like to find out whether the antagonisms between Spain and Portugal that played out on the literary landscape following the Restoration, can also be detected in Spanish works published during the annexation. Were there Catalonian authors (or other Iberian peripheral identities) who felt bonded to their Portuguese contemporaries by their common struggle against Spanish hegemony? These questions, and others, follow quite naturally from the work that has taken place in this book.

Whereas all texts produced in Iberia during the early modern period reflect the distinct social, political, and cultural realities sweeping across the peninsula to some degree, Portuguese literature written in Spanish offers a unique vantage point from which to see these converging landscapes. This study reads these works through an Iberian lens that rejects either/or criticism that would make superficial what is rich and multifaceted. Through such a reading we begin to see the impossibility of traditional canons to account for the heterogeneous nature of Peninsular identities and cultures during the sixteenth and seventeenth centuries. Hence, the story of the Portuguese authors writing in Spanish during the late sixteenth and early seventeenth centuries is a story worth telling; a story with many more characters and many more twists and turns than I have identified here. It is a narrative that reminds us that border-crossings, hybridity, code-switching, and many other frequently-studied aspects of twentieth- and twenty-first-century literature are not entirely recent phenomena. There has never been a better time to commit to a serious study of Portuguese-authored works written in Spanish during the Iberian Union.

Notes

Introduction

1. From his 1970 study of polyglot poetry in early modern Europe, *The Poet's Tongues* (28).

2. Benito Caldera's was published in Alcalá de Henares by Juan Gracián, and Luis Gómez de Tapia's was published in Salamanca by Joan Perier.

3. "Portugal gozaba, según la constitución filipina, de una amplísima autonomía" (Asensio, "España" 66). As Jean Frédéric Schaub explains, it is not as though Portugal was recolonized by the Spanish empire: "durante todo el período en que dura la unión (1580–1640) la lengua castellana no tiene ningún valor jurídico en Portugal, que la moneda de Castilla no circula allí, que los magistrados castellanos no pueden ejercer allí su jurisdicción, que la legislación de los reyes de Portugal sigue siendo la única utilizable, etc." (28). In his analysis of the revolutionary flavor of 1640 *Restauração*, David Tengwall identifies six ways in which the Spanish crown would go on to violate the terms of the *carta patente*.

4. Unless otherwise noted, all translations are by the author. The punctuation and spelling of book titles and author names sometimes vary given the lack of standardization in the past.

5. For a broader consideration of the persistence of these characteristics in early modern Iberian literature, see José Manuel Pedrosa's "El otro portugués: tipos y tópicos en la España de los siglos xvi al xviii."

6. For more on the many editions and translations that emerged during the Iberian Union, see Anastácio ("Leituras"), Dasilva ("Líneas maestras" and "La evolución"), Asensio ("Fortuna"), Martínez, Serra, Namora, and Alonso.

7. In response to centuries of disparaging comments about Portuguese annexation literature, Hernani Cidade advanced a nationalist view of said works, grouping them beneath the banner of resistance literature in his work, *A literatura autonomista sob os Filipes* (*Autonomous Literature under the Philips*), to which this study refers many times. Cidade orients his work around three specific genres from the time: epic, historiography, and essay. His analysis shows how several Portuguese writers employed their pens to articulate some form of objection to the Spanish takeover. He makes his intentions clear from the outset: "Não é outra senão a piquena [sic] Casa Lusitana, de que fala Camões, a que enche este livro. É a Nação inteira, na totalidade dos seus valores, que eu procuro mostrar como reagiu, numa crise mais grave da sua história" (7; "It is none other than the small Lusitanian House, of which Camões speaks, that fills this book. It is the entire Nation, in the totality of her values, which I mean to reveal as she dealt with the most serious crisis of her history"). In his article, "España en la época filipina," Eugenio Asensio explains that Cidade's work "provoca en el lector del otro lado de la raya fronteriza la reflexión y no pocas veces la contradicción" (66). Asensio's study attempts to correct those parts of Cidade's text that tend to hyperbole. The point is not that Cidade got it all wrong and that Asensio has all the answers. In concert, the two works have a lot to say about Portuguese-authored works of the Dual Monarchy. By walking back some of the more outrageous claims within Cidade's work, Asensio demonstrates how easy it is to get carried away in representing the underrepresented.

8. An international colloquium in 2016 at the Casa de Velásquez in Madrid titled "La literatura áurea ibérica: La construcción de un campo literario peninsular (siglos XVI y XVII)," exemplifies the kinds of scholarly activities taking place in the twenty-first century.

Chapter 1

1. Nearing the completion of this book, I obtained a copy of Onésimo Almeida's recent work, *A obsessão da portugalidade: identidade, língua, saudade & valores* (2017). Unfortunately, I was not able to incorporate the study into my discussion of *portugalidade* in this chapter. On the other hand, many of the ideas expressed in his new work are familiar given how much he has previously written on the subject.

2. Cidade speaks confidently of Portugal during the annexation as "uma inconfundível personalidade colectiva" (37; "an unmistakable collective personality"). Mattoso, however, warns of the tendency to falsely attribute the characteristics of one group to another by virtue of their proximity or other shared features: "não é lícito atribuir simultaneamente a todos os habitantes de um país as operações de diferenciação, de significação e de valorização quando envolvem apenas um determinado grupo" (6; "it is not right to simultaneously attribute to all inhabitants of a country the operations of differentiation, signification and valorization when they involve only certain groups").

3. Birmingham does not shy away from speaking of Portugal as a transcendent collectivity in his short history on the Portuguese nation. He resists calling the 1640 Restoration a popular revolution, but points out that such an uprising occurred three years previous in Évora: "The lack of popular initiative in launching the Portuguese independence movement does not mean that there was not a degree of popular enthusiasm for liberation from the Spanish union. Centuries of war with Castile had created deep antagonism between the Portuguese and their only land neighbors" (36). While Birmingham may overstate the rivalry between the two countries, there was indeed a rivalry. Daviken Studnicki-Gizbert's *A Nation upon the Ocean Sea* demonstrates the ways in which many Portuguese merchants of the Atlantic world identified with their native Portugal. The author, however, struggles to come up with a definition for the Portuguese nation that adequately encompasses the many merchants within his study.

4. For more information on *theatrum mundi*, see Bernheimer, Hawkins, and Righter's studies.

5. My view of nationalism is informed by Ernest Gellner's definition: "It is nationalism which engenders nations, and not the other way around. Admittedly, nationalism uses the pre-existing, historically inherited proliferation of cultures or cultural wealth, though it uses them very selectively, and it most often transforms them radically" (54).

Chapter 2

1. Both the Fundación Biblioteca Virtual Miguel de Cervantes's online portal "Literatura hispano-portuguesa" and Pilar Vázquez Cuesta's essay "La lengua y la cultura portuguesas," for example, identify Pedro de Portugal as the first of the Portuguese authors to publish in Spanish.

2. The full passage reads: "Que si la muy insigna magnificencia vuestra demandare qual fue la causa que a mi movio dexar el materno vulgar e la seguiente obra en este catellano romance proseguir Vos responderé que como la rodante fortuna con su tenebrosa rueda me visitasse venido con estas partes me di a esta lengua mas costrenido de la necesidad que de la voluntad" (9). It is worth noting that while Pedro de Portugal explains his exceptional use of Spanish in the prefatory pages of his work, by the time the writers listed above were on the literary scene such clarifications were less common because writing in Spanish had become normative. As I will detail in subsequent chapters, during the Dual Monarchy, when the use of Spanish by Portuguese authors reached its apex, language-based apologetics were once again a common occurrence within the introductory sections of published works.

3. The titles of Vicente's plays often appear with subtle differences from one publication to the next. This is primarily due to the various ways in which they have been grouped over the centuries (e.g., comédias, farsas, etc.), beginning with the *Copilacam de todalas obras de Gil Vicente* (1562). For the sake of consistency and simplicity, this study uses the titles and texts of the online versions put out by the Universidade de Lisboa's Centro de Estudos de Teatro under the direction of José Camões (who also directed the Imprensa Nacional-Casa da Moeda's publication of *As obras de Gil Vicente* [2002]).

4. It is worth noting that while the verse in these works appears in Spanish, the stage directions are in Portuguese. Hence, many of the works that traditionally fall into the category of Vicente's *teatro castellano* still maintain a certain degree of polyglotism. This is especially true when considering that Spanish and Portuguese are not singular, cohesive languages in Vicente's plays in the first place. In fact, Vicente employs various Peninsular dialects in his works (e.g., sayagués), as well as both common and cultured variations of Spanish and Portuguese. For these reasons and others, the language of Vicente's first plays as well as those that follow are difficult to classify as Spanish, Portuguese, or both (see Sletsjöe's "Las lenguas de Gil Vicente" for a sustained treatment of these issues).

5. There is some question whether *Auto da festa* was ever even performed. See José Augusto Cardoso Bernardes's article for more information.

6. Manuel Calderón insists that there is no clear criteria for evaluating the significance of Vicente's switches between languages (xxviii). It should be noted that Roig's observations come from published conference proceedings and are not, therefore, as exhaustive as a full-length article. What is more, the examples of *salvajes*, *ruines*, and *seductores* that he identifies comprise only part of his broader interest in how the Spanish show up in Vicente's plays. Roig's paper is more suggestive than conclusive, inviting others to pick up where he left off. The most balanced treatment of Vicente's Spanishness and Portugueseness that I am aware of comes from Marie-France Antunes-Fernandes, whose article "Gil Vicente: Un espagnol portugais du debut du XVIème siècle" concludes that, on the whole, his works are best classified as Iberian, with an awareness of and preference for Portugal's singularity.

7. In these humorous scenes, Vicente's French and Italian are heavily influenced by Spanish, especially in the case of French where there is only a smattering of common linguistic markers embedded therein (e.g., le, par, vu, moi).

8. This being Manuel, Prince of Portugal (1531–37), the fifth child of João III of Portugal and Catarina of Austria.

9. This plot summary is in prose and not numbered as part of the play (which is in verse).

10. See Hobsbawm's introduction in *The Invention of Tradition* for more information on the relationship between myth and history.

11. In Vicente's *Romagem dos Agravados*, for example, we see the idiomatic use of *ventura* when Frei Paço asserts, "impossível é vencer / batalha contra ventura / quem ventura nam tiver" (1048–50; "it is impossible to win / battles vs. luck / if you do not have any"). In another instance, this one depicting the divinization of *ventura*, the Ermitão in his *Tragicomedia Pastoril da Serra da Estrela* explains that "de Deos vem a ventura" (468; "good luck comes from God"). In *Floresta d'Enganos* we discover perhaps the most striking case of *ventura* as personified deity, with *Ventura pelegrina* among the characters. As Ventura pelegrina explains, she is on God's errand (God in this case being Apollo): "No es cordura / quexaros de la Ventura: / con Apolo esta demanda; / que naquello que Dios manda / no erró nada la Ventura" (1173–77). Only a few lines later, she continues: "Yo os guío por la vía / que Dios quiere que vayáis" (1180–81). From these examples we can see some of the varied ways in which *ventura* appears in Vicente's plays.

12. One of the earliest manifestations of Camões's importance to Portugal and the Portuguese identity is the proliferation of translations and editions of *Os Lusíadas* in the decades following his death (see chapter three for more information). One of Lisbon's oldest and most recognized plazas, Praça de Luís de Camões, bears a statue of the poet that was inaugurated in 1867. The centenary celebrations dedicated to Camões in 1880 (and again in 1980) are also indicative of his sustained importance to the Portuguese. Reflecting on the centenary celebrations of the late nineteenth century, Teófilo Braga anticipates what will eventually become a national holiday decades later: "O Centenario de Camões devia ser a festa da nacionalidade portugueza" (*Os centenarios* 6–7; "The Centenary of Camões should be the holiday of Portuguese nationality").

13. Because *Os Lusíadas* is a touchstone of this entire study, especially chapter three, I will not elaborate on specific passages from the poem in

this chapter as I have done with Gil Vicente's works (and will subsequently do with some of António Ferreira's writings).

14. Camões likewise composed a handful of poems in Spanish: "[su] producción en castellano abarca por lo menos siete sonetos, doce redondillas y el llamado *Monólogo de Aónia*—traducción de su *Écogla I*—por no citar a los personajes en sus Autos que se expresan en esta lengua" (Vázquez Cuesta, "Lengua" 602).

15. Although not published until 1587, Ferreira would have written *Castro* during the mid–1550s, when it also would have reached the stage for the first time (Martyn 59, 84). It would have then circulated widely in manuscript form thereafter (84–85).

16. His complete works include 19 epitaphs, 102 sonnets, 13 odes, 10 epigrams, 9 eulogies, 14 eclogues, 26 letters, and the tragedy *Castro*. All of these, as well as a eulogy by Diogo Bernardes and a response by Pêro de Andrade Caminha, appear in *Poemas lusitanos* (1598).

17. The introductory essays of John R. C. Martyn's edition of *The Tragedy of Ines de Castro* are a rich source of bibliographic material and literary criticism on the subject of Inês de Castro.

18. Vázquez Cuesta cites one such example in "O bilinguismo castelhano-português na época de Camões" (820). The footnote explains that she pulled the reference from Eugenio Asensio's edition of *Comédia Eufrosina* (1951).

Chapter 3

1. Faria e Sousa died in Madrid on June 3, 1649, and was initially interred at the Convento de Mostenses in the same city. In 1660, however, his wife had his remains transferred to the Igreja de Santa Maria do Pombeiro where he had been baptized as an infant.

2. The entry on "Españolado" in the *Diccionario de la lengua española* (2014) is nearly identical: "Dicho de un extranjero: Que en el aire, traje y costumbres parece español." Since at least the nineteenth century, it is not uncommon to read descriptions of Faria e Sousa that label him *hispanizado* or *estrangeirado*. While these are used pejoratively as a character attack, *españolado* (at least according to Covarrubias's definition) appears to be more affirmative in nature, highlighting a person's cross-cultural knowledge.

3. The two works by Faria e Sousa that were published in 1624—*Noches claras* and *Divinas y humanas flores*—are sometimes confused as being one in the same. The former, however, is a work in prose while the latter consists of poetry. Both texts were apparently reviewed and approved at the same time, the approbations by Vicente Espinel and Fr. Lucas de Montoya reading exactly the same in each work. Whereas *Noches claras* includes a third approbation and the quoted *décima* by Lope, *Divinas y humanas flores* offers a laudatory sonnet by Lope. The confusion probably results from the 1674 edition of *Noches claras* that was titled *Noches claras, divinas y humanas flores*, which, contrary to what one might expect, is not an edition of both works.

4. Demosthenes is best-known for his Philipic Orations, in which he urges his people to rise up and defend their country from Philip II of Macedon.

5. Faria e Sousa's first exposure to Lope came through his *comedias*, which Faria e Sousa read in his youth (*Fortuna* 136). While we do not know how or when they first met, the paper trail they left clearly suggests a strong friendship between the two men of letters. For a more detailed discussion of their relationship see Marín's "Camoens, Faria y Cervantes," Rodríguez Cepeda's "La relación Camoens, Lope de Vega y Faria y Sousa," Glaser's "Lope de Vega e Manuel de Faria e Sousa," and my own "Manuel de Faria e Sousa and *Comedia* Culture: Resituating Portugal on the Early Modern Spanish Stage."

6. A similar idea comes up in the conclusion of his prologue to *Epítome de las historias portuguesas* (1628) where he explains that by living abroad and writing primarily for non-Portuguese readers "puedo librarme de los propios naturales." These words reiterate the fact that things were not pleasant for Faria e Sousa back in Portugal; the problem not being the *patria* per se, but the apparent vitriol he faced from his compatriots.

7. Although he never refers to them by name in *Informacion*, Faria e Sousa singles out two of his accusers: "de los Acusadores, los màs declarados son dos … que son enemigos patentes del Acusado" (4). Hélio Alves identifies those two as Agostinho Manuel de Vasconcelos and Manuel Pires de Almeida ("Faria" 371).

8. Faria e Sousa organizes his defense into *luces* and *rayos* (the former refers to the section, of which there are thirteen, and the latter refers to the number of paragraphs in each section). Rather than follow this particular organizing principle, I refer instead to the column number in my quotations (which only begin after the preliminary sections [e.g., Advertencias]).

9. Francisco Moreno Porcel's *Retrato de Manuel de Faria y Sousa* (1650) includes a very comprehensive listing of Faria e Sousa's earliest admirers.

10. Sir Richard Fanshawe's English translation *The Lusiad, or Portugal's Historical Poem* (1655), for example, relied heavily on Faria e Sousa's edition, and may have been based entirely on Faria e Sousa's Spanish prose translation and not on the original Portuguese at all (see Roger Walker and Tiago Sousa Garcia's respective articles for more information).

11. Glaser sees this as a "major contribution to the legend of Faria e Sousa" and an "effort to clear an admired author of a possible charge of treason" (*Fortuna* 9), but doubts its veracity considering the absence of correspondence between João IV and Faria e Sousa (10). Taking up the same question, Hélio Alves considers the connection between Faria e Sousa and João IV quite plausible given the positive relationships between many prominent members of João IV's court and the author. He also acknowledges the harmony between Faria e Sousa's commentary on *Os Lusíadas* and the propaganda machine supporting the *Restauração* ("Faria" 371–72). Jorge de Sena, recalling both Castelo Branco and Teófilo Braga's words on the subject, leaves the matter open, ultimately rejecting the importance of even

establishing a link between Faria e Sousa and João IV, seeing such efforts as missing the point (16–17).

12. In "A violência literária contra Manuel de Faria e Sousa," Joaquim Luís Costa provides additional context and numerous examples of how Faria e Sousa's legacy was damaged during the nineteenth and early twentieth centuries.

13. A few passages from Costa e Silva's study reveal the homogenizing effect on literature that the nineteenth century inherited to future generations. This can be seen in the separation, for example, of Portuguese literature written in Spanish from that written in the mother tongue. Speaking of Faria e Sousa's four historiographical texts—*Europa portuguesa, Asia portuguesa, África portuguesa,* and *América portuguesa*—he makes the following observation: "sam em lingoa castelhana, que este grande engenho erradamente, e não sei porque motivo, preferia ao idyoma patrio, e que por essa mesma razão pertencem mais á historia da literatura hespanhola, que a da nossa" (7:105; "they are in the Castilian tongue, which this great talent mistakenly, and I do not know why, preferred to his native language, and for that same reason they belong more to the history of Spanish literature than to ours"). In Costa e Silva's narrow view, there is no room within the Portuguese canon for these works because of the language in which they are written, even though both the author and the content of his works is clearly Portuguese. I also find it incredible that Costa e Silva would feign ignorance regarding the personal and Peninsular circumstances that caused Faria e Sousa to write in Spanish at all. Another illustrative passage from Costa e Silva's work follows: "diremos agora alguma cousa a respeito dos seus Sonetos, porque o juizo das suas outras poesías pertence de direito aos Criticos da nação visinha, em cujo idyoma se acham escriptos" (7:145; "we will say something now regarding his Sonnets, because the consensus on his other poetry pertains directly to critics of the neighboring nation, in whose language they are written"). Here, Costa e Silva explains that his consideration of Faria e Sousa's poetry ends where Spanish begins, contending that such works pertain to Spanish philology. Related to this passage is another in which he extols the purity of Portugal's literary golden age: "Camões, Ferreira, João de Barros, e Diogo do Couto, sem alguma dúvida os melhores Escriptores do seculo de ouro das nossas letras, sam tão recommendavis pela belleza, e elevação dos seus pensamentos, como pela sua linguagem sempre castiça, sempre pura, elegante, e correcta" (7:150; "Camões, Ferreira, João de Barros, e Diogo do Couto, without a doubt the best writers of our golden age of letters, are so commendable for the beauty, and elevated thought, as well as for their high-quality language, always pure, elegant and correct"). Given the values governing this kind of criticism, there is no way that a period as hybrid as the Iberian Union could ever satisfy the purity standard of the nineteenth century.

14. While there is evidence that he held literary criticism and history of the nineteenth-century in general disregard, Jorge de Sena may have saved his most poignant jab for Storck and Michaëlis de Vasconcelos, whom he accuses of wanting to out-Portuguese the Portuguese in their disdain for seventeenth-century Portuguese bilingualism (42).

15. In the 1970s, Jorge de Sena described Costa e Silva as the "último crítico a tratá-lo [Faria e Sousa] com consideração e estima inteligente" (40; "the last critic to treat him with consideration and intelligent praise").

16. Even though he tears apart Faria e Sousa's eclogues and maintains little regard for the baroque aesthetic overall, Costa e Silva remains positive about his poetry: "As composições poeticas de Manoel de Faria e Sousa, apesar dos seus defeitos de estylo, me parecem superiores ás da maior parte dos Poetas, que floresceram naquelle tempo tanto em Portugal, como em Castella, e tenho para mim, que mereciam ser mais conhecidas" (7:145; "The poetic compositions of Manoel de Faria e Sousa, despite their style defects, seem superior to me compared to the majority of Poets who flourished at that time in Portugal as well as in Castile, and I contend that they deserve to better be known").

17. As Asensio explains, "Glaser había iniciado la rehabilitación de Faria y Sousa en sus *Estudios hispano-portugueses*" ("Autobiografía" 630). Since at least the late nineteenth century, many scholars have argued that Faria e Sousa deserves a better place within Iberian letters, including Pierce (121), Flasche (7), Pires (163), García Peres (209), and Glaser (Preface 6).

18. In addition to his critical edition of the autobiography, Glaser's publications on Faria e Sousa include articles on the mythological apparatus of Faria e Sousa's commentary on *Os Lusíadas* and the relationship between Faria e Sousa and Lope de Vega, as well as a critical edition of the *Cancionero* often attributed to Faria e Sousa.

19. As was the case for most of the twentieth century (see Costa Pimpão, Pierce, Flasche, Hart, Lemos, Glaser, Askins), the critical spotlight has continued to shine brightest on Faria e Sousa's literary criticism during the last twenty-five years (see Oliveira e Silva, Leyva, Martínez, Vitali, Alves, Boto, Laferl, Núñez Rivera, Fouto and Weiss, Bass, Sousa Garcia). To a much lesser extent, recent articles have focused on his autobiographical writings (see Gonçalves Pires, Ramada Curto), poetry (see Hatherly, Heiple), and historiography (see Wade, "Manuel").

20. See Javier Núñez Cáceres (275) and Felipe C. R. Maldonado (11).

21. Quantity was never an issue for Faria e Sousa, as the author exhausted the various subjects of his works. That he dedicated a quarter century to his critical commentary of *Os Lusíadas* reveals his painstaking approach to writing, especially literary criticism.

22. Here, I am not merely thinking of Portugal's population, which only numbered around two million, but an even smaller group we might refer to as the Portuguese learned elite.

23. Neither the *Licencias* nor the dedications that follow are numbered in any way. Both the "Advertencias" and "Elogio al comentador" sections, however, include numbered paragraphs. From the prologue through the end of the work, each paragraph is assigned a number in ascending order.

24. Jorge de Sena refers to the monumentality of Faria e Sousa's work seven times in his introduction, including three times on the first page. Other examples include Glaser ("Manuel" 135), Valle de Figueiredo (8), Martínez (80), Asensio ("Fortuna" 317, 318), Sousa Garcia (1), Marcos de Dios (41), Bass (183, 184, 188, 199), Fouto and Weiss (1), and Alves ("Manuel de Faria" 290; "Faria e Sousa" 371). Perhaps most curious of all is that Faria e Sousa himself speaks of his works as "monumentos / … de la Patria generosa" in his autobiographical poem, "Patria i vida del autor" (stanza 144, lines 1–2).

25. Sena calls the work "a obra máxima do príncipe dos poetas das Espanhas" (56; "the greatest work on the prince of poets of the Iberian Peninsula"). Oliveira e Silva states, "For sheer volume, his discussion of these stanzas (or any stanzas in the work, for that matter) is unequaled, the first stanza alone taking up seven and a half pages of commentary alone. In all, his discussion of these four stanzas entails some seventeen pages of text" ("Exile" 70). As depicted by the following passages, Frank Pierce likewise sees Faria e Sousa as the culmination of criticism on *Os Lusíadas*: "Faria has not been surpassed in his formidable undertaking to meet squarely and faithfully the critical problems presented by the roving fantasy of the poet" (108); "As it stands, Faria's four-volume work remains the most substantial piece of Camões scholarship. It came out a bare sixty years after the first edition and, apart from being a magnificent tribute, crowns the critical appreciation of a generation that took its poetry very seriously" (100). José V. de Pina Martins describes it as "um manancial inexaurível para o estudo da poesia camoniana e do Universo intelectual do poeto e do seu tempo" (xii; "an inexhaustible wellspring for the study of Camonian poetry and the intellectual universe of the poet and his time").

26. Although this section does not include pagination, "Elogio" continues for ten pages and consists of twenty-six numbered sections of varying lengths. The numbers in the parenthetical references, therefore, correspond to the sections.

27. His critical edition of Camões's lyric poetry is similarly titled: *Rimas varias de Luis de Camões. Príncipe de los poetas heroycos, y lyricos de España* (1685).

28. A nineteenth-century translation of Faria e Sousa's commentary alters the title: *Os Lusiadas de Luiz de Camões Principe dos Poetas Portuguezes Commentados em castelhano por Manuel de Faria e Souza, traduzidos por Manuel Nunes Godinho e feito a penna pelo calligrapho Domingos Nunes Godinho*. The change to "poetas portugueses" is a poor alternative considering how it diminishes the scope of the original. Without some kind of reference to the entire peninsula the translation lacks the punch of the 1639 title page.

29. According to Laura Bass, Faria e Sousa's work "fue concebida como una superación de las *Lecciones solemnes* de Pellicer" (188). By 1630 (the year *Lecciones solemnes* was published), however, Faria e Sousa's commentary had been through multiple drafts (which is to say, well beyond the point of conception). The poor quality of extant commentaries on *Os Lusíadas*, especially when compared to Herrera's edition of Garcilaso's work, motivated Faria e Sousa to erect his own monument to Camões. That said, Bass is convincing in linking Pellicer's work to Faria e Sousa's; the former setting a new standard for literary commentaries that Faria e Sousa would do everything to surpass. One might even argue that Pellicer's work had a hastening effect on Faria e Sousa's commentary not unlike the influence of Alonso Fernández de Avellaneda's "False *Quixote*" (1614) on Cervantes's second part (1615).

30. All parenthetical references to Faria e Sousa's commentary, aside from the preliminary sections, will be configured as follows: canto.stanza.column. References to *Os Lusíadas*, on the other hand, will appear as canto.stanza.line.

31. Pedro Calderón de la Barca's *El príncipe constante* (1628) dramatizes Fernando's preservation of Ceuta as a Portuguese colony at the expense of his own life. This and other Portuguese-themed *comedias* are part of the focus of chapter three. For more information, see Wade "Manuel de Faria e Sousa and *Comedia* Culture."

32. Apparently there are two variations of the final four verses in this stanza. Faria e Sousa looks at both without attempting to resolve the matter (2.332).

33. All English translations of *Os Lusíadas* are by Landeg White.

34. God's successive reduction of Gideon's army (Judges 6–8) is one such example. The point is made even more clear in 2 Kings 6, when Elisha demonstrates that those favored of God always have the advantage.

35. This passage comes from the "Argumento general" that precedes canto 1. The number refers to the number assigned to that column of text. All quotes from this section will include "Argumento" in the parenthetical reference.

36. This may seem contradictory, as many critics argue—Maldonado (11), Asensio ("Autobiográfia" 631), and Núñez Cáceres (268, 275–76)—but this concession was necessary in order to spread the glories of Portugal while living in Spain.

37. In contrast to Spain's more than seven-hundred-year struggle with the Arabs, Portugal established religious autonomy by the late twelfth century through the papal Manifestis Probatum of 1179 which officially recognized Afonso I as King of Portugal. While conflicts certainly continued thereafter, Portugal was a named kingdom comprising, from the late thirteenth century onward, nearly the exact same geographic area it maintains today.

38. José Eduardo Franco titled his critical edition of Olivieira's work *O mito de Portugal* instead of maintaining *História de Portugal*.

39. Oliveira's antagonistic feelings toward Castile are also manifest in his historiographical work *Viagem de Fernão de Magalhães*, wherein he emphasizes Magalhães's Portuguese roots in an apparent effort to distance the famed navigator from his ties to Spain.

40. João de Barros was to Faria e Sousa's historiography what Camões was to his poetry (Costa 62). Diogo do Couto, Fernão Lopes de Castanheda, Gaspar Correia, and Damião de Goes were also influential.

41. Unfortunately, Manuel de Faria e Sousa's *América portuguesa* was never published nor did it survive in manuscript form. Apparently, it covered the years between Portugal's discovery of Brazil and the Restoration of 1640. Rocha Pita's widely published and celebrated work could be considered the completion of the four-part series.

42. In the prologue to *Epítome* he alludes to the fact that some would have him translate all of his historiographical works to Spanish (which he eventually does), but not apparently because he was fond of translation.

43. It is fitting that the author never completed the larger historiographical project. According to Faria e Sousa, a comprehensive look at Portuguese history is impossible; the project will always outlive the author, the former being too great for the latter to capture in any number of lifetimes.

44. Faria e Sousa's response to the allegation appears in *Información en favor de Manoel de Faria y Sousa Cavallero de la Orden de Christo e de la Casa Real*. The Portuguese author was exonerated of all charges.

45. A similar conception defines his approach to his commentary on *Os Lusíadas*. That he dedicated twenty-five years of his life to the composition of this work served as a fitting tribute, at least in the author's mind, to the unmatched worth of Camões's national epic.

46. One example of Faria e Sousa's concern with the extent of his work occurs in his analysis of Alonso's reign: "En seis horas que durò el conflito, hizo Alonso tales suertes que el abreviarlas fuera osadia, i el escrivirlas salir de nuestra brevedad" (3.2.354).

47. In the Licenças section of the 1733 edition of Francisco Moreno Porcel's *Retrato de Manuel Faria y Souza* is a multi-page approbation by a certain João Col, "da Congregação do Oratorio, Qualificador do Santo Officio, Examinador das Tres Ordens Militares, e Academico do Numero da Academia Real da Historia Portugueza." Among the praise he showers upon the Portuguese author, he explains that were a grammarian to describe the historiographer, he would call him *Superlativo*.

Chapter 4

1. Given the improbability that he wrote a *comedia* at the young age of fifteen, there is some question as to whether Cordeiro was actually born in 1606. Jaime Cruz-Ortiz summarizes the critical conversation around this issue well in the introduction to his edition of Cordeiro's *El juramento ante Dios, y lealtad contra el amor* (11–12).

2. During the latter stages of the writing of this book I have learned of Valerie Hegstrom and Catherine Larson's bilingual edition *El muerto disimulado/Presumed Dead*. The edition is by Hegstrom, translation by Larson, with a critical introduction by both authors.

3. For more on the decadent view of seventeenth-century Portuguese drama that scholars have long maintained, see Jaime Cruz-Ortiz (18–20).

4. The best approximation of the total number of *comedias* penned by the Portuguese can be found in García Peres's 1890 bibliography, which names two hundred sixty-six works by sixty-eight playwrights (Cruz-Ortiz 33).

5. In the critical introduction of his edition of Cordeiro's *El juramento ante Dios*, Cruz-Ortiz also explores the topic of the Portuguese *comedia*. While he initially defines the Portuguese *comedia* according to the various ways that it gives voices to nationalist expression (19), the way he actually uses the category thereafter would suggest that what defines the Portuguese *comedia* is the origin of its author (i.e., if the playwright is Portuguese then it is a Portuguese *comedia*). I approach the same category in terms of authorship and content. Thus, what I designate "Portuguese *comedia*" not only includes all of the *comedias* written by Portuguese dramatists, but also the Lusocentric *comedias* by Lope, Tirso, and other Spanish playwrights.

6. The framing of Castillejo's chapter on Portuguese playwrights, titled "El imperio hispanoportugués: Cubillo, Remón, Cordero, Araujo de Castro," is more valuable than the framed, as it offers little more than a snapshot of each author and, by his account, their best works.

7. *Rua Nova* appears frequently in the literature of the time, including Gil Vicente's theater, Camões's *El-rei Seleuco*, Tirso's description of Lisbon in *El burlador de Sevilla*, Francisco Manuel de Melo's *Apólogos Dialogais*, and António Vieira's *Cartas* (Davies).

8. This point is too rich and complex to treat at length presently. While there is much to say about the difference between Spanish and Portuguese concepts of nationhood and how they are represented on the stage, such a rich topic requires more attention than this study affords. Such a work would take as its basic premise the static nature of dramatizations depicting the Portuguese nation in comparison to the dynamic views of Spain; the former much more stable than the latter.

9. For a general survey of this trend, see Ares Montes's "Portugal en el teatro español del siglo XVII." For studies specifically related to Lope, see Edward Glaser's *El lusitanismo de Lope de Vega*, Fidelino de Figueiredo's "Lope de Vega: alguns elementos portugueses na sua obra," and Hipólito Raposo's chapter "O sentimento português em Lope de Vega" from his critical work *Aula régia*. For a look at this same phenomenon in Tirso's canon, see Alonso Zamora Vicente's "Portugal en el teatro de Tirso de Molina," Manoel de Sousa Pinto's *Portugal e as portuguezas em Tirso de Molina*, and Edwin Morby's "Portugal and Galicia in the Plays of Tirso de Molina."

10. For more information on the impact of *Epítome* on the *comedia*, see Wade "Manuel de Faria e Sousa and *Comedia* Culture."

11. A. E. Sloman locates Calderón's work at the end of 1628, while Tirso scholars have not been able to situate *Las quinas* any earlier than the decade following the publication of Faria's *Epítome*. At the end of the *Las quinas* manuscript, Tirso specifically identifies *Epítome* as one of the primary sources of his play. Margaret Wilson's "The Last Play of Tirso de Molina" offers a close look at Faria e Sousa's contribution to *Las quinas*.

12. Morby, for example, speaks of Tirso's "extremely flattering conception" of Portugal (269).

13. The seven Luso-centric works are *El vergonzoso en palacio, Averígüelo Vargas, Doña Beatriz de Silva, El amor médico, Escarmientos para el cuerdo, Siempre ayuda la verdad* y *Las quinas de Portugal.*

14. The numbers within the parenthetical reference correspond to the line number of the *comedia.*

15. According to Covarrubias, it is "el papel que ha decorado el farsante para recitar en la comedia" (470). *Dicho* is probably the best word to describe this selection, although its playfulness recalls the *entremés* and its moralization hearkens to the *loa.*

16. "Never a prophet was valued in his native country" (see Matt. 13.57, Mark 6.4, Luke 4.24, John 4.44). This biblical trope is an important subtext for much of what is written by the Portuguese during the Dual Monarchy, particularly in cases where authors (e.g., Manuel de Faria e Sousa) speak of a certain hostility at home that contributed to leaving or not returning to Portugal.

17. Bouza dedicates all of chapter 6 of his *Portugal no tempo dos Filipes: política, cultura, representações, 1580–1668* (2000) to the topic of Lisbon; not just how it was esteemed throughout the peninsula, but also how it evolved from an aspiring location of the Spanish court, to an afterthought of the Hapsburg Dynasty.

18. The lines dedicated to Violante do Céu read,

Aqui Fénix reservo una Syrena
Cuya voz celestial, cuya armonia,
Muchos laureles á su pluma ordena
Debidos por razon, no en cortesia:
Que es Violante deidad, cuya Camena
A valientes ingenios desafia,
Con tanta admiracion, que alçando el vuelo,
Las letras hurta el insigne abuelo. (qtd. in García Peres 131)

19. Maroto Camino, Doménech, and Mujica give some attention to her Portuguese identity. For a more complete treatment of the subject, see Wade "Patriotism and Revolt: Uncovering the Portuguese in Ângela de Azevedo."

20. Regarding their maritime past, one scholar notes "Portugal foi a primeira nação a aproveitar-se totalmente da tecnologia, melhorando ou aperfeiçoando alguns aspectos, inventando outros e colocando o todo na práctica numa escala global enorme, até então desconhecida" (Williams 40; "Portugal was the first nation to completely take advantage of technology, improving or perfecting certain features, inventing others and situating everything within the practice of an enormous global scale, previously unknown"). Camões's work chronicles Vasco da Gama's famous journey to India. Through his pen Camões immortalizes the famous voyage, which created an unprecedented passage to the Orient and inspired Portugal's greatest season of economic prosperity.

21. While the overlap between Faria e Sousa's account and Azevedo's play is interesting, perhaps even more fascinating are the points of contrast, which may result from the sources themselves or from the dramatist's artistic license.

22. Audience may not be the right word to use in conjunction with Azevedo, whose *comedias*, if staged at all, would have been performed for very small audiences at Court, where she served as a lady-in-waiting for Isabel of Borbón.

23. Pablo Neruda affirms the untranslatability of the word in his poem "Saudade," found in the collection "Los crepúsculos de Maruri" from *Crepusculario* (1921–23). The opening line admits, "Saudade—¿qué será? ... yo no sé" (136). In *Tala* (1938), Gabriela Mistral titles the sixth section of her collection "Saudade," which consists of five poems and a brief explanation of the title. There are still many other examples of *saudade* in Spanish American poetry.

24. Polyptoton = "Repetition of words from the same root but with different endings" (Lanham 117).

25. For more information, see Wade "Patriotism and Revolt: Uncovering the Portuguese in Ângela de Azevedo."

Chapter 5

1. Sousa de Macedo briefly takes up the matter of the title in his words to the reader, where he anticipates the complaint that the title mentions Spain but the text only highlights Portugal, to which he reinforces his previous contention that as a part of the empire, any praise of Portugal indirectly elevates Spain.

2. This translation is by Frederick G. Williams and appears in his *Poetas de Portugal: Uma selecção bilingue de poemas do século XIII ao século XX* (2005).

Conclusion

1. Fernando Bouza Álvarez's *Corre manuscrito* (2001) and Gwyn Fox's *Subtle Subversions* (2008) are bright examples of the kind of work I am describing. In general, early modern scholars studying women writers tend to show greater openness to the mutual consideration of Spanish and Portuguese writers, although in some cases this is due to the fewer number of female-authored works available among the Spanish. This, of course, would go against the point I am trying to make. Critics should not turn to Portuguese authors as a last resort, but instead consider them coterminously with their Spanish contemporaries.

Works Cited

Albuquerque, Martim de. *A consciência nacional portuguesa: ensaio de história das ideias políticas.* 1974.

Almeida, Onésimo Teotónio. *National Identity—a Revisitation of the Portuguese Debate.* NUI Maynooth Papers in Spanish, Portuguese, and Latin American Studies, no. 5, National University of Ireland, 2002.

———. *A obsessão da portugalidade: identidade, língua, saudade & valores.* Quetzal, 2017.

Alonso, Dámaso. "La recepción de 'Os Lusíadas' en España (1579–1650)." *Obras completas*, vol. 3, Gredos, 1974, pp. 9–40.

Alves, Hélio J. S. "Faria e Sousa, Manuel de." *Dicionário de Luís de Camões*, coordinated by Vítor Aguiar e Silva, Caminho, 2010, pp. 371–78.

———. "Manuel de Faria e Sousa e Manuel Pires Almeida: Uma contenda fundamental em torno de Camões." *Homenagem ao Professor Augusto da Silva*, edited by F. M. Ramos et al., U de Évora, 2000, pp. 283–300.

Anastácio, Vanda. "Leituras potencialmente perigosas. As traduções castelhanas de Os Lusíadas no tempo da União Ibérica." *Portugal und Spanien: Probleme (k)einer Beziehung = Portugal e Espanha: encontros e desencontros*, edited by Tobias Brandenberger and Henry Thorau, Peter Lang, 2005, pp. 93–105.

———. Prefácio. *Teatro completo*, by Luís de Camões, edited by Anastácio, Edições Caixotim, 2005, pp. 7–73.

Anderson, Benedict. *Imagined Communities.* Verso, 1991.

Anedotas portuguesas e memórias biográficas da corte quinhentista. Edited by Christopher C. Lund, Almedina, 1980.

Antunes-Fernandes, Marie-France. "Gil Vicente: Un espagnol portugais du debut du XVIème siècle." *Les Cahiers du CRIAR: Langues et identités dans la péninsule ibérique*, no. 9, 1989, pp. 23–50.

Ares Montes, José. "Los poetas portugueses, cronistas de la Jornada de Felipe III a Portugal." *Filología Románica*, vol. 7, 1990, pp. 11–36.

———. "Portugal en el teatro español del siglo XVII." *Filología Románica*, vol. 8, 1991, pp. 11–29.

Asensio, Eugenio. "La autobiografía de Manuel de Faria y Sousa." *Arquivos do Centro Cultural Português*, vol. 13, 1978, pp. 629–37.

———. "España en la épica filipina." *Revista de Filología Española*, vol. 33, 1949, pp. 66–109.

213

Asensio, Eugenio. "La fortuna de *Os Lusíadas* en España." *Estudios portugueses*, Fundação Calouste Gulbenkian, Centro Cultural Português, 1974, pp. 303–24.

Askins, Arthur. "Os inéditos camonianos de Manuel de Faria e Sousa." *Critique textuelle portugaise; actes du colloque, Paris, 20–24 octobre 1981*, edited by Eugenio Asensio, Fondation Calouste Gulbenkian, Centre culturel portugais, 1986, pp. 219–26.

———. "Manuel de Faria e Sousa's *Fuente de Aganipe*: The Unprinted Seventh Part." *Florilegium Hispanicum: Medieval and Golden Age Studies*, edited by John S. Geary, Hispanic Seminary of Medieval Studies, 1983, pp. 245–77.

Atkinson, William C. Introduction. *Os Lusíadas*, by Luis Vaz de Camões, translated by Atkinson, Penguin, 1952, pp. 7–36.

Azevedo, Ângela de. *Dicha y desdicha del juego y devoción de la Virgen. Women's Acts: Plays by Women Dramatists of Spain's Golden Age*, edited by Teresa Scott Soufas, UP of Kentucky, 1997, pp. 4–44.

———. *La margarita del Tajo que dio nombre a Santarén. Women's Acts: Plays by Women Dramatists of Spain's Golden Age*, edited by Teresa Scott Soufas, UP of Kentucky, 1997, pp. 45–90.

———. *El muerto disimulado. Women's Acts: Plays by Women Dramatists of Spain's Golden Age*, edited by Teresa Scott Soufas, UP of Kentucky, 1997, pp. 91–132.

Baranda, Nieves. "Violante do Céu y los avatares políticos de la Restauração." *Iberoamericana*, vol. 7, no. 28, 2007, pp. 137–50. dx.doi.org/10.18441/ibam.7.2007.28.137-150.

Barbosa Machado, Diôgo. *Biblioteca Lusitana histórica, crítica e cronológica*. Com. Nac. para as comemorações dos descobrimentos portugueses, 1930–35, vol. 1–3.

Barros, João de. *Diálogo em louvor da nossa linguagem*. 1540. Edited by Luciana Stegagno Picchio, Società tipografica modenese, 1959.

Bass, Laura R. "Poética, imperio y la idea de España en época de Olivares: las *Lusíadas comentadas* de Manuel de Faria e Sousa." *Poder y saber: bibliotecas y bibliofilia en la* época del conde-duque de Olivares, edited by Oliver Nobel Wood et al., Centro de Estudios Europa Hispánica, 2011, pp. 183–205.

Beardsmore, Hugo Baetens. "Polyglot Literature and Linguistic Fiction." *International Journal of the Sociology of Language*, vol. 15, 1978, pp. 91–102.

Bernheimer, Richard. "*Theatrum Mundi*." *The Art Bulletin*, vol. 38, no. 4, 1956, pp. 225–47.

Bessa-Luis, Agustina. Commemorative Speech. *Camões e a identidade nacional*, Imprensa Nacional-Casa de Moeda, 1983, pp. 113–24.

Bhabha, Homi K. "Narrating the Nation." Introduction. *Nation and Narration*, edited by Bhabha, Routledge, 1990, pp. 1–7.

The Bible. Authorized King James Version, Hendrickson, 2003.

Birmingham, David. *A Concise History of Portugal*. Cambridge UP, 2003.

Bloom, Harold. *The Anxiety of Influence*. Oxford UP, 1997.

Borges, Jorge Luis. "Pierre Menard, autor del *Quijote*." *Ficciones*, Alianza, 1999.

Botelho, Afonso, and António Braz Teixeira. *Filosofia da saudade*. Imprensa Nacional-Casa da Moeda, 1986.

Boto, Sandra. "'Os príncipes dos poetas': Teorização nos coméntarios de Fernando de Herrera e de Faria e Sousa." *La lengua portuguesa*, vol. 1, *Estudios sobre literatura y cultura de expresión portuguesa*, edited by Ángel Marcos de Dios, U de Salamanca, 2014, pp. 381–96.

Bouza Álvarez, Fernando. *Corre manuscrito: Una historia cultural del Siglo de Oro*, Marcial Pons, 2001.

———. *Portugal no tempo dos Filipes: política, cultura, representações, 1580–1668*. Translated by Ângela Barreto Xavier and Pedro Cardim, Cosmos, 2000.

Braga, Marquez, editor. *Poesias castellanas y autos*. by Luís de Camões, Imprensa Nacional, 1929.

Braga, Teófilo. *Os centenarios como synthese affectiva nas sociedades modernas*. Porto, 1884.

———. *História da literatura portuguesa: Os Seiscentistas*. vol. 3, Imprensa Nacional-Casa da Moeda, 1984.

Brandenberger, Tobias. "Literature at the Crossroads of Politics: Spain and Portugal, 1580." *A Comparative History of Literatures in the Iberian Peninsula*, vol. 1, edited by Fernando Cabo Aseguinolaza, Anxo Abuín Gonzalez, and César Domínguez, John Benhamins, 2010, pp. 595–600.

Brasil, Reis. *Gil Vicente e a Cidade de Lisboa*. Livraria Portugal, 1968.

Brown, Jonathan, and J H Elliott. *A Palace for a King. The Buen Retiro and the Court of Philip IV*. Yale UP, 1980.

Bustamante, Ciriaco Pérez. Introducción. *Historias portuguesas*. by Manuel de Faria e Sousa, Atlas, 1943, pp. 9–10.

Calderón, Manuel. Prólogo. *Teatro Castellano*. by Gil Vicente, edited by Calderón, Crítica, 1998, pp. xxiii–liii.

Calderón de la Barca, Pedro. *El príncipe constante.* Edited by Fernando Cantalapiedra and Alfredo Rodríguez López-Vázquez, Cátedra, 1996.

Camões, José. *Festa.* Quimera, 1992.

Camões, Luís de. *Lusíadas de Luís de Camões, comentadas por Manuel de Faria e Sousa.* 1639. Edited by Manuel de Faria e Sousa, Imprensa Nacional-Casa de Moeda, 1972.

———. *Teatro completo.* Edited by Vanda Anastácio, Edições Caixotim, 2005.

Carabias Torres, Ana María. "Castilla y Portugal: el trajín de la cultura académica." *Castilla y Portugal en los albores de la edad media,* Varona, 1997, pp. 31–53.

Cardoso Bernardes, José Augusto. "O *Auto da festa* e a (rica) oficina de Gil Vicente." *Uma coisa na ordem das coisas: Estudios para Ofélia Paiva Monteiro,* edited by Carlos Reis et al., Coimbra UP, 2012, pp. 227–39.

Castillejo, David. *Guía de ochocientas comedias del Siglo de Oro: para el uso de actores y lectores.* Ars Milleni, 2002.

———. *El otro siglo de oro: cuarenta dramaturgos recuperados.* Funcación Olivar de Castillejo, 2007.

Cervantes, Miguel de. *El ingenioso hidalgo don Quijote de la Mancha.* Edited by Tom Lathrop, Juan de la Cuesta, 2005.

———. *Numancia.* Edited by Robert Marrast, Cátedra, 1990.

Céu, Violante do. *Rimas varias.* Edited by Margarida Vieira Mendes, Presença, 1994.

Cidade, Hernani. *A literatura autonomista sob os Filipes.* Livraria Sá da Costa, 1950–1959.

Cisneros, Luis Jaime. "La polémica Faria-Espinoza Medrano: Planteamiento crítico." *Lexis,* vol. 6, no. 1, 1987, pp. 1–62. revistas.pucp.edu.pe/index.php/lexis/article/view/5413.

Coelho Muniz, Márcio Ricardo. "De Castela … casamento: festa e política no teatro de Gil Vicente." *Portugal und Spanien: Probleme (k)einer Beziehung = Portugal e Espanha: encontros e desencontros,* edited by Tobias Brandenberger and Henry Thorau, Peter Lang, 2005, pp. 79–91.

Contente Domingues, Francisco. Prefácio. *O mito de Portugal: a primeira história de Portugal e a sua função política,* by Fernão de Oliveira, edited by José Eduardo Franco, Fundação Maria Manuela e Vasco de Albuquerque d'Orey, 2000, pp. 9–11.

Cordeiro, Jacinto. *Los doze de Inglaterra. Segunda parte de las Comedias.* Lisboa, 1634, pp. 60–78.

———. *Elogio de Poetas Lusitanos.* 1631. *Catálogo razonado, biográfico y bibliográfico de los autores portugueses que escribieron en castellano,* edited by Domingo García Peres, Madrid, 1890, pp. 124–37.

———. *La entrada del Rey en Portugal.* Lisboa, 1621.

———. *Prospera e adversa fortuna de Duarte Pacheco em duas Comedias.* Lisboa, 1630.

Costa, Joaquim Luís. "A violência literária contra Manuel de Faria e Sousa." *Las violencias y la historia,* edited by Paula Hernández Rodríguez et al., Asociación de Jóvenes Historiadores, 2016, pp. 511–25.

Costa e Silva, José Maria da. *Ensaio biographico-critico sobre os melhores poetas portuguezes.* Lisboa, 1850–55. 8 vols.

Costa Pimpáo, A. J. da. "A lírica camoniana no século XVII." *Brotéria,* vol. 35, 1942, pp. 14–27.

Covarrubias Orozco, Sebastián de. *Tesoro de la lengua castellana o española.* Edited by Martín de Riquer, Alta Fulla, 2003.

Cruz-Ortiz, Jaime. Introduction *El juramento ante Dios, y lealtad contra el amor.* By Jacinto Cordeiro, edited by Jaime Cruz-Ortiz, Peter Lang, 2014, pp.1–37.

Dasilva, Xosé Manuel. "La evolución histórica de las traducciones españolas de *Os Lusíadas.*" *Revista de Letras,* vol. 54, no. 1, 2014, pp. 193–207.

———. "Líneas maestras en la historia de la difusión de Camões en España." *Rumbos del hispanismo en el umbral del Cincuentenario de la AIH,* vol. 3, coordinated by Patrizia Botta, Bagatto Libri, 2012, pp. 32–40.

Davies, Mark. *Corpus del Español: Genre/Historical.* Brigham Young University. www.corpusdelespanol.org/hist-gen/. Accessed 13 Nov. 2008.

———. *Corpus do Português: Genre/Historical.* Brigham Young University. www.corpusdoportugues.org/hist-gen/. Accessed 13 Nov. 2008.

Dias, Jorge. *Estudos do carácter nacional português.* Junta de Investigações do Ultramar, Centro de Estudos de Antropologia Cultural, 1971.

Doménech Rico, Fernando. Introducción. *La margarita del Tajo que dio nombre a Santarén; El muerto disimulado,* by Ângela de Azevedo, edited by Doménech, Publicaciones de la Asociación de Directores de Escena de España, 1999, pp. 5–31.

Earle, T. F. "António Ferreira, *Castro.*" *A Companion to Portuguese Literature,* edited by Stephen Parkinson, Cláuda Pazos Alonso, and T. F. Earle, Boydell and Brewer, 2009, pp. 68–71.

Estruch Tobella, Joan. Introducción. *Historia de los movimientos, separación y guerra de Cataluña*, by Francisco Manuel de Melo, edited by Estruch Tobella, Fontamara, 1982, pp. 7–41.

Faria e Sousa, Manuel de. *África portuguesa*. Lisboa, 1681.

———. *Asia portuguesa*. Edited by Pedro Faria e Sousa, 1666. Civilização, 1945–47. 6 vols.

———. *The Cancionero de Manuel de Faria*. Edited by Edward Glaser, Aschendorff, 1968.

———. *Epítome de las historias portuguesas*. Madrid, 1628.

———. *Europa portuguesa*. Lisboa, 1678.

———. *The "Fortuna" of Manuel de Faria e Sousa: An Autobiography*. Edited by Edward Glaser, Aschendorff, 1975.

———. *Informacion en favor de Manuel de Faria i Sousa*. Lisboa, 1640.

———, editor. *Lusíadas de Luís de Camões, comentadas por Manuel de Faria e Sousa*. 1639. Imprensa Nacional-Casa de Moeda, 1972.

———. *Narciso e Echo*. Lisboa, 1623.

———. *Noches claras*. Madrid, 1624.

———. "Patria i vida del autor." *Fuente de Aganipe*, vol. 2, Madrid, 1644.

———, editor. *Rimas varias de Luis de Camoens Principe de los Poetas Heroycos y Lyricos de España*. Lisboa, 1685, vol. 1–2.

Faria e Sousa, Pedro. "Aos que lerem." *Asia Portuguesa*, by Manuel de Faria e Sousa, edited by Pedro Faria e Sousa. 1666. Vol. 1, Civilização, 1945, pp. 15–26.

Ferreira, António. *Castro*. Edited by F. Costa Marques, Atlântida, 1967.

———. *Poemas Lusitanos*. Edited by F. Costa Marques, Atlântida, 1961.

Ferreira, Vergílio. "Da ausência, Camões." *Camões e a identidade nacional*, Imprensa Nacional-Casa de Moeda, 1983, pp. 13–21.

Figueiredo, Fidelino de. *História literária de Portugal (séculos XII–XX)*. Nobel, 1944.

———. *Lope de Vega: Alguns elementos portugueses na sua obra*. U de Santiago, 1936.

———. Prefácio. *Comedia trofea*, by Bartolomé de Torres Naharro. U de São Paulo, 1942, pp. 7–46.

Flasche, Hans. *O método de comentar de Manuel de Faria e Sousa*. Comissão Executiva do IV Centenário da Publicação de *Os Lusíadas*, 1973.

Forster, Leonard W. *The Poet's Tongues: Multilingualism in Literature*. Cambridge UP, 1970.

Fouto, Catarina, and Julian Weiss. "Reimagining Imperialism in Faria e Sousa's *Lusíadas comentadas*." *Bulletin of Spanish Studies*, vol. 93, no. 7–8, 2016, pp. 1243–70. doi:10.1080/14753820.2016. 1219526.

Fox, Gwyn. *Subtle Subversions: Reading Golden Age Sonnets by Iberian Women*. Catholic U of America P, 2008.

Franco, José Eduardo, editor. *O mito de Portugal: a primeira história de Portugal e a sua função política*. by Fernão de Oliveira, Fundação Maria Manuela e Vasco de Albuquerque d'Orey, 2000.

Frèches, Claude Henri. Introduction. *Comedias portuguesas*, by Simão Machado, edited by Frèches, O Mundo do Livro, 1971, pp. 9–49.

Freitas, William John. *Camoens and His Epic: A Historic, Geographic and Cultural Study*. Institute of Hispanic American and Luso-Brazilian Studies, 1963.

García Peres, Domingo, editor. *Catálogo razonado, biográfico y bibliográfico de los autores portugueses que escribieron en castellano*. Madrid, 1890.

Gascón, Christopher. "Female and Male Mediation in the Plays of Ángela de Azevedo." *Bulletin of the Comediantes*, vol. 57, no. 1, 2005, pp. 125–45.

Gellner, Ernest. *Nations and Nationalism*. Blackwell, 2006.

Gimeno Ugalde, Esther. "El giro ibérico: panorama de los Estudios Ibéricos en los Estados Unidos." *Informes del Observatorio / Observatorio Reports*, 2017. doi:10.15427/OR036-12/2017SP.

Glaser, Edward. Introducción. *Estudios hispano-portugueses: Relaciones literarias del Siglo de Oro*, Castalia, 1957, pp. v–xii.

———. Introduction. *The "Fortuna" of Manuel de Faria e Sousa: An Autobiography*, by Manuel de Faria e Sousa, edited by Glaser, Aschendorff, 1975, pp. 5–122.

———. "Lope de Vega e Manuel de Faria e Sousa: Achegas para o estudo das relações literárias entre Portugal e Espanha." *Colóquio*, vol. 8, 1960, pp. 57–59.

———. "O lusitanismo de Lope de Vega." *Boletín de la Real Academia Española*, vol. 34, 1954, pp. 387–411.

———. "Manuel de Faria e Sousa and the Mythology of *Os Lusíadas*." *Portuguese Studies*, Fundação Calouste Gulbenkian, Centro Cultural Português, 1976, pp. 135–57.

———. "On Portuguese *Sprachbetrachtung* of the Seventeenth Century." *Studia Philológica: Homenaje ofrecido a Dámaso Alonso*, Gredos, 1961, pp. 115–26.

Gloël, Matthias. "Los autores portugueses entre 1580 y 1640: una lucha literaria por la preeminencia en la monarquía hispánica." *Revista de Historia*, vol. 23, no. 1, 2016, pp. 29–51.

Gonçalves Pires, Maria Lucília. *Xadrez de palavras: Estudos de literatura barroca*. Cosmos, 1996.

Góngora, Luis de. "Soneto CLXVI." *Renaissance and Baroque Poetry of Spain*, edited by Elias L. Rivers, Waveland, 1988, p. 168.

Haberly, David T. "Colonial Brazilian Literature." *The Cambridge History of Latin American Literature*, edited by Roberto González Echevarría and Enrique Pupo-Walker, vol. 3, Cambridge UP, 1996, pp. 47–68.

Hart, Thomas R. "The Literary Criticism of Manuel de Faria e Sousa." *Kentucky Romance Quarterly*, vol. 21, 1974, pp. 31–41.

Hatherly, Ana. "A égloga *Toledo* que Manuel de Faria e Sousa fez com versos de Garcilaso." *Revista de Filología Románica*, vol. 9, 1992, pp. 191–206.

———. "Laberintos da parte VII da *Fuente de Aganipe* de Manuel de Faria e Sousa." *Arquivos do Centro Cultural Português*, vol. 21, 1985, pp. 439–67.

Hawkins, Harriet Blocker. "'All the World's a Stage' Some Illustrations of the *Theatrum Mundi*." *Shakespeare Quarterly*, vol. 17, no. 2, 1966, pp. 174–78.

Hegstrom, Valerie, and Catherine Larson, editors. *El muerto disimulado / Presumed Dead*. By Ângela de Azevedo, translated by Catherine Larson, Liverpool UP, 2018.

Heiple, Daniel L. "Political Posturing on the Jewish Question by Lope de Vega and Faria e Sousa" *Hispanic Review*, vol. 62, no. 2, 1994, pp. 217–34.

Helgerson, Richard. *Forms of Nationhood: The Elizabethan Writing of England*. U of Chicago P, 1995.

Herrera, Fernando de, editor. *Obras de Garcilaso de la Vega con anotaciones de Fernando de Herrera*. Sevilla, 1580.

Hobsbawm, E. J. "Introduction: Inventing Traditions." *The Invention of Tradition*, edited by Hobsbawm and Terence Ranger, Cambridge UP, 1992.

———. *Nations and Nationalism since 1780*. Cambridge UP, 2006.

Jorge, Ricardo d'Almeida. *A intercultura de Portugal e Espanha no passado e no futuro*. Araujo & Sobrino, 1921.

Juana Inés de la Cruz. *Carta Atenagórica. Sor Juana Inés de la Cruz e o Padre António Vieira, ou, A disputa sobre as finezas de Jesús Cristo*. Edited by Joaquim de Montezuma de Carvalho, Vega, 1998, pp. 117–38.

Laferl, Christopher F. "Góngora, Espinosa Medrano y la defensa del hipérbaton." *Iberoromania* vol. 75–76, 2012, pp. 41–58. doi: 10.1515/ibero-2012-0019.

Lanham, Richard A. *A Handlist of Rhetorical Terms.* U of California P, 1991.

Lemos, Esther de. "Faria e Sousa, comentador das rimas de Camões." *Boletim da Academia Portuguesa de Ex-Libris,* vol. 11, 1966, pp. 1–17.

Lewis, Christopher T. "The Sea and the Shield: Lacan and Epic Mirrors in Luís de Camões's *Os Lusíadas* and Torquato Tasso's *Gerusalemme Liberata.*" *Romance Notes,* vol. 52, no. 3, 2012, pp. 353–61.

Leyva, Aurelia. "La *preceptiva* de un comentador barroco: A propósito de Manuel de Faria y Sousa." *Homenaje al profesor Antonio Gallego Morell,* edited by C. Argente del Castillo, A. de la Granja, J. Martínez Marín, and A. Sánchez Trigueros, U de Granada, 1989, pp. 201–12.

Literatura hispano-portuguesa. Directed by José Miguel Martínez Torrejón, *Fundación Biblioteca Virtual Miguel de Cervantes.* www.cervantes-virtual.com/portales/literatura_hispanoportuguesa/.

Livermore, H. V. *Portugal: A Short History.* Edinburgh UP, 1973.

López Castro, Armando. Introducción. *Lírica,* by Gil Vicente, Cátedra, 1993, pp. 9–68.

Lourenço, Eduardo. *O labirinto da saudade: Psicanálise mítica do destino português.* Gradita, 2000.

Machado, Simão. *Comedias portuguesas.* Edited by Claude Henri Frèches, O Mundo do Livro, 1971.

Magalhães Godinho, Vitorino. *Portugal: a emergencia de uma nação: das raízes a 1480.* Colibri, 2004.

Maldonado, Felipe C. R. "'Fortuna de Manuel de Faria e Sousa': Cronica de un resentimiento." *La estafeta literaria,* no. 585, 1976, pp. 10–13.

Manuel de Melo, Francisco. *Epanáforas de vária história portuguesa.* U de Coimbra, 1931.

———. *O fidalgo aprendiz.* Edited by José Camões, *Centro de Estudos de Teatro,* Faculdade de Letras da Universidade de Lisboa. www.helenabarbas.net/BiblioLus/Textos/ffm.pdf.

———. *Historia de los movimientos, separación y guerra de Cataluña.* 1645. Edited by Joan Estruch Tobella, Castalia, 1996.

———. *O Hospital das Letras. Apólogos Dialogais,* vol. 2, edited by Pedro Serra, Angelus Novus, 1999, pp. 39–140.

Marcos de Dios, Ángel. "Libros y lecturas portuguesas en la España de los siglos XVI y XVII." *Aula Ibérica Online*, 2010, pp. 1–57. www.filologiaportuguesa.es/aulaIbericaBuscar.asp

Marín, Nicolás. "Camoens, Faria y Cervantes." *Homenaje a Camoens; estudios y ensayos hispano-portugueses*, U de Granada, 1980, pp. 239–46.

Maroto Camino, Mercedes. "Transvestism, Translation and Transgression: Angela de Azevedo's *El muerto disimulado*." *Forum for Modern Language Studies*, vol. 37, no. 3, 2001, pp. 314–25. doi:10.1093/fmls/37.3.314.

Martínez, Miguel. "A Poet of Our Own: The Struggle for *Os Lusíadas* in the Afterlife of Camões." *Journal for Early Modern Cultural Studies*, vol. 10, no. 1, 2010, pp. 71–94. doi.10.1353/jem.0.0046.

Martínez-Almoyna, Julio, and Antero Viera de Lemos. *La lengua española en la literatura portuguesa*. Imnasa, 1968.

Martínez Torrejón, José Miguel. Prologue. *La littérature d'auteurs portugais en langue castillane*, Centro Cultural Calouste Gulbenkian, 2002, pp. 3–10.

Martyn, John R. C. Introduction. *The Tragedy of Inés de Castro*, by António Ferreira, edited and translated by John R. C. Martyn, U de Coimbra, 1987, pp. 1–157.

Mattoso, José. *A Identidade Nacional*. Gradiva, 1998.

Michaëlis de Vasconcelos, Carolina. Prefácio. *A intercultura de Portugal e Espanha no passado e no futuro*, by Ricardo d'Almeida Jorge, Araujo & Sobrinho, 1921, pp. xviii–xxxiv.

Molina, Tirso de. *Las quinas de Portugal*. Edited by Celsa Carmen García Valdés, Instituto de Estudios Tirsianos, 2003.

Morby, Edwin S. "Portugal and Galicia in the Plays of Tirso de Molina." *Hispanic Review*, vol. 9, 1941, pp. 266–74. doi:10.2307/470222.

Moreno Porcel, Franciso. *Retrato de Manuel de Faria y Sousa*. Madrid, 1650.

Mujica, Bárbara Louise. *Women Writers of Early Modern Spain: Sophia's Daughters*. Yale UP, 2004.

Namora, Fernando. "A pretexto de Camões." *Camões e a identidade nacional*, Imprensa Nacional-Casa de Moeda, 1983, pp. 43–61.

Nascentes, Antenor. *Diccionario etimológico resumido*. Instituto Nacional do Livro, Ministério da Educação e Cultura, 1966.

Nebrija, Antonio de. *Gramática de la lengua castellana*. 1492. Madrid, 1984.

Neruda, Pablo. *Obras completas*, vol. 1, edited by Hernán Loyola, Galaxia Gutenberg, 1999.

Nunes de Leão, Duarte. *Leal conselheiro*. 1438. Imprensa Nacional-Casa de Moeda, 1983.

Nunes Godinho, Manuel, translator. *Os Lusiadas de Luiz de Camões, Principe dos poetas portugueses, comentados em espanhol por Manuel de Faria e Souza.* 1639. Lisboa, 1886. www.loc.gov/item/33032639/.

Núñez Cáceres, Javier. "Las anotaciones bilingües de Manuel de Faria y Sousa." *Boletín de la Real Academia Española*, vol. 60, 1980, pp. 261–98. web.frl.es/BRAE_DB.html.

Núñez Rivera, José Valentín. "Sobre géneros poéticos e historia de la poesía. Los *Discursos* de Faria e Sousa (de la *Fuente de Aganipe* a las *Rimas* de Camoens)." *Edad de Oro*, vol. 30, 2011, pp. 179–206.

Oliveira, Fernão de. *Grammatica de linguagem portugueza.* 1536. Porto, 1871.

———. *O mito de Portugal: a primeira história de Portugal e a sua função política.* Edited by José Eduardo Franco, Fundação Maria Manuela e Vasco de Albuquerque d'Orey, 2000.

Oliveira Marques, A. H. de. *História de Portugal.* Vol. 1. Palas Editores, 1976.

Oliveira e Silva, John de. "Exile Under Fire: Reassessing the Poetics and Practice of Manuel de Faria e Sousa." *Global Impact of the Portuguese Language*, edited by Asela Rodriguez de Laguna, Transaction, 2001, pp. 61–76.

———. "Reinventing the Nation: Luís De Camões' Epic Burden." *Mediterranean Studies*, vol. 9, 2000, pp. 103–22. www.jstor.org/stable/41166914.

Oriente, Fernão Alvares do. *Lusitânia transformada.* 1607. Imprensa Nacional, Casa da Moeda, 1985.

Pap, Leo. "On the Etymology of Portuguese SAUDADE: An Instance of Multiple Causation?" *Word. Journal of the International Linguistics Association*, vol. 43, no.1, 1992, pp. 97–102.

Parker, Jack Horace. *Gil Vicente.* Twayne, 1967.

Payne, Stanley G. *A History of Spain and Portugal.* Vol. 1. U of Wisconsin P, 1973.

Pedro (Condestable de Portugal). *Satira de felice e infelice vida.* 1468. *Biblioteca Digital Hispánica*, Biblioteca Nacional de España. bdh.bne.es/bnesearch/detalle/bdh0000048140.

Pedrosa, José Manuel. "El otro portugués: tipos y tópicos en la España de los siglos xvi al xviii." *Iberoamericana*, vol. 28, 2007, pp. 99–116. doi:dx.doi.org/10.18441/ibam.7.2007.28.99-116.

Pérez Isasi, Santiago. "Entre dos tierras y en tierra de nadie: el reflejo del multilingüismo peninsular en la historiografía literaria ibérica." *Revista de Filología Románica*, vol. 30, no. 1, 2013, pp. 137–48. doi.org/10.5209/rev_RFRM.2013.v30.n1.42606.

Pérez Isasi, Santiago. "Iberian Studies: A State of the Art and Future Perspectives." *Looking at Iberia: A Comparative European Perspective*, edited by Santiago Pérez Isasi and Ângela Fernandes, Peter Lang, 2013, pp. 11–26.

———. "Literaturas nacionales, literaturas supranacionales: el lugar del los Estudios Ibéricos." *Interlitteraria*, vol. 19, no. 1, 2014, pp. 22–32. doi.org/10.12697/IL.2014.19.1.2.

Pérez Isasi, Santiago, and Ângela Fernandes. "Looking at Iberia in/from Europe." *Looking at Iberia: A Comparative European Perspective*, edited by Santiago Pérez Isasi and Ângela Fernandes, Peter Lang, 2013, pp. 1–8.

Pierce, Frank. "The Place of Mythology in the *Lusiads*." *Comparative Literature*, vol. 6, no. 2, 1954, pp. 97–122. doi:10.2307/1768486.

Pina Martins, José V. de. Preface. *Portuguese Studies*, by Edward Glaser, Fundação Calouste Gulbenkian, Centro Cultural Português, 1976, pp. vii–xvii.

Rama, Angel. *La ciudad letrada*. Ediciones del Norte, 2002.

Ramada Curto, Diogo. "Por una Historia de las formas de toma de conciencia de la cultura escrita. Notas en torno a *Fortuna* de Manuel de Faria e Sousa." *Cultura Escrita y Sociedad*, vol. 2, 2006, pp. 183–228.

Raposo, Hipólito. "O sentimento português em Lope de Vega." *Aula Régia*, by Raposo, Civilização, 1936. pp. 299–367.

Reed, Cory A. "Identity Formation and Collective Anagnorisis in *Numancia*." *Theatralia*, vol. 5, 2003, pp. 67–76.

Renan, Ernest. "What is a Nation?" *Nation and Narration*, edited by Homi K. Bhabha, Routledge, 1990, pp. 8–22.

Rennert, Hugo Albert. *The Spanish Stage in the Time of Lope de Vega*. Dover, 1963.

Resina, Joan Ramon. *Iberian Modalities: A Relational Approach to the Study of Culture in the Iberian Peninsula*. Liverpool UP, 2013.

Ribeiro, Orlando. *A formação de Portugal*. Instituto de Cultura e Língua Portuguesa, 1987.

Righter, Anne. *Shakespeare and the Idea of the Play*. Barnes & Noble, 1963.

Rodríguez Cepeda, Enrique. "La relación Camoens, Lope de Vega y Faria y Sousa." *Quaderni Portoghesi*, vol. 7–8, 1980, pp. 207–22.

Roig, Adrien. "Los españoles en el teatro de Gil Vicente." *Encuentros y desencuentros de culturas desde la edad media al siglo XVIII*, edited by Juan Villegas, Regents of the U of California, 1994, pp. 129–38.

Schaub, Jean-Frédéric. "España y la cuestión portuguesa." *Ábaco*, no. 16, 1998, pp. 22–32. www.jstor.org/stable/20796301.

Sena, Jorge de. Introdução. *Lusíadas de Luís de Camões, comentadas por Manuel de Faria e Sousa*. 1639. Imprensa Nacional-Casa de Moeda, 1972, pp. 9–56.

Serra, Pedro. "Recepção de Luís de Camões em Espanha." *Dicionário de Camões*, edited by Vítor M. Aguiar e Silva, Caminho, 2011, pp. 772–93.

Shakespeare, William. *As You Like It*. Edited by Michael Hattaway, Cambridge UP, 2000.

Silveira Bueno, Francisco da. *Grande diccionario etimológico-prosódico da língua portuguesa*. Vol. 7, Saraiva, 1967.

Sletsjöe, Leif. "Las lenguas de Gil Vicente." *XI Congreso Internacional de Lingüística y Filología Románcias*, vol. 2, 1968, pp. 989–1002.

Sloman, Albert E. *The Sources of Calderón's* El príncipe constante. Oxford UP, 1950.

Smith, Anthony. *The Antiquity of Nations*. Polity, 2004.

Soufas, Teresa Scott. "Angela de Azevedo: Introduction." *Women's Acts: Plays by Women Dramatists of Spain's Golden Age*, edited by Soufas, UP of Kentucky, 1997, pp. 1–3.

———, editor. *Women's Acts: Plays by Women Dramatists of Spain's Golden Age*. UP of Kentucky, 1997.

Sousa de Macedo, António de. *Eva y Ave, o, Maria triunfante [...]*. Madrid, 1731.

———. *Flores de España, Excelencias de Portugal*. Lisboa, 1631.

———. *Lusitania liberata ab injusto Castellanorum dominio*. London, 1645.

Sousa Garcia, Tiago. "How *The Lusiad* Got English'd: Manuel Faria y Sousa, Richard Fanshawe and the First English Translation of *Os Lusíadas*." *Literature Compass*, vol. 14, no. 4, 2017, pp. 1–18. doi:10.1111/lic3.12387.

Sousa Pinto, Manoel de. *Portugal e as portuguezas em Tirso de Molina*. Aillaud, 1914.

Stegagno Picchio, Luciana. *História do teatro português*. Portugália, 1969.

Stevens, John. Preface. *The History of Portugal*, by Manuel de Faria e Sousa, translated by Stevens, London, 1698.

Studnicki-Gizbert, Daviken. *A Nation upon the Ocean Sea: Portugal's Atlantic Diaspora and the Crisis of the Spanish Empire, 1492–1640*. Oxford UP, 2007.

Surtz, Ronald E. "Gil Vicente's *Auto da Lusitânia.*" *Creation and Re-creation: Experiments in Literary Form in Early Modern Spain*, edited by Ronald E. Surtz and Nora Weinerth, Juan de la Cuesta, 1983, pp. 41–48.

Talvet, Jüri. "How to Research Iberian Literatures from a European Perspective? Premises and Contexts." *Looking at Iberia: A Comparative European Perspective*, edited by Santiago Pérez Isasi and Ângela Fernandes, Peter Lang, 2013, pp. 87–97.

Tengwall, David. "The Portuguese Revolution of 1 December 1640: A Reappraisal." *eHumanista*, vol. 17, 2017, pp. 448–59.

Teyssier, Paul. *La Langue de Gil Vicente*. Klincksieck, 1959.

Torres Naharro, Bartolomé de. *Comedia trofea*. Edited by Fidelino de Figueiredo, U de São Paulo, 1942.

———. *Comedias: Soldadesca, Tinelaria, Himenea*. Edited by D. W. McPheeters, Castalia, 1973.

Valle de Figueiredo, José. Prefácio. *Manuel de Faria e Sousa: Cidadão do mundo e das letras ao serviço de Portugal*, by Joaquim Costa, Centro de Estudos do Românico e do territorio, 2012, pp. 8–9.

Vázquez Cuesta, Pilar. "O bilinguismo castelhano-português na época de Camões." *Arquivos do Centro Cultural Português*, vol. 16, 1981, pp. 807–27.

———. "La lengua y la cultura portuguesas." *Historia de la Cultura Española: El siglo del* Quijote. Vol. 2, *Las Letras. Las Artes*, Espasa, 1996, pp. 577–680.

Vega, Lope de. *Arte Nuevo de hacer comedias*. Edited by Enrique García Santo-Tomás, Cátedra, 2006.

———. "Elogio al comentador." *Lusíadas de Luís de Camões, comentadas por Manuel de Faria e Sousa*. 1639. Imprenta Nacional-Casa de Moeda, 1972.

———. *Laurel de Apolo*. Edited by Antonio Carreño, Cátedra, 2007.

———. *El marido más firme. Parte veinte de las Comedias de Lope de Vega*. Madrid, 1627, pp. 275–98.

Vicente, Gil. *Fama*. Directed by José Camões, *Centro de Estudos de Teatro*, Faculdade de Letra da Universidad de Lisboa. www.tmp.letras. ulisboa.pt/images/stories/Documentos/Centros/Teatro/fama.pdf.

———. *Festa*. Directed by José Camões, *Centro de Estudos de Teatro*, Faculdade de Letra da Universidad de Lisboa. www.tmp.letras. ulisboa.pt/images/stories/Documentos/Centros/Teatro/festa.pdf.

———. *Floresta d'Enganos*. Directed by José Camões, *Centro de Estudos de Teatro*, Faculdade de Letra da Universidad de Lisboa, www.fl.ul. pt/centros_invst/teatro/pagina/Publicacoes/Pecas/Textos_GV/floresta_denganos.pdf.

———. *Lusitânia*. Directed by José Camões, *Centro de Estudos de Teatro*, Faculdade de Letra da Universidad de Lisboa. www.tmp.letras.ulisboa.pt/images/stories/Documentos/Centros/Teatro/lusitania.pdf.

———. *Romagem dos Agravados*. Directed by José Camões, *Centro de Estudos de Teatro*, Faculdade de Letra da Universidad de Lisboa, www.fl.ul.pt/centros_invst/teatro/pagina/Publicacoes/Pecas/Textos_GV/romagem_dos_agravados.pdf.

———. *Templo de Apolo*. Directed by José Camões, *Centro de Estudos de Teatro*, Faculdade de Letra da Universidad de Lisboa, www.fl.ul.pt/centros_invst/teatro/pagina/Publicacoes/Pecas/Textos_GV/templo_dapolo.pdf.

———. *Tragicomedia pastoril da Serra da Estrela*. Directed by José Camões, *Centro de Estudos de Teatro*, Faculdade de Letra da Universidad de Lisboa, www.fl.ul.pt/centros_invst/teatro/pagina/Publicacoes/Pecas/Textos_GV/serra_da_estrela.pdf.

Vieira, António. *Sermão do mandato*. *Sor Juana Inés de la Cruz e o Padre António Vieira, ou, A disputa sobre as finezas de Jesús Cristo*, edited by Joaquim de Montezuma de Carvalho, Vega, 1998, pp. 95–115.

Wade, Jonathan. "Manuel de Faria e Sousa and *Comedia* Culture: Resituating Portugal on the Early Modern Spanish Stage." *Miríada Hispánica*, vol. 4, 2012, pp. 109–21. www.miriadahispanica.com/revista/5cc8c3e753e561d11ee5c945a8b7bb2351d30300.pdf.

———. "Patriotism and Revolt: Uncovering the Portuguese in Ângela de Azevedo." *Bulletin of the Comediantes*, vol. 59, no. 2, 2007, pp. 325–44. doi:10.1353/boc.2007.0026.

Walker, Roger. "Sir Richard Fanshawe's *Lusiad* and Manuel de Faria e Sousa's *Lusíadas Comentadas*: New Documentary Evidence." *Portuguese Studies*, vol. 10, no. 1, 1994, pp. 44–64. www.jstor.org/stable/41105001.

White, Hayden. *Tropics of Discourse: Essays in Cultural Criticism*. Johns Hopkins UP, 1978.

White, Landeg, translator. *The Lusíads*. By Luís Vaz de Camões, Oxford, 2001.

Williams, Frederick G. *Poetas de Portugal: Uma selecção bilingue de poemas do século XIII ao século XX*. Instituto Camões, 2005.

Wilson, Margaret. "The Last Play of Tirso de Molina." *Modern Language Review*, vol. 47, no. 4, 1952, pp. 516–28. www.jstor.org/stable/3719703.

———. *Spanish Drama of the Golden Age*. Pergamon, 1969.

Zimic, Stanislav. "Nuevas consideraciones sobre el *Auto da Lusitânia* de Gil Vicente." *Homenaje a Alonso Zamora Vicente*, edited by Pedro Peira, vol. 3.1, Castalia, 1991, pp. 359–69.

Index

About the Book

Jonathan William Wade
Being Portuguese in Spanish: Reimagining
Early Modern Iberian Literature, 1580–1640
PSRL 78

Among the many consequences of Spain's annexation of Portugal from 1580 to 1640 was an increase in the number of Portuguese authors writing in Spanish. One can trace this practice as far back as the medieval period, although it was through Gil Vicente, Jorge de Montemayor, and others that Spanish-language texts entered the mainstream of literary expression in Portugal. Proficiency in both languages gave Portuguese authors increased mobility throughout the empire. For those with literary aspirations, Spanish offered more opportunities to publish and greater readership, which may be why it is nearly impossible to find a Portuguese author who did not participate in this trend during the dual monarchy.

Over the centuries these authors and their works have been erroneously defined in terms of economic opportunism, questions of language loyalty, and other reductive categories. Within this large group, however, is a subcategory of authors who used their writings in Spanish to imagine, explore, and celebrate their Portuguese heritage. Manuel de Faria e Sousa, Ângela de Azevedo, Jacinto Cordeiro, António de Sousa de Macedo, and Violante do Céu, among many others, offer a uniform yet complex answer as to what it means to be from Portugal, constructing and claiming their Portuguese identity from within a Castilianized existence. Whereas all texts produced in Iberia during the early modern period reflect the distinct social, political, and cultural realities sweeping across the peninsula to some degree, Portuguese literature written in Spanish offers a unique vantage point from which to see these converging landscapes. *Being Portuguese in Spanish* explores the cultural cross-pollination that defined the era and reappraises a body of works that uniquely addresses the intersection of language, literature, politics, and identity.

About the Author

Jonathan Wade is an Associate Professor of Spanish at Meredith College. He specializes in early modern Spanish and Portuguese literature, with particular emphasis on the comedia, *Don Quixote* and Cervantes, and Iberian Studies (1580–1640). He has published articles in the *Bulletin of the Comediantes, Hispania,* and *Comedia Performance*, among other journals, as well as essays in various book-length studies. Overall, it is the crossing of borders (linguistic, national, genre) within literature that propels his scholarly inquiry. Originally from California, he currently resides in Raleigh, NC, with his wife and two daughters.

This important book makes a commendable contribution to the field of Iberian literary studies. It offers readers a panoramic and intricate understanding of the cross-cultural production and reception of an often-misunderstood period and set of texts— work written in Spanish by Portuguese authors during the Iberian Union. The author shows how this hybrid cultural production that crosses linguistic and cultural boundaries creates nonetheless a coherent national discourse and an intelligible rhetoric of nationhood.

Estela Vieira, Indiana University

Printed in the United States
By Bookmasters